Social Policy and Human Development in Zambia

By

Ndangwa Noyoo

Published by
Adonis & Abbey Publishers Ltd
P. O. Box 43418
London
SE11 4XZ
http://www.adonis-abbey.com
Email: editor@adonis-abbey.com

Second Edition, January 2010
First published by UNZA Press 2008

Copyright 2010 © Ndangwa Noyoo

British Library Cataloguing-in-Publication Data
A catalogue record for this book is available from the British Library

ISBN: 9781906704681(HB)/ 9781906704568(PB)

The moral right of the author has been asserted

All rights reserved. No part of this book may be reproduced, stored in a retrieval system or transmitted at any time or by any means without the prior permission of the publisher

Layout Artist/Technical Editor, Jan B. Mwesigwa

Printed and bound in Great Britain

Social Policy and Human Development in Zambia

By

Ndangwa Noyoo

Dedication

This work is dedicated to the thirty-two University of Zambia (UNZA) students who were detained in 1990 by the one-party regime and who had helped to unshackle Zambia from the chains of dictatorship. It is also dedicated to all Zambians who were incarcerated under the state of emergency laws for political reasons.

CONTENTS

Acknowledgments .... *vii*
Acronyms .... *ix*
List of Figures, Tables and Boxes .... *xiv*
Postscript .... *xv*

Preamble 1

Chapter 1
Conceptual Grounding and Theoretical Perspectives 21

Chapter 2
Social Change and Development in Zambia 47

Chapter 3
The Development and Evolution of Social Policy in Zambia 83

Chapter 4
Social Policy and Human Development in a Least Developed Country (LDC): Zambia 115

Chapter 5
Zambia's Human Development Imperatives 149

Chapter 6
Monitoring and Evaluation: Outcomes, Impacts and Policy Analysis for Human Development 183

Chapter 7
The Social Work Profession and Human Development in Zambia 209

Chapter 8
Concluding Notes on Social Policy and Human Development in Zambia 231

Epilogue 255

Bibliography 269
Index 287

ACKNOWLEDGMENTS

This book is a crystallisation of my ideas and work that I have undertaken in the areas of development studies, politics of development, social development, social policy, social welfare, and social work in the last twelve years. More important, I was enabled to follow through some of my thoughts on socio-political and economic issues when I was pursuing a Post-doctoral Research Fellowship with the Maison des Science de L'Homme (MSH) in Paris between 2005 and 2006. This period also helped me to lay the foundation for most of the discussions in the text. Furthermore, this work owes much to people who helped me to arrive at this final product. I would first like to thank the late Professor Bill Mitchell, who was Professor of Social Work, at the University of Johannesburg, and Dr Kenneth Mwenda, Senior Counsel at the World Bank, for agreeing to referee the book manuscript. Their insights, critical comments and words of encouragement were cardinal in helping me to fine-tune my thoughts. Thanks also to Mr Akashambatwa Mbikusita-Lewanika for agreeing to write the Foreword to this book, which eventually was reworked into an Epilogue. I would like to particularly extend my gratitude to Mr Joseph Kayumba Chiseyengi, who helped with most of the logistical arrangements for the research in Zambia. I also would like to thank my family, specifically my brothers Ikanuke and Noyoo, who provided invaluable perspectives that helped to shape some of the book's points of departure. Lastly, I would like to pay tribute to my son Thabo, who brought me much joy and needed frivolity when I was finalising this manuscript.

Furthermore, the following people are worth mentioning, in the light of the vital roles that they had played in my data collection endeavours:

Ms Francine Davies – Lecturer, Department of Human and Community Development, University of the Witwatersrand, South Africa.

Mr John Zulu – Director (Child Affairs), Ministry of Sport, Youth and Child Development, Lusaka.

Mrs Dorith Kasambala – Assistant Permanent Secretary (HIV/AIDS Focal Point), Ministry of Community Development and Social Services, Lusaka.

Mr P. Chinkanda – Assistant Director (Department of Community Development), Ministry of Community Development and Social Services, Lusaka.

Ms Ester Ng'ambi – Social Welfare Officer (Co-ordinator, HIV/AIDS), Ministry of Community Development and Social Services, Lusaka.

Mr Edmond Mwakalombwe – Programmer (Planning Unit – Desk Officer HIV/AIDS), Ministry of Community Development and Social Services, Lusaka.

Ms Ntasheni Makambi – United Nations Volunteer (HIV/AIDS), Ministry of Community Development and Social Services, Lusaka.

Ms Nangana Simwiinji – Director (Community Response to HIV/AIDS, CRAIDS), Mongu, Zambia.

Mr Mubyana Kakenenwa – Programme Officer (HIV/AIDS and Youth), Young Women's Christian Association (YWCA), Mongu, Zambia.

Mrs N.S. Imwiiko – Regional Director (Western Region), Young Women's Christian Association (YWCA), Mongu, Zambia.

ACRONYMS

AB	Asset Building
ACF	Agricultural Consultative Forum
ANC	African National Congress
ART	Antiretroviral Therapy
ARVs	Anti-retrovirals
AU	African Union
BSAC	British South Africa Company
CBOs	Community Based Organisations
CCUP	Child Care and Upgrading Programme
COS	Charity Organisation Society
COZ	Credit Organisation of Zambia
CPI	Corruption Perception Index
CSO	Civil Society Organisation
CSWE	Council on Social Work Education
DACs	District Agricultural Committees
DRC	Democratic Republic of the Congo
DSWO	District Social Welfare Officer
ECCED	Early Childhood Care Education and Development
EBZ	Export Board of Zambia
EPZs	Export Processing Zones
FBOs	Faith-Based Organisations
FDI	Foreign Direct Investment

FNDP	Fifth National Development Plan
FNDP	First National Development Plan
FSP	Food Security Programme
GDP	Gross Domestic Product
GDR	German Democratic Republic
GNI	Gross National Income
HBC	Home Based Care
HDA	Human Development Approach
HDI	Human Development Index
HIPC	Heavily Indebted Poor Country
HPI	Human Poverty Index
IFSW	International Federation of Social Workers
ILO	International Labour Organisation
IMF	International Monetary Fund
IMR	Infant Mortality Rate
IRHS	Indoor Residual House Spraying
JCTR	Jesuit Centre for Theological Reflection
LASF	Local Annuities Superannuation Fund
LDC	Least Developed Country
LME	London Metal Exchange
MAP	Millennium Partnership for African Recovery Programme
MCC	Member of the Central Committee
MDGs	Millennium Development Goals

MLGH	Ministry of Local Government and Housing
MMD	Movement for Multiparty Democracy
MSMEs	Micro, Small and Medium Enterprises
MTEF	Medium Term Expenditure Framework
NAPSA	National Pensions Scheme Authority
NCDP	National Commission for Development Planning
NCZ	Nitrogen Chemicals of Zambia
NEPAD	New Partnership for Africa's Development
NGOs	Non-Governmental Organisations
NGOCC	Non-Governmental Organisations Co-ordinating Committee
NIEC	National Import and Export Corporation
NRANC	Northern Rhodesian African National Congress
NSSN	National Social Safety Net
OAU	Organisation of African Unity
OECD	Organisation for Economic Co-operation and Development
OPS	Occupational Pension Scheme
OVC	Orphans and Vulnerable Children
OZA	Organisation of Zambians Abroad
PAM	Programme Against Malnutrition
PMCT	Prevention of Mother-to-Child Transmission
PMS	Paris Missionary Society
PPPs	Public Private Partnerships

PRSP	Poverty Reduction Strategy Paper
PSPF	Public Service Pension Fund
PSRP	Public Service Reform Programme
PUSH	Project Urban Self Help
RDA	Road Development Agency
RIF	Rural Investment Fund
RISDP	Regional Indicative Strategic Development Plan
SAP	Social Action Programme
SAP	Structural Adjustment Programme
SADCC	Southern African Development Co-ordinating Conference
SADC	Southern African Development Community
SEDB	Small Enterprise Development Board
SLF	Sustainable Livelihoods Framework
SWAP	Social Welfare Assistance Programme
TDCF	Tourism Development Credit Facility
TFSP	Targeted Food Security Pack
TIZ	Transparency International Zambia
TNDP	Transitional National Development Plan
UBZ	United Bus Company of Zambia
UDI	Unilateral Declaration of Independence
UNIP	United National Independence Party
UP	United Party
UPP	United Progressive Party

USAID	United States Agency for International Development
VCT	Voluntary Counselling and Testing
WCA	Washington Consensus on Agriculture
WHA	World Health Assembly
WSSD	World Summit on Sustainable Development
YWCA	Young Women's Christian Association
ZAFOD	Zambia Federation of the Disabled
ZANC	Zambia African National Congress
ZAPD	Zambia Agency for Persons with Disabilities
ZCTU	Zambia Congress of Trade Unions
ZDA	Zambia Development Agency
ZEPZA	Zambia Export Processing Zone Authority
ZHDR	Zambia Human Development Report
ZIC	Zambia Investment Centre
ZNBC	Zambia National Broadcasting Co-operation
ZNS	Zambia National Service
ZPA	Zambia Privatisation Agency

Currency conversion

Zambia's currency is the Kwacha. The current rate is 1 US $ = K 4,740 (as of September 2009).

LIST OF FIGURES, TABLES AND BOXES

Figure 1: Maslow's Hierarchy of Needs – Adapted from Boeree, 1998.. 7

Table 1: Three definitions of social policy relevant to LDCs and Zambia 26

Table 2: The scope of social policy adapted from Devereaux and Cook (2000) 26

Table 3: Key findings and recommendations of the 'drivers for change' study 108

Table 4: Approaches to policy analysis, adapted from Weiner and Vining (1992:4) 193

Box 1: The Public Welfare Assistance Scheme (PWAS) 102

Box 2: Case study 109

POSTSCRIPT

As this book was going to print, the Zambian President, Levy Patrick Mwanawasa, passed away in France at the age of 59, two months after suffering a stroke and collapsing at an African Union summit in Cairo, from which he was flown to Percy Military Hospital in Paris where he received medical attention. For Zambia this was a first, as the nation had not had an incumbent president dying before. Moreover, the country's two former presidents are still alive. The nation was traumatised and mourned its president for twenty-one days. In his last term, Mwanawasa had endeared himself to a cross-section of the Zambian society. With the economy on the upswing and hovering around 5 per cent annual growth (this was against a favourable global climate that saw the prices of copper rising to unprecedented levels), a zealous campaign against corruption unfolding and the president's genuine desire to see Zambians free from poverty, Mwanawasa's popularity ratings were at their highest prior to his death. On the question of Zimbabwe, Mwanawasa had broken ranks with other African leaders and vociferously criticised Mugabe's megalomaniac rule. The usual complicity of silence from African leaders while their compatriots plundered their countries and wantonly abused their people was seriously challenged by Mwanawasa.

Five months after Mwanawasa's passing, Mugabe continued to run Zimbabwe into the ground, with thousands of Zimbabweans dying from a cholera epidemic due to collapsed health, water and sanitation systems. He has continued to do so, and it remains to be seen how much the power-sharing arrangement with the opposition Movement for Democratic Change (MDC) will improve matters. What is sad about the Zimbabwean debacle is that the region is shouldering the problems of that country's failed politics and economic organisation. Diseases, vices like prostitution and crime, and much else have spilled over into neighbouring countries. African leaders, especially those of the Southern African Development Community (SADC), went on for long pussyfooting around Mugabe whilst Zimbabweans died unnecessarily, and then did no more than insist on the power-sharing arrangement leaving Mugabe with most of the power. True, perhaps Mugabe was once a respected icon of the liberation struggle, but he has now become a pariah, a human rights abuser and a moribund dictator. Whatever little respect he had from progressive Africans has been eroded. In essence, Mugabe is an embarrassment to Africa and it is high time that he goes.

It will not be just fanciful to suggest that Mugabe and his cronies must be indicted for crimes against humanity for what they have done to the Zimbabwean people. But Zimbabweans are partly to blame for this untenable situation. Where is the student movement? Where is the voice of organised labour? Where are the church and other faith-based organisations? Where is the groundswell of civil society? Instead of fighting Mugabe's regime, Zimbabweans simply run away from their country and expect the region to fight their battles. In Zambia, citizens had fought against the excesses of the one-party state and Kenneth Kaunda as well as Chiluba's Third Term Campaign. It is therefore a pity that Mwanawasa died before he could effectively engage Mugabe on his misrule. Mwanawasa was at the time of his death Chairperson of the SADC.

Mwanawasa's passing also had repercussions for the country's nascent democracy and the rule of law. As stipulated in the Zambian Constitution, elections had to be held within ninety days after the death of the country's president. With the nation in mourning and minimal resources at its disposal, the country went ahead and prepared for presidential elections. Mwanawasa's ruling Movement for Multiparty Democracy (MMD) had eight candidates that vied for the presidency, with the former Vice-President and acting president Rupiah Banda and the former Minister of Finance Ng'andu Magande emerging as front runners. Eventually, Rupiah Banda won the internal MMD contest. The opposition candidates were merely one-man shows with no internal democratic processes taking place in their parties. Michael Sata of the main opposition, the Patriotic Front (PF), Hakainde Hichilema of the United Party for National Development (UPND), and Godfrey Miyanda of the Heritage Party all threw in their candidacies for the presidency without having conventions in their own parties. In fact some of these parties remain quite autocratic as independent thinking is treated as treasonous amongst their ranks. Michael Sata expelled a number of his Members of Parliament because they had 'defied' him and participated in the National Constitutional Conference (NCC). This body aims to solicit views from all sections of Zambian society in order to arrive at an inclusive Constitution.

The elections were gruelling and almost followed the same pattern as those of 2006. The only difference was that Sata's PF almost gained an upper hand. The message was clear during the campaigns. Zambians were not given policy alternatives but outright hooliganism, mudslinging and name-calling. Sadly, the more these antics were exhibited, the more the supporters of both the ruling party and opposition parties, especially the PF, were amused. The idle youths seemed to be the most impressed with the unfolding election drama. It was quite chaotic as PF cadres hijacked trucks of the Independent Electoral Commission (IEC), supposedly to check for rigged ballot papers. In all such cases, it turned out that the trucks were carrying lamps and other equipment needed for the rural areas where basic infrastructure is simply inexistent. Now this is not acceptable at all. The PF's penchant for anarchy and disregard for the rule of law in the name of elections has got to end. These mobs cannot undermine the democratic processes at will and jeopardise the country's democracy that progressive Zambians fought so long for, with some paying the ultimate price of incarceration. Who are these self-appointed advocates of democracy who only emerge when it is election time? Where were they when the one-party state had oppressed the nation? What did they do when Chiluba was pillaging the nation's wealth?

It is important that some of these people who come to the fore to vie for leadership positions should be scrutinised in the light of their track records. For instance, did they ever volunteer any time for their country? Have they ever been engaged in any civic initiatives to better their country? Were they ever Cadets, Boy Scouts, Girl Guides, student leaders, young pioneers, religious and engaged youths, or have they ever put their lives on the line for their country? These are questions Zambians need to ask of their political leaders and cadres. In fact this discussion would like to venture and propose that certain political positions should not come with perks and hefty salaries. They should relate to citizens' responsibilities whereby their passion and love for their country are taken as cardinal attributes for such positions. For instance, Members of Parliament should only be provided logistical support by the state for development work in their constituencies. Then the country will be able to see who its true leaders are: people who are change agents and serve their constituencies and country selflessly.

After the elections it emerged that some young men and women really believed that Sata and the PF would give them money and houses. Obviously, outlandish promises were made by the PF during its campaigns. The youth are a captive audience as many remain semi-literate, idle, lazy or illiterate. These young people are mainly referred to as the 'lost generation' or 'Chiluba's children'. They grew up when education was not celebrated in the country and when standards in the sector had regressed to appalling levels, with many young people unable to read or write, even though some of their parents had gone to school. The former are now the present voters and, as things stand, they are the ones that are driven by mob rule and politics of the belly. Many of these young men and women celebrate Sata's promises of a better future; promises not backed up by any solid policy positions. However, the MMD also had not done enough to turn the tide of poverty around, especially the glaring inequalities that began to emerge with the country's positive economic growth. Pro-poor economic policies have not so far been implemented in the country, despite the successes in the economy.

In the end, Rupiah Bwezani Banda won the presidency with a slim margin of 40 per cent in comparison to Sata's 38 per cent. On 2 November he was sworn in as Zambia's fourth president. On his rule the jury is still out and until the next elections (2011) it would be futile to have an objective and systematic score-card for the new president. Banda has been in government before, during the reign of Kenneth Kaunda and the United National Independence Party (UNIP). Banda had an illustrious career as a diplomat. He was Zambia's Ambassador to Egypt in the late 1960s and the country's Permanent Representative to the United Nations in the 1970s. He also held the position of General Manager for certain parastatal companies, and was a Minister of Foreign Affairs as well as District Governor of Lusaka. He later resigned from UNIP and joined the MMD. He had retired to his farm in Chipata, in the Eastern Province of Zambia, when he was called up by Mwanawasa after the 2006 elections and appointed Vice-President of Zambia. Rupiah Banda was born in 1937 in Gwanda in Zimbabwe where his parents were migrant workers. Hailing from the Eastern Province, Banda is Zambia's second intellectual president. He studied Economic History at the University of Lund in Sweden and also obtained a Postgraduate Diploma in Development Studies at the University of Cambridge (actually the present MPhil in Development Studies that Cambridge is offering). All eyes are on Rupiah Banda to turn the country's fortunes around.

Another notable development (or policy blunder to be precise) during this period was the withdrawal of Zambia from hosting the All Africa Games because of 'lack of funds' and because the country could not 'build' infrastructure 'in time' before the onset of the games. Again, it must be reiterated here that there was even no need for the country and the government of the day to compete to host this continental event. Zambian politicians just do not seem to learn. They fail to understand the fact that a country cannot hold any major event if it does not have proper infrastructure. In addition, the road network is still below par; certain cities have perpetual traffic jams because of too few roads and outdated road systems, with no elevated highways or off-ramps for example. Dilapidated buildings and sport infrastructure are still the order of things.

However, this is not to say that nothing can be done. But without the right planning, innovative thinking and passion for the country's beauty, the task will remain monumental. For instance, Livingstone as the tourist capital could have been earmarked as the venue for this showpiece. It has comparative advantage and can still be developed at a faster rate without the headache of slums getting in the way. The ultra-modern stadium that has been designated for Ndola could have been built in Livingstone. Several other facilities could have been erected as auxiliaries of this modern stadium. The All Africa Games would have served as a critical platform for the country to offer itself as a regional gateway for the 2010 World Cup to be held in South Africa. For example, some teams could have been enticed to come to Zambia in order to acclimatise to the region's weather and train in Livingstone before the start of the World Cup. In the process, the country's tourism would have been boosted as Livingstone would also have been turned into a springboard for tourist activities in other regions of the country. Now what can Ndola offer comparatively in this regard? It seems planning and innovation will continue to elude Zambian politicians.

One major issue that also came to the fore in this recent period was the candid and forthright report of the Auditor General relating to Zambian missions abroad. It noted disapprovingly the misapplication and misappropriation of funds in these missions. This was indeed a very laudable exercise and a breath of fresh air in regard to this matter. However, the rot had set in a long time ago in the UNIP era, when people were sent to head missions not because of their competencies, but because they were either relatives or friends of political leaders. Therefore, most Zambian diplomats were and are still unable to understand what their main roles are supposed to be in such settings. Rarely does one hear of Zambian missions abroad showcasing the country's potential in mining, tourism, sport, or the arts and culture. One never hears of educational or cultural exchanges being sought after by mission officials, for instance. Further, officials in these missions have not been known to strike deals with universities abroad relating to student exchanges where young Zambians could go overseas on short visits and get the needed exposure to help them build their country and, conversely, international students could also be encouraged to come to the country and have firsthand experience of the issues that confront a developing country like Zambia. However, the truth of the matter is that these missions need to be reduced.

When this book was going to press, the world began to experience unprecedented upheavals in the financial sector that had a domino effect on the social, economic and political arenas of various countries. Since then, Zambia's economy has come under threat. The ripple effects of the global financial crisis have led to the plummeting of revenue from the country's main export, copper, and also the closing down of various mines. The resultant job losses also mean severe declines in human development as various households grapple with the prospect of no income. Thus far, the minimal economic gains that were made with the help of the 'copper boom' are on the verge of being wiped out as the financial meltdown continues to unravel. It is almost déjà vu, recalling the financial crunch of 1973. The question to ask therefore is: how many times is the song of diversifying the economy going to be sung in Zambia?

In concluding this section, it must be re-emphasised that Zambia needs a total transformation in order to move from its state of decay and lethargy. A developmental state that is executed by competent people is the surest way of taking Zambia forward in matters of development. Until that time when the country's institutions are fortified, when policies are well thought-out and followed through, when some mediocre citizens and pirates are completely removed from the political arena; and when Zambians, especially young people, work hard and exhibit an unyielding work ethic, the country's challenges are not going to diminish at all. Levy Mwanawasa tried his best to redeem Zambia from hopelessness and despair. May his soul rest in peace.

I must record with sadness that Professor Bill Mitchell passed away when this book had just been printed. Prof. Mitchell was indeed a motivator and scholar par excellence. He had enthusiastically embraced this project every step of the way. He will be sorely missed; may his soul rest in peace.

Finally, when this book's re-print was taking place, former President Frederick Chiluba, was cleared of all counts of corruption and of embezzling the country out of US$ 500 000 while he was in office. This was after a six year legal battle that had been instituted by Mwanawasa's administration. His two accomplices were not lucky as they were both imprisoned for five years respectively. This judgment did not go well with many people and raised a lot of ire amongst the populace. Since Chiluba was found guilty by the London court that was held in circuit in Zambia, Zambians were of the view that his exoneration by a Zambian court was purely on a technicality. He had been ordered by the London court to repay the US$ 46 million of public money he had misappropriated during his rule. Some Zambians felt that the Zambian government was not so enthusiastic in registering the judgment in the Zambian High Court. This issue has raised eyebrows and is making people fear that something sinister is afoot. Despite Chiluba's flimsy remonstrations that the judgment is not binding because it is driven by so-called imperialistic designs and undermines Zambia's sovereignty, many Zambians still take comfort from the fact that it had taken a Briton to hand down a just and fair judgment in the country's favour. Indeed, Judge Peter Smith had responded to the cries of many Zambians, who had suffered Chiluba's misrule, which was characterised by an audacious plunder of national resources.

PREAMBLE

Social Policy and Human Development in Zambia is a book intended to contribute towards a growing body of knowledge on development-related issues in the country. It begins by delving into the theoretical debates relating to social policy and human development, before situating the two processes in the context of a Least Developed Country (LDC). Through this undertaking, attempts are also made to show how social policy and human development take on unique features in these environs, by comparison with other societies such as emerging economies or developed countries. Zambia is an LDC and, because of this reality, is confronted by specific development challenges, notably related to meeting citizens' needs. Of critical importance, and as a point of departure, it is necessary to note that Zambia is in Africa, a continent covered with socio-economic and political hurdles. Although many of these impediments are a direct result of colonial domination, a good number are self-inflicted. In the main, Zambia is typified by various forms of social deficit. Overriding all existing social problems in the country is poverty that has become extremely entwined with the livelihoods of many Zambians, especially in the preceding two decades.

Recently, Zambia experienced a surge of energy in the economy after decades of negative economic growth. After almost thirty years, the country even managed to exhibit a single digit inflation rate of 7.9 per cent (as of October 2006) as well as 6 per cent growth rate in the Gross Domestic Product (GDP). The local currency, the kwacha, also strengthened in value against major convertible currencies, such as the United States dollar. Furthermore, Zambia managed to attain what is known as the Heavily Indebted Poor Countries (HIPC) completion point in April 2005, making it possible for the bulk of the country's external debt to be written-off altogether, in line with the benchmarks set by the G8 nations, the IMF and the World Bank. This meant that money which serviced Zambia's external debt (running into billions of US dollars), could now be used to shore up the country's social services, especially health and education services. To this end, health 'user-fees' in the rural areas have been abolished and primary school education is now free. There has also been an inflow of Foreign Direct Investment (FDI) into the country in the areas of mining, agriculture and tourism. In real terms, GDP growth increased from 3.3 per cent in 2002 to 5.1 per cent in 2003, exceeding the Poverty Reduction Strategy Paper (PRSP) target of 4 per cent. Consequently, real per capita income increased by 2.6 per cent in 2003 from 2.2 per cent in

2002. Economic activity continued to improve in the first half of 2004, with output in the key sectors of agriculture, mining, manufacturing, construction and tourism registering an increase (Government of the Republic of Zambia, 2004).

Politically, the country seems to have stabilised and has successfully conducted its fourth consecutive multi-party elections without major upheavals. With regard to governance, the former president and certain government officials were charged with corruption and abuse of office shortly after President Levy Mwanawasa took over office in 2002. The said individuals are still answering to these charges in the courts of law. Also, at the time of writing, the Zambian president announced that oil and gas deposits had been discovered in the North-Western Province, close to the Angolan border.[1] However, it should be borne in mind that although there is a positive swing in the economic sphere, the benefits have not as yet percolated down to the mass of the people. It may take several years to reverse the prevailing negative economic tide in the country.

As a starting-point, social policy in this work is regarded as a vehicle that can be used by governments to uplift people's standards of living, while human development is taken as both an operational framework and a desired end – a state devoid of social distress due to poverty, hunger, destitution, homelessness, disease and other ills. As an operational framework, human development can be articulated by both governments and organs of civil society. In this way, the Human Development Approach (HDA) is taken as a process that can also inform social policy and proffer solutions aimed at reducing life-threatening situations in a country. It is suggested that once a country's human development profile has been raised, through instruments like social policy among others, its citizens will have significantly risen above social deprivation and allowed to function at higher levels of existence. Furthermore, social policy and human development are pitted as springboards for the attainment of social justice and equality, for without them, people's wellbeing will simply remain a pipedream. This work also places great emphasis on the role of social policy and human development in bolstering public institutions that will in turn guarantee both social and economic justice, particularly in LDCs. Needless to say, it is not merely the creation of conditions for raising of people's living circumstances that should matter in these contexts, but also an ability to sustain them over generations. Usually, this will depend on a country's available resources or assets.

Indeed, society's ability to enhance human wellbeing through time depends on choices made by individuals, firms, communities and governments on how to use and transform their assets (World Bank, 2003). Arriving at these choices is not an easy feat at all. Rational and logical choices are quite difficult to attain in LDCs, for instance, where there are high levels of maladministration, illiteracy, poverty, ignorance and disease. In most cases, the majority of people are either not enlightened enough to easily make such choices or else so encumbered by poverty that they remain occupied with only one task: survival. Thus an anomaly arises, where many people wrongly believe that governments (which in most cases remain ineffectual due to bad governance) should provide a panacea to all prevailing social ills in society. Unfortunately, people do not see that it is their initial responsibility to chart their own destinies, even though it is recognised in this work that the state[2] should complement individual efforts by strongly intervening in the social sector.

Rarely do people in such settings prudently and steadfastly organise themselves in order to better their lives. With such prevailing attitudes people may, for instance, not strive to educate themselves or their children, work hard and learn to save for a rainy day. This understanding then brings into focus the question of citizenship. Aristotle (384-322 BC) observed that citizenship was the power to take part in the deliberative or judicial administration of any state. Citizens were distinguished from other inhabitants, such as resident aliens and slaves. Following his mentor, Plato, Aristotle regarded *education* and *mental development* as crucial in moulding citizenship.

Nevertheless, countries like Zambia have huge armies of illiterates for myriad reasons, with poverty taking the lead. These masses cannot effectively execute their citizenry duties owing to poor intellectual capacities because of, among other things, lack of education. Also, in least developed societies such as Zambia, individuals still heavily subscribe to primordial or parochial identities as opposed to affiliations based upon logic or rational thought. For example, when citizens are accorded an opportunity to choose political leaders such as a president, many still feel that the person from their tribe or region will be best suited for the position. Thus, tribalism and not the merit system is still the preferred yardstick in choosing political leaders in many LDCs like Zambia. The driving force in this equation still remains illiteracy. Electoral processes are somehow window-dressing exercises as the electorate is unenlightened.

What is called a 'crisis of post-colonial citizenship' remains a real threat to nation-building in Zambia and other African countries. In many respects, the post-colonial citizen has continuities with the colonial order's categorisation of the 'natives'. In this way, an individual pays more allegiance to the tribe than the nation-state. Thus, the identities that were constructed by colonial state-formations actually shape the dilemmas of post-colonial citizenship (Mamdani, 1986). It is also questionable whether people in LDCs or Zambia can truly execute their rights as citizens when they are constantly weighed down by social stress. For example, hungry people may not always see beyond their hunger and probably should not be expected to become critical examiners of intricate policy matters, or even engage politicians on substantive development issues.

Thus, in most cases, politicians take advantage of this situation in LDCs like Zambia, as there remains little room for critical engagement on the part of the hungry masses. Jean-François Bayart's (1993) insightful work *L'Etat en Afrique: La politique du ventre* – literally translated as *The State in Africa: the Politics of the Belly* – lucidly captures the brazen greed and corruption in African politics which have become deciding factors in the manner in which a country is governed. The overriding legitimising element in the political arena is 'the power of the big man' which depends to some extent on his ability to 'feed' his supporters. In Zambia, the Second and Third Republics[3] epitomised this form of politics, whereby presidents ingeniously crafted a system of patronage in order to entrench themselves in power, whilst impoverishing many Zambians in the process. Therefore, food or promises of better opportunities to a selected few became indispensable political weapons. Politics of this nature still exist in Zambia and it is only hoped that they could be rooted out.

The arguments in this book primarily rest on an analysis of Zambia's socio-economic and political factors, and how they influence the human development situation in the country. Attempts are also made to show how these circumstances impinge upon the way ordinary people are able to cope with social problems or function optimally. It is from this position that discussions unfold, basically from an understanding that a country's social wellbeing is essentially heavily influenced by its prevailing economic and political systems. It is further argued that, among other things, socio-economic and political forces are critical in determining the way in which social policy also takes root in a country. Encapsulated in the political domain is also the notion of ideology. In this work, ideology is perceived as a very important tool aimed at charting the development course of a particular country. Arguably, many governments' development plans are guided by some form of ideology, which is usually informed by the values of the ruling party. Zambia's post-colonial history cannot be separated from the heavy influences of ideology and this book will touch on the issue, so as to highlight the manner in which it shaped matters of national development.

Ideally, human wellbeing should always remain a critical component of any country's development designs and pursuits. To this end, serious and caring governments will constantly be preoccupied with finding appropriate strategies that support human development in their countries. When people's needs[4] are not met by governments (taken here as custodians of citizens' wellbeing), social discord will inevitably ensue. Therefore, it is imperative that governments ensure that satisfactory conditions exist in society, where people can make use of available opportunities to live fulfilling lives. Where these living circumstances are non-existent, then institutions have to be created in order to empower ordinary people so that they take charge of their lives. How can this be done? It goes without saying that elected governments (though this is not always the case in Africa) must create enabling environments in the true sense of the word, for all citizens to engage effectively in their country's productive processes. Building of schools (so that people are educated and guaranteed upward social mobility, and unshackled from ignorance), as well as hospitals and clinics (to combat diseases so that people are healthy and participate in wealth-creating activities), and expanding the agricultural base (to fight hunger so that the nation is healthy and productive), all need to be prioritised by governments in LDCs.

The foregoing could be used as linchpins of human development that envisages, *inter alia*, the strengthening of people's capabilities. A government's ability in meeting people's basic needs is a delicate and intricate assignment that requires adroitness and commitment from both politicians and technocrats. For too long the problems of LDCs, Africa and Zambia in particular, have seemingly remained intractable solely because of the incompetence of politicians and policy-makers. All too often, their mediocrity has been reflected in the manner in which society deals with social problems. Therefore, these people's responsibilities in the light of national development should not be taken lightly at all.

Clearly, the decisions made by politicians are critical in determining a country's human development trajectory because they have the power to regulate, to legislate, to tax, to set and enforce the 'rules of the game'. Politicians control this power and discharge the fundamental responsibilities of the state. Similarly, policy-makers are also influential as they exercise the power of the state by regulating entry, enforcing standards, and determining the conditions under which providers receive public funds (World Bank, 2003). Fundamentally, politicians' and policy-makers' interventions should be geared towards elevating and sustaining people's livelihoods. Sadly, this has not been the case in LDCs, in most parts of Africa and in Zambia.[5] The view upheld in this text is that the primary responsibility of politicians and policy-makers is to create conditions that allow citizens to live meaningful and fruitful lives in their country. Once this precondition has been met, citizens will be enabled to obtain most of their basic needs and begin functioning optimally. In short, people will be unencumbered by social maladies and also be allowed to effectively participate in their country's development. They can become more innovative and dwell on some of the aesthetic aspects of life, instead of constantly struggling to put food on the table.

Without a doubt, when a country's populace is unable to meet its needs, then it will become susceptible to social perils that will make it vulnerable and dysfunctional. A country in this state of existence, resulting from lack of social resources or assets, cannot be expected to make any headway in socio-economic development. It is thus imperative that there exists a critical mass of individuals in a country like Zambia who maintain living standards above the threshold of want and deprivation. In short, they should be able to meet their needs. It is only after this situation has transpired that citizens can become active and energetic drivers of their country's progress. In the classic work of Abraham Maslow (1908-70), needs were presented as preceding each other in terms of importance and were visualised through a pyramid. One of the many interesting things Maslow noticed while working with monkeys, early in his career, was that some needs take precedence over others. For example, if you are hungry and thirsty, you will tend to try to take care of the thirst first (Boeree, 1998). The following illustration highlights Maslow's explication of needs.

Figure 1: Maslow's Hierarchy of Needs – Adapted from Boeree, 1998

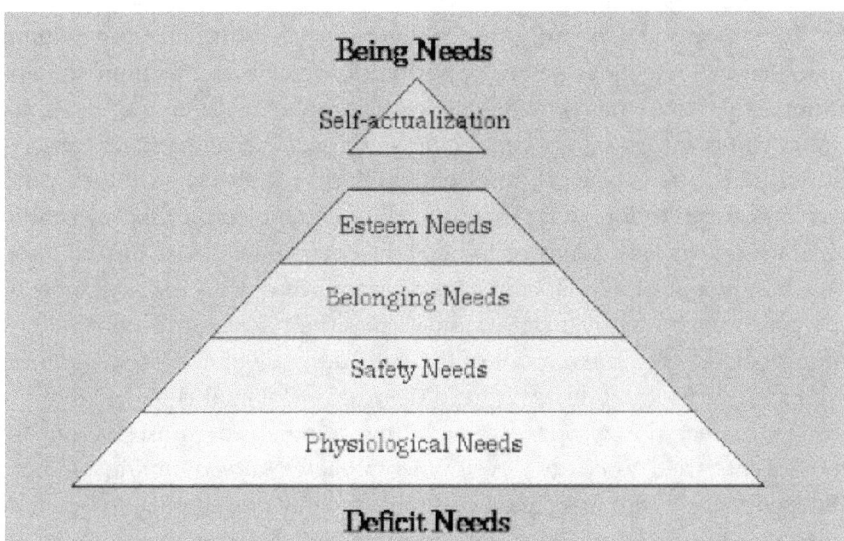

Accordingly, the *physiological needs* will include those we live for such as oxygen, water, protein, salt, sugar, calcium, and other minerals and vitamins. When the physiological needs are largely taken care of, the *safety and security needs* come into play. People then become increasingly interested in finding safe circumstances, stability and protection (Boeree, 1998). The *love and belonging needs* will emerge when physiological needs and safety needs are, by and large, taken care of. People begin to feel the need for friends, a sweetheart, children; affectionate relationships in general, even a sense of community. Next, they begin to look for a little self-esteem. Furthermore, Maslow identified two forms of *esteem needs:* a lower need and a higher one. The lower one results in the respect of others, for status, fame, glory, recognition, attention, reputation, appreciation, dignity, and even dominance (Boeree, 1998). The higher form involves the desire for self-respect, including such feelings as confidence, competence, achievement, mastery, independence, and freedom. Note that this is the 'higher' form because, unlike the respect of others, once you have self-respect, it is a lot harder to lose (Boeree, 1998). *Self-actualisation needs* are those that do not involve balance or homeostasis. Once engaged, they continue to be felt. In fact, they are likely to become stronger as we 'feed' them. They involve the continuous desire to fulfil potential, to 'be all that you can be'. They are a matter of becoming the most complete, the fullest, 'you', hence the term 'self-actualisation'

(Boeree, 1998). Many people are still grappling with the first set of needs in LDCs such as Zambia.

Needs can only be fully met if there is an existing and functioning state that can engender ample opportunities for citizens to flourish. Unfortunately, Africa has only been good at producing a litany of dysfunctional states: *failed states, kleptocratic states and predatory states*, among others. The pitfalls of most post-colonial African states should then prod us to ask the question: what should be the roles and responsibilities of the African state as it endeavours to meet the needs of citizens? In partly answering the question, this book takes cognisance of the historical roots of the post-colonial African state. It notes that the roles and responsibilities of most states were carved out of the political struggle for independence, when various formations sought to overthrow colonial rule. In attempting to correct the wrongs wrought by colonialism, most nationalist movements tried to create developmental states[6] after winning political independence. What this meant was that the state played an active part in the social and economic development of the nation. The state also became the main provider of social services aimed at raising the quality of life of the people. At the time, the modern private sector barely existed in Africa, and where it was present, it neither had the capacity nor the will to embark on huge social and economic development projects. Zambia also followed this same path to freedom and later on embraced socialism as its guiding ideology.[7]

It is well known that colonialism disadvantaged African people in socio-economic development. For generations, they were neglected and did not have access to health care, education and other forms of social protection. Owing to this situation, a statist approach was virtually unavoidable in many African countries after independence. The state had to intervene heavily in the economy so as to change the deplorable living conditions of ordinary people. Independence was the dawn of a new era for many Africans, and governments responded to the people's expectations by fast-tracking development projects in their respective countries, Zambia included. But along the way, after military coups, tribal/ethnic conflicts, corruption, nepotism and outright greed, Africa began to slide backwards in matters of human development. Single-party regimes (such as Zambia adopted) took their toll and led to bad forms of governance that ultimately created negative living conditions in Africa. In this quagmire, visionary or quality leadership[8] was a rare commodity. A direct product of this chaotic political situation in Africa was the rise of neo-colonialism in the guise of 'development aid', primarily from multilateral development agencies and governments in the West. Many countries in Africa, including LDCs like Zambia, had unwisely borrowed money from the international lending institutions and then accumulated huge foreign debts that bound them in servile types of relationships. This meant that the same 'donors' could dispense their 'adjustment prescriptions' willy-nilly. The infamous Structural Adjustment Programme (SAP) propagated by the World Bank and the IMF wreaked havoc in most of sub-Saharan Africa. By the beginning of the 21st century, the roles and responsibilities of the African state had been greatly reduced.[9]

The role of the state in development cannot be understated. It is held responsible for the wellbeing of its citizens,[10] and traditionally this responsibility takes the form of social services (Mafeje, 2001). Even though citizens should be the ones to first develop themselves, it would be unjust for a state to abdicate its obligation of guaranteeing social welfare in a country. Thus, states have a profound role to play in meeting the needs of citizens. Dasgupta (1990), cited in Hawthorn (1993), points out that a standard expectation from states is that they should provide not only for the security of their subjects against attack from each other and from other states, but also furnish the conditions in which citizens can maximise their wellbeing. It is these conditions, of security and wellbeing more generally, that we can expect any modern state to try to maximise. The state can also be perceived as an arena in which conflicting interests compete for scarce resources. It then becomes a means of managing competition so that the state is recognised as a legitimate way to settle such disputes (Smith, 1996). But when a state becomes predatory or kleptocratic, like Zaire (now the Democratic Republic of the Congo, DRC), under Mobutu, this creates another situation, whereby citizens have to fend for themselves and lead extremely perilous lifestyles.

The 20th century passed with resounding progress for most of the African LDCs and for Zambia individually, especially in the 1960s, but its final years were eclipsed by their dismal failures in the social, economic and political arenas. Africans in general, and Zambians in particular, have been crying out for a new order: one that is charted by a visionary and committed leadership and epitomises functioning states, abiding by the tenets of good governance, centred around a common vision of progress and human dignity. The crystallisation of the New Partnership for Africa's Development (NEPAD)[11] by key African political actors, and its subsequent endorsement by the African Union (AU) and civil society formations on the continent, as well as the call for an African Renaissance (primarily from the former South African President Thabo Mbeki), all underline the desire for a new progressive dispensation in Africa, on both the political and economic fronts. This position echoes the Pan-Africanist rallying call of early independence protagonists like Kwame Nkrumah, the first President of Ghana. It also mirrors the desire for regional co-operation and development, and the quest for international solidarity in an increasingly polarised and unequal global climate. The above mentioned factors are treated in this work as critical requisites for Africa's development and its eventual emancipation from the bondage of neo-colonialism. Further, the importance of regional groupings in helping shape internal conditions of wellbeing in specific countries is taken into account. Therefore, the role of the SADC in propelling Zambia's human development goals is regarded as very important by this discussion. Other exogenous forces, for instance globalisation, also have profound influences over local developments, and this process will be given some attention in the present examination.

This book has also been written at a time when the international community, via the United Nations, has ratified the Millennium Development Goals[12] in recognition of the need for global social and economic justice. Zambia is signatory to the MDGs and over the past two years there has been an increasing level of commitment on the part of the Zambian government,[13] Civil Society Organisations (CSOs) and co-operating partners to create a conducive environment aimed at realising the MDGs (Government of the Republic of Zambia, 2005). However, there are already indications that the country will not realise the MDGs in the set time. Nevertheless, strategies aimed at enhancing social and economic wellbeing took heavy flak towards the end of the last century when scholars, multilateral aid agencies, and some governments attacked the centrality of the state in socio-economic matters. Such positions were heavily influenced by an ascending neo-liberal doctrine around the globe, signalling what some overzealously referred to as the end of history (see Fukuyama, 1992).[14]

In the same period there was also fast-paced globalisation that was not favourable to poor countries, but only exacerbated their exploitation by the already rich and developed North. With rising waves of antipathy towards the interventionist state, other global trends emerged: unchecked privatisation of national industries, the rolling back of the state in social service provision and the introduction of user-fees for social services such as education and health. There were also attendant cutbacks in social investments and the liberalisation of trade regimes. Zambia and other LDCs could barely manage to protect citizens against the shocks that emanated from economic austerity measures imposed by Western financial institutions and globalisation. Despite this unfair situation, LDCs, especially in Africa, were not resolute enough in breaking their dependency on the West that was initially created by colonialism. The main problem with Africa's post-independence regimes was that there was little attention paid to growth and productive forces. Almost everywhere in Africa, the post-independence experience has been associated with declining productivity by national economies, which were ignored by rhetoric or placed at the door of foreign forces (Turock, 1991).

Zambia has had its fair share of human tragedies and perhaps the country has now come full circle in matters of human development. With hundreds of thousands of people dying from curable diseases like malaria and many decimated by the HIV/AIDS pandemic in the last century, the untold miseries experienced by Zambians cannot even be quantified. Furthermore, wrong-headed policies, corruption, tribalism and nepotism, outright plunder of national resources, perpetrated by politicians and policy-makers, slid the economy into the doldrums, and resulted in countless deaths due to hunger, disease and depression.

As Zambians begin to settle down, after participating in the elections of September 2006, the crucial question to be posed is: are they willing to collectively take stock of their past and ascertain which route they want to follow in rebuilding their shattered economy and, just as important, the social fabric, whilst unified by a common purpose and not by sectarian interests? Probably, through self-reflection, the citizenry, civil society structures and government could begin to offer workable alternatives in order to move the country forward. A proactive citizenry that is well informed or has access to information and is able to process that information so as to make the right choices would be ideal for a country like Zambia. Sadly, this has not been the case so far.[15] As certain issues are elucidated in the book, it is hoped that the reader will be able to arrive at a clear understanding of the critical importance of social policy and human development processes, and also the manner in which these can bolster the quality of life of Zambians. It is envisaged that the individual will also be provided with some theoretical tools so as to understand the three-pronged relationship of: social, economic and political forces, and how these three can either support or hinder human development.

In most of the book's arguments there flows one theme: 'prudent policy decisions are needed to steer Zambia from its current socio-economic crisis'. For instance, the nature of the Zambian economy requires urgent remedying. Zambia's economy is so distorted that all of the commodities that sustain life are very expensive and beyond the reach of the ordinary masses. There is no reprieve at all when it comes to the pricing of essential commodities. Even in Western Europe, the cradle of neo-liberalism, food is still subsidised by the state via the farmers that produce the commodity. Even in expensive cities like Paris, London or Geneva it is possible to find affordable food that the majority of people can purchase. Added to this distortion is the question of tax.[16] Zambian workers pay up to 30 per cent in personal income tax while corporate tax is pegged at 35 per cent and value added tax at 17.5 per cent. Customs duty on imported equipment is in the high twenties per cent (Reuters, 2006). To add insult to injury, the revenue collected from tax is not even visible in terms of improved social services or infrastructure development. Also, by comparison with neighbouring countries, most basic commodities like food, transport, accommodation and even fuel are just unrealistically expensive.[17] Food, which is an important catalyst for human development, is too expensive for most Zambians. Many people remain hungry, malnourished and unable to play any important role in developing Zambia. So, despite policy pronouncements made at the political level, the test is how these will be translated into tangible actions aimed at addressing these human development dilemmas. In response to these concerns, the Zambian President, in an address to the National Assembly after his re-election, promised a tax review in 2007 that would be driven by tax incentives for rural investment with a bias towards agriculture as well as enterprises employing women and the young.

No sooner had these assertions been made by the president than the IMF announced some disturbing news in the light of Zambia's taxation. The IMF's Fiscal Affairs Department (FAD) argued in its October 2006 report that there were several weaknesses in Zambia's tax system that needed to be corrected. It recommended that the exemption from Value Added Tax (VAT) of *books, magazines, newspapers, food and agricultural products, water and sewerage, domestic transportation* and *mosquito nets* (emphasis added), among others, should be ended. There was also a proposal to change the Pay As You Earn (PAYE) income tax (*The Post*, 2006). Many Zambians condemned this short-sighted proposal by the IMF which again wants to increase the misery of Zambians at a time when they should be rewarded, after their severe belt-tightening to achieve the HIPC completion point. Arguably, the IMF and the World Bank are partly to blame for Zambia's present haemorrhaged socio-economic state. Does the IMF want to erase the minimal gains that have been made in the last couple of years? As observed earlier, the European Union is still subsidising agriculture and thus food prices are still very low in these countries. Now, why should a country such as Zambia, with so much hunger and unemployment, be told to do otherwise? This is simply not fair. The country has strictly adhered to the IMF conditions for over fifteen years and has only poverty and destitution to show for it.

This book is patterned in the following manner: Chapter 1 begins with discussions that focus on theoretical debates pertaining to social policy and human development, in order to ground forthcoming chapters in an analytical framework. Chapter 2 picks up on the issue of social change and examines its transformative qualities. It also tries to illustrate how social change can become an important catalyst in the development process, especially for impoverished countries like Zambia. The chapter also introduces selected theories of development for scrutiny. Chapter 3 highlights the historical development of social policy in Zambia. Chapter 4 then contextualises social policy and human development processes in an LDC set-up, so as to enable the reader to have a firm grasp of the complex nature of least developed settings, especially when it comes to meeting people's needs. Also, the chapter begins to locate Zambia in its regional context, Southern Africa. Chapter 5 pays particular attention to Zambia's human development imperatives such as social services, rural development, civil liberties and equal opportunities, as well as focusing on vulnerabilities and populations at risk. Chapter 6 begins to look at the process of monitoring and evaluation by highlighting its outcomes and impacts in regard to human development. It also introduces a dimension of policy analysis. Chapter 7 is more concerned with issues of praxis and how certain helping professions such as social work can implement strategies that bring about human wellbeing in Zambia. Chapter 8 then concludes the discussion with summaries and considerations for the future.

Notes

[1] These political announcements must be treated with caution. Even if the oil deposits are commercially viable and drilling kicks off, it remains to be seen how the oil revenues will be used for human development and the fight against poverty. The African story of oil turning into a curse is all too familiar and therefore, there is need for prudent decisions on the part of the Zambian government, as regards this issue, once it materialises.

[2] In this work, the state is taken as an entity that uses government to effect development, and also meets the needs of citizens. It is not this

work's intention to engage in a discussion regarding the existence or non-existence of the state in Africa. In this regard, government is seen as superimposed by the state. The government becomes one of several instruments that the state relies on to govern a country.

3   See chapter 2.

4   *Human needs* are those resources people require to survive as individuals and to function appropriately in their society. Needs vary, depending on the specific individual and the situation, and include the following: sufficient food, clothing and shelter for physical survival; a safe environment and adequate health care for treatment, protection from illness and accidents; relationships with other people that provide a sense of being cared for, of being loved and belonging also play an important role in this regard. Opportunities for emotional, intellectual, and spiritual growth and development, including opportunities for individuals to make use of their innate talents and interests, are also critical. Lastly, opportunities for participation in making decisions about the common life of one's own society, including the ability to make appropriate contributions to the maintenance of life, are important factors in the meeting of needs (Johnson et al., 1997:4).

5   Political power is important as it can also be used to affect another's behaviour by some form of coercion or inducement: the carrot or the stick may back power and it may be exercised in a positive or negative fashion (Ball, 1993). Thus, political leaders may acquire compliance with their wishes by promising wealth or honours to their supporters, or they may threaten to deny such rewards to their opponents *(Ibid.)*. Hence the state's political machinery will be at the disposal of politicians, to control and define state agendas on behalf of the citizens. This line of thought can be traced back to the thesis of the *Social Contract* articulated by Jean-Jacques Rousseau, in which such a contract becomes the foundation of political association. In this regard the Social Contract is necessary and sufficient for establishing a society capable of sustaining moral agency. Politics are therefore an indispensable basis for a distinctively human existence (Levin, 1987).

6   The developmental state is conceived as a state able to marshal resources aimed at creating equitable social and economic systems in Africa. Mkandawire (1998:1) is of the opinion that the 'developmental state' has two components, *ideological* and *structural*. It is this

ideology-structure nexus that distinguishes developmental states from other forms of state. In terms of ideology, such a state is essentially one whose ideological underpinning is 'developmentalist' in that it conceives its 'mission' as that of ensuring economic development, usually interpreted to mean high rates of accumulation and industrialisation.

7. Zambia's brand of Socialism was known as Humanism. It was a blend of the Scientific Socialism of Eastern Europe and African Socialism propagated in the 1960s, notably by Tanzania's President Julius Nyerere. The state controlled most of the economic activities in the country, and also guaranteed free social services as well.

8. Mwaipaya (1980) has an interesting thesis based on identification of quality leadership and how this type of leadership can effect national development. He makes the following observation: 'The significance of quality leadership is that it engages in rational and objective thinking and tries to make policies that are not far removed from the reality of human nature. Indeed, where as it is often consistent in its deliberations, mediocre leadership usually acts either without following any kind of objective manner or reasoning or simply follows the dictates of feelings, passions, and sentiments of special vested interests.' Quality leadership is extremely important in offering solutions to Africa's development challenges. It is disconcerting to note that most African countries have been led for decades by mediocre leaders, who lack intellectual depth and political will. This thesis was extended by Noyoo (1999), who also linked it to the notion of good governance and national social development in Zambia: 'Good governance is not only essential but pivotal to the processes of economic and social development. It has to be organic and intrinsic to a country's socio-political, cultural, psychological and economic environs.'

9. If the state was given a central role in earlier views of the process of development in Africa, the situation changed dramatically in the late 1970s and 1980s. The African state is today the most demonised social institution in Africa, vilified for its weaknesses, its over-extension, its interference with the smooth functioning of the markets, its repressive character, its dependence on foreign powers, its ubiquity, its absence, etc. The state, once the cornerstone of development, is now the millstone around otherwise efficient markets (Mkandawire, 1998).

10. For Mafeje (2001:15), it is the whole issue of poverty alleviation. 'Putting aside the question of whether we can with equanimity speak of

the state in sub-Saharan Africa, it would appear that what is at stake, is poverty alleviation and the role therein of the powers that be, irrespective of whether in common parlance they pass as states or governments.'

11 NEPAD is a pledge by African leaders, based on a common vision and a firm, shared conviction that they have a pressing duty to eradicate poverty and to place their countries, both individually and collectively, on a path of sustainable growth and development and, at the same time, to participate actively in the world economy and body politic. The programme is anchored on the determination of Africans to extricate themselves and the continent from the malaise of underdevelopment and exclusion in a globalising world (NEPAD, 2001:1). NEPAD was adopted as Africa's development framework in 2001 by the then Organisation of African Unity (OAU), which changed to the African Union (AU) in the following year. Initially, NEPAD was conceived as two separate development strategies known as the Millennium Partnership for the African Recovery Programme (MAP), which was driven by Presidents Thabo Mbeki of South Africa, Olusegun Obasanjo of Nigeria and Abdelaziz Bouteflika of Algeria, and the OMEGA plan for Africa that was spearheaded by President Abdoulaye Wade of Senegal. These two plans were merged into one strategy known as the New African Initiative at the OAU Summit in Lusaka, in July 2001.

12 The eight Millennium Development Goals (MDGs), with a target date of 2015, form a blueprint agreed to by all the world's countries and leading development institutions. They have galvanised unprecedented efforts to meet the needs of the world's poorest (United Nations, 2005). Specifically, they aim to:

• Reduce by half the proportion of people living on less than a dollar a day.

• Reduce by half the proportion of people who suffer from hunger.

• Ensure that all boys and girls complete a full course of primary schooling.

• Eliminate gender disparity in primary and secondary education preferably by 2005, and at all levels by 2015.

• Reduce by two-thirds the mortality rate among children under five.

• Reduce by three-quarters the maternal mortality ratio.

- Halt and begin to reverse the spread of HIV/AIDS.
- Halt and begin to reverse the incidence of malaria and other major diseases.

[13] For instance, in the area of poverty reduction, the Zambian government tries to create what it terms as *a supportive environment* and sees the following as crucial steps towards poverty reduction:

- Integrate the principles of sustainable development into country policies and programmes, and reverse loss of environmental resources.
- Reduce by half the proportion of people without sustainable access to safe drinking water.
- Develop further an open trading and financial system that is rules-based, predictable and non-discriminatory, including a commitment to good governance, development and poverty reduction, nationally and internationally.
- Address the least developed countries' special needs, including tariffs, and quota-free access for their exports; enhanced debt relief for heavily indebted poor countries; cancellation of official bilateral debt; and more generous official development assistance for countries committed to poverty reduction.
- Address the special needs of landlocked and small-island developing states.
- Deal comprehensively with developing countries' debt problems through national and international measures to make debt sustainable in the long term.
- In co-operation with the developing countries, develop decent and productive work for the youth.
- In co-operation with pharmaceutical companies, provide access to affordable essential drugs in developing countries.
- In co-operation with the private sector, make available the benefits of new technologies, especially information and communications technologies.
- An expressed commitment to address the high levels of poverty through various initiatives including the Poverty Reduction Strategy Paper (PRSP), the Transitional National Development Plan (TNDP), and the Fifth National Development Plan (FNDP).

- The establishment of and adherence to a Medium Term Expenditure Framework (MTEF), which programmes expenditure prioritisation on a three-year basis, developed through a consultative process to ensure transparency and ownership of the budgeting process.

- The Sectoral Development Plan (SDP), which emphasises the importance of the decentralised approach in development and is likely to reduce poverty among Zambians.

- The willingness of the creditor nations to forgive 100 per cent of Zambia's debt, as announced at the Gleneagles Summit in July 2005. Since the Heavily Indebted Poor Countries (HIPC) completion point has been attained, it is hoped that some funds will be allocated to other socio-economic activities aimed at improving the welfare of Zambians, especially the very poor.

- NEPAD is an important strategy, which Zambia's government has adopted. If domesticated and harmonised properly within the FNDP, NEPAD is likely to make a significant contribution towards Zambia's economic growth and development within the broader framework of reducing poverty (Government of the Republic of Zambia, 2005:3-4).

14 Fukuyama (1992) argues that a remarkable consensus concerning the legitimacy of liberal democracy as a system of government has emerged throughout the world over the past few years, as it conquered rival ideologies like hereditary monarchy, fascism, and most recently communism (p. 1). More than that, however, he argues that liberal democracy may constitute the 'end point of mankind's ideological evolution' and the 'final form of human government', and as such constitutes the 'end of history'. That is, while earlier forms of government were characterised by grave defects and irrationalities that led to their eventual collapse, liberal democracy was arguably free from such fundamental internal contradictions. This is not to say that today's stable democracies, like the United States, France, or Switzerland, were not without injustice or serious social problems. But these problems were ones of incomplete implementation of the twin principles of liberty and equality on which modern democracy is founded, rather than of flaws in the principles themselves. While some present-day countries might fail to achieve stable liberal democracy, and others might lapse back into other, more primitive forms of rule like theocracy or military dictatorship, the ideal of liberal democracy could not be improved on. *(Ibid.)*

15 At the time of writing, Zambians had gone to the polls for the fourth and consecutive time since multi-party democracy had been re-introduced in 1991. The emerging pattern was that some voters' preferred candidates were chosen on the basis of their tribe. Michael Sata was overwhelmingly voted in the Northern Province, where he originates, and the Copperbelt where there is a huge presence of his tribe. In Lusaka Province, where he also had support, the issue was quite different as tribe or region could not be cited as having been the only contributing factors. Sata's populist rhetoric was warmly received by the urban idle and poor populace in Lusaka. This could have also tilted the scales in his favour. The other opposition candidate, who came third to the incumbent, Levy Mwanawasa, was Hakainde Hichilema who won all the seats in his home area, the Southern Province, again confirming the hypothesis of tribal or regional voting. The incumbent was mainly voted by the rural dwellers and seemed to command a national appeal as he did not depend on the tribal factor.

What is critical, however, is the fact that most voters still remain ignorant and illiterate. Even though democracy is slowly gaining ground in the country, unfortunately the ignorant and illiterate are in the majority in Zambia and cannot be trusted to make rational choices. This is quite dangerous for democracy as such an electorate could simply be swayed by a fellow illiterate. Unless certain mechanisms are instituted, whereby the minimum requirement for the presidency is a first degree, the problem of mediocre leadership will remain unchecked. This issue was raised by the Constitutional Review Commission in 2004 and there was a huge uproar from a cross-section of Zambians. If the manner in which the issue became emotive can be used as a barometer to determine how many people were educated in the political arena, then most politicians, later on Zambians, are illiterates and do not even possess a basic degree. This is a very serious problem for Zambia's fledgling democracy.

16 At the time of writing, President Mwanawasa had announced in his inaugural speech to Parliament, after being re-elected for the second and last term of office, that there would be a re-evaluation of the country's tax regime in the 2007 budget. Mwanawasa also promised that firms investing in rural areas and also employing more women and youths would be awarded special tax rebates. This move seems to have been inspired by criticisms made by the opposition, relating

to high taxes, during the election campaigns. Taxes, which the main opposition party (the Patriotic Front) flagged in order to highlight the plight of poor Zambians, were extremely contentious.

[17] These assertions are based on the author's personal experiences, during travels around Southern Africa.

Chapter 1

CONCEPTUAL GROUNDING AND THEORETICAL PERSPECTIVES

Introduction

During the last decade of the 20th century the world experienced colossal transformations that also culminated in significant shifts in social policy trends. Key among these were, *inter alia*, the fall of the Soviet Empire and the re-configuration of the Eastern bloc into a democratic sphere, and the rejection of undemocratic regimes in Africa. These developments, coupled with the rise of the Right in Western Europe, all profoundly contributed towards the emergence of a new global world order. In place of a previously bipolar, geopolitically balanced equation, the United States of America emerged as the sole superpower. During this period, traditionally held views of social policy were also challenged by scholars from alternative schools of thought. Before and during the said years, social policy had not remained static or insulated against the turbulent forces of social change.[1] Therefore this chapter attempts to arrive at a working definition of social policy and also highlight its various functions in society.

Social policy's historical roots can first be traced to Europe and then to North America. Western governments began searching for appropriate ways to deal with social deprivation centuries ago, as in the Poor Laws of England.[2] By the 19th century, some countries were already establishing social security systems, for example, the German social insurance programmes under Count Otto von Bismarck. For generations, the social policy pendulum has swung from a residual-minimalist type of intervention to one of incremental provision or otherwise known as universalism. With the former, state intervention was temporary and used as a 'stopgap' while the institutions of the family and the economy 'recovered' to meet the needs of individuals. State aid, through residual provisions, was mostly perceived as an aberration and thus led to a stigma. In the latter case, social policy was institutionalised and geared towards a comprehensive redress of social maladies in society. Universal access to social services therefore underpinned the institutional social policy perspective. Spurred on by the Keynesian model of economic growth and the call for full employment, the state's intervention in the economy, to create jobs among other things, became a justifiable objective, which again legitimised the institutional model's cause.

After the 1960s and 1970s the redistributive aspects of social policy, dramatically changed, because social policy in these decades was mainly driven by growth strategies.[3] Thus, by the 1980s, when the Right's macroeconomic policies dubbed *Thatcherism* or *Reaganomics* gained momentum in Britain and the USA, residual intervention was again on an upswing. This was also the time when universal social policy coverage was being questioned and perceived as a burden on the economy. This thinking resulted in what came to be known as the period of 'stabilisation'.

During the first wave of adjustment programmes in the early 1980s, most attention was focused on developing the appropriate combination of policies to achieve stabilisation and structural reform, and little attention was paid to the question of social costs (Graham, 1997). First, a consensus gradually developed on the appropriate policy mix: the reduction of fiscal deficits, the elimination of price controls and trade restrictions, the introduction of realistic and unified exchange rate regimes and positive real interest rates, and a shift to relying on the private sector rather than the state to run most productive enterprises. After this period, the debate shifted somewhat, from an emphasis on short-term safety nets to one on appropriate macroeconomic policies, coupled with longer-term investment in health and education (Graham, 1997). For Zambia, this situation led to the introduction of the Structural Adjustment Programme (SAP). On the insistence of the International Monetary Fund (IMF) and the World Bank, the Zambian government in the late 1980s and the rest of the 1990s cut back on social service spending in the name of 'adjustment' and 'stabilisation'. The harsh economic prescriptions of the IMF and World Bank resulted in many social problems and also in countless deaths, as many poor Zambians were now unable to access medical care, which had been free in the past. Furthermore, fees for education were reintroduced in the country, while subsidies on food and agricultural implements and inputs such as fertiliser were scrapped. Social policy shifted into crisis mode with 'safety-nets' encouraged as the alternative to state intervention. The results were dismal.

Social policy and societal institutions have also evolved in a time of fast technological and social change. Socio-economic factors, demographic trends, communications technology, and cultural as well as political changes have left their imprints on the family, the roles ascribed to the market and the state, and the organisations of civil society. Social policy thus faces challenges to address the impact of these changes (United

Nations, 2001). For the family (which is taken here as the primary institution in society and the first line of defence against deprivation) these changes have had a significant impact on its roles and functions. In LDCs like Zambia, the family has been changing drastically as the extended family quickly became eroded as a result of economic austerity measures employed by states in response to changing global economics and the rise of neo-liberalism. Further, new patterns of families began to emerge, especially after the continued onslaught of the HIV/AIDS pandemic on the family, such as child-headed and single-parent households. Linked to this scenario was also the ever-increasing number of orphans. Owing to these forces, the family's role as an economic unit of production has been declining. Despite this, it has somehow still managed to remain a pivotal institutional arrangement providing support and care to members, including the young and old and the infirm and disabled, on a reciprocal basis, without expectation of reward. The consequences of the changes in the family call for policy measures to protect the welfare of the vulnerable in society (United Nations, 2001).

Every historical period has its own societal challenges that also beg for unique solutions. This outlook on social reality and the need to stem social problems have also mirrored the formulation of social policy around the globe. In the colonial era, for example, the imperial powers' agendas gave specific meaning to social policy formulation in the occupied territories. For Zambia, British colonial interests and the wellbeing of settler populations superseded those of the indigenous people, when it came to the country's social policy. Owing to the various motives, definitions and practicalities ascribed to social policy, it becomes crucial that a definition of the term is clearly spelt out. The manner in which the concept is defined will also delineate its roles in society. This chapter intends to arrive at a conceptual definition of social policy and determine its utility in LDCs and in the Zambian context. The section also discusses the roles of social policy in development and then examines the whole notion of human development in the manner that it affects human wellbeing. An elucidation of the role of social welfare and how it ties in with both social policy and human development then follows.

Social policy conceptualised

In conceptualising social policy, it is important first to consider its multifaceted nature. The concept is diverse in application and takes on various nuances depending on a number of factors, chief among these being the country's socio-economic and political conditions. Social policy's raison d'être will depend on numerous societal variables, for instance the level of economic development, political stability and the availability of skilled personnel for its shaping and implementation. It should also be borne in mind that the definition of social policy involves making a basic distinction between social policy as an applied policy arena, relating to government and other institutional interventions that affect people's welfare, and as an academic field of inquiry (Hall and Midgley, 2004). In making this distinction, a broader viewpoint would be achieved, in that these two aspects are closely related, since theory feeds directly into practice. Moreover, theory is of critical importance in social policy formulation and implementation as it provides a coherent framework from which governments can operate. Thus, governments or practitioners can only discard theory at their own peril. Inevitably, the conceptualisation of social policy and its eventual adoption for use will be guided by normative positions. Recognition of theoretical issues also reveals that particular social programmes can be linked to different normative orientations in order to give expression to varying objectives. For example, policymakers with different ideological inclinations may view the implementation of social programmes differently (Midgley, 2003).

In Zambia, during the 1960s and 1970s, Humanist or Socialist principles gave direction to social policy's programmatic interventions.[4] Therefore, normative stances – which are, needless to say, ideological positions – remain profoundly important to social policy formulation and implementation. Hence there exists a wide array of social policy definitions. Moser (2005) observes that a spectrum of social policy approaches can be categorised as ideal types along a continuum from residual welfare, through incremental policies and basic needs, to compensatory measures and, most recently, agendas relating to social justice, citizenship and human rights.

The rationale for social policy formulation rests on an assumption of change and, in this respect, positive change. Social policy must then be perceived as a change agent. It also recognises the factor of deliberate planning because the different instruments that back up its operationalisation are usually deliberately thought out and then tested for efficacy. It is this notion that makes social policy both an intellectual and practical activity. Nonetheless, social policy's mandate will be context-driven, with socio-economic, political and cultural forces (of a particular country) having a bearing on how it is conceptualised and then utilised. The process of formulating and implementing social policy goes a long way in translating the development objectives of a given society. When looking at the dynamics of social policy-making, one issue to note is that it is the institutional forces of society – ideological, political, social, economic, and cultural, for instance – that combine to influence its promulgation. Therefore, social policy will not exist in a vacuum as it will again be shaped by those forces.

To have a better understanding of policy perspectives in general, and social policy in particular, it is necessary to adopt a holistic viewpoint. Thus, a multi-pronged theoretical analysis is needed, whilst bearing in mind that society and its processes are complex. It would be futile and dangerous to engage in a one-dimensional type of analysis when undertaking an exercise of this nature. This study concurs with the position of George and Wilding (1985:1): 'Theories of society, of the state, of social problems and of social policy are inter-related. The views a social scientist holds of societal organisation and of the nature of the state will affect the explanation he or she gives of the incidence of social problems and of the government's response, if any, in the form of social policy measures.'

Social policy plays important roles in various countries. From time immemorial, societies have sought ways and means of protecting their less fortunate members from distress. In more closely-knit and communal societies such as pre-colonial Africa or medieval Europe, the family was highly instrumental in seeing to it that vulnerable members were looked after. With the advent of industrialisation, especially in Europe, more formalised ways of looking after members of society became popular in the wake of changed family patterns. Like 'development', the concept of 'social policy' is subject to various explanations and cannot be easily unpacked. For Noyoo (2000), social policy is taken as an overarching framework that is used by nations to guide different social interventions towards the ideal of social wellbeing. This text will be guided by three definitions of social policy, because they touch on certain aspects that are closely related to the terrain of LDCs like Zambia. In this case, after an inventory of different definitions of social policy, the following three in the table on the next page will guide further discussions in this book.

Table 1: Three definitions of social policy relevant to LDCs and Zambia

Source	Definition
Hall and Midgley (2004)	Social policy regards social analysis as ultimately concerned with people's wellbeing and the main objective of planned development. Therefore, social policy becomes a multi-institutional exercise, whether pursued by the state, through civil society or through international organisations. In the light of poverty reduction, actions may take the form of one or a combination of other social welfare interventions and/or broader social and economic interventions designed to promote livelihoods strengthening.
Mkandawire (2004)	Social policy is a collective intervention in the economy to influence the access to and the incidence of adequate and secure livelihoods and income. As such, social policy has always played redistributive, protection and transformative or developmental roles. In the context of development, there can be no doubt that the transformative role of social policy needs to receive greater attention than it is usually accorded in the developed countries and much more than it does in the current 'safety nets'.
Siamwiza et al. (1993)	Social policy is defined holistically and inclusively. Its broad objective is development of a just, equal and prosperous society. Its concern is more equitable wealth distribution and poverty reduction through active participation of different social groups in the satisfaction of both their economic and social rights. This definition means that not only is it concerned with sectors usually defined as 'social', such as Education, Health, Social Welfare and Social Security, but also includes sectors more commonly identified as 'economic', such as Employment, or 'infrastructure' such as Housing, Water, Transportation Infrastructure and Services, and Electricity.

Table 2: The scope of social policy adapted from Devereaux and Cook (2000)

Social sectors	Health, education, water and sanitation, housing.
Social insurance	Pensions, unemployment benefits, disability allowances.
Social protection	Food subsidies, targeted safety nets (e.g. public works projects, supplementary feeding, income transfers).
Social services	Care for vulnerable groups (people with disabilities, elderly, orphans).
Social rights	Child labour, women's rights, labour codes.

The scope and nature of social policy

It can be seen from Table 1 that social policy has certain features or characteristics that determine its scope. To begin with, all the three definitions emphasise human wellbeing. For the developing world or Zambia in particular, social policy becomes an extremely important intellectual and practical exercise as it attempts to offer solutions to the existing poverty and destitution in these areas. LDCs like Zambia exhibit high levels of poverty, and thus social policy helps to give government actors the necessary blueprints to intervene in the social sector, so as to arrest human deprivation. The second common thread flowing through the three definitions is the collective nature of social policy. The formulation of social policy stems from a cross-section of society: government, non-governmental bodies, Faith-Based Organisations (FBOs) and the broad spectrum of civil society. It is therefore all-embracing, bringing to the centre issues that affect various sections of society. The entities mentioned work in tandem to define social policy and then arrive at ways geared to its implementation. In addition, social policy's interventions are applied cross-sectorally and multi-dimensionally. Social policy addresses the needs of various sectors relying on a multiplicity of tools to effect change. An examination of the scope of social policy may perhaps prove instructive in that it will also show the different applications of the concept and then how it is eventually defined (see Table 2).

It has been argued that many LDCs' social policies remain ineffectual, in most cases owing to their heavy reliance on foreign 'recipes' and borrowed tools that simply fail because they are products of assumptions and conditions from outside, and are totally different from existing ones. Inappropriate transfers of fundamentally Northern concepts and programmes to LDCs also lead to instruments and interventions that reflect Northern priorities rather than local realities and thereafter meet assumed rather than identified needs (Nyirenda, 1977; Devereaux and Cook, 2000). This discrepancy can be attributed to colonialism and neo-colonialism/neo-imperialism (where Western models are thrust onto developing countries in the guise of *conditional aid*, with these countries having no say over the matter because the same 'aid' would be withdrawn by the foreign masters if there was any dissent). Rarely has the policy arena in LDCs been immune to outside interference, in the name of donors etc. For example, in Zambia, during the implementation of the World Bank and the IMF's SAP, social policy was the purvey of 'donors' who prioritised what they deemed important for Zambia's social development, in terms of which areas received funding or not (Siamwiza et al., 1993).

Social policy has been formulated under the aegis of a wide range of political regimes: elitist/populist, democratic/authoritarian, right-fascist/-Stalinist, colonialist/nationalist, etc. The scope for popular pressure for the institution has varied in these arrangements (Mkandawire, 2001). Different political regimes will gravitate towards certain forms of social policy, primarily because public policy or social policy concerns essentially become normative issues. It should be noted that the choice of social policy does not entirely depend on its instrumental efficacy or intrinsic value. Consequently, social policy is an intensely contested political project and an important arena in which ideologies clash. Thus, politics matters a great deal and political activity is afforded no little significance in the formulation of social policy (Lavalette and Pratt, 1997). It is this political dimension that brings to the surface the ideological factor, which is, in most cases, overwhelmingly powerful. It will also legitimise government intentions and justify its actions in society.

The role of ideology in social policy

It will be difficult to give political direction to social policy and human development initiatives if there is no existing ideology in a country. Ideology in this case determines the goals of social policy, which in turn clarify programmatic interventions. Ideology has been used over time to guide social policy formulation and development planning in various countries. However, things seem to have changed globally after the Communist camp in Eastern Europe was disbanded. The rise of neo-liberalism and globalisation also meant that certain discourses were relegated for those who justified less state action in matters relating to social wellbeing. Ideology has in most instances been likened to indoctrination or infringement of free thought, and such views seem to be supported by some of the world's most gruesome atrocities committed against humanity in the name of ideology. Hitler's Germany, Mussolini's Italy and Franco's Spain are just some of the stark reminders in modern history of how far ideology can be used to propagate hate and oppression of certain peoples.[5] However, it is also important to note that there is a positive side to ideology that engenders progress and development. It is this progressive slant that will be the centre of the present discussion.

It is argued here that ideology is a crucial vehicle that can be used to guide a country's development pursuits, because it has an ability to imbue social policy and development planning with certain values. Initially coined by the French philosopher Destutt de Tracy in 1795 to denote the general science of ideas, which was to clarify and improve the public mind, and later on given currency by the French Revolution and then by Marx, the term 'ideology' had developed in many directions (Scruton, 1982). Ideology refers to:

> Any systematic and all-embracing political doctrine, which claims to give a complete and universally applicable theory of man and society, and to derive there from a programme of political action. An ideology in this sense seeks to embrace everything that is relevant to man's political condition, and to issue doctrine whenever doctrine would be influential in forming or changing that condition. In Marxist and Marxian theories 'ideology' denotes any set of ideas and values which have the social function of consolidating a particular economic order, and which is explained by that fact alone, and not by its inherent truth or reasonableness (Scruton, 1982:212-13).

Ideology justifies the actions that men and women take to support or to oppose the prevailing political and social order. Contemporary ideologies emerged in modern times as elements among the forces which undermined the traditional societies (Stadler, 1991). In effect, political ideas and ideologies set goals, which inspire political activity. Also, they provide perspectives through which the world is understood or explained (Heywood, 1992).

Stadler (1991), while paying particular attention to contemporary ideologies, cites *liberalism* as the oldest ideology in this category. The central values which liberals uphold are individual rights and liberties that emerged in the English, American and French Revolutions as the ideological basis of resistance to absolutism from the 17th century onwards. Stadler (1991) then refers to *Conservatism, Nationalism, Socialism, Marxism,* and *Fascism* as other forms of contemporary ideologies. All these ideologies would also take on varying forms and meanings in different contexts. But what is significant about them all is that they have the all-powerful ability to define as well as chart, *inter alia*, society's historical tangents.

Ideology and social policy in Zambia

In Zambia, ideology was critical in shaping social policy and development planning especially in the first decade of independence (1964-74). The country's official ideology in this period was referred to as Zambian Humanism (see Mebeelo, 1973). Molteno (1977) cited in Kandeke

(1977:212) shows how Zambian Humanism was explained by different circles in the country:

> One view is that it is a formalisation and systematisation of values and social principles which were live realities in pre-colonial society: the absence of exploiting classes, egalitarianism, communalism and inclusiveness, self-reliance balanced by mutual aid, hospitality together with generosity, politeness and respect. A second view is that Zambian Humanism is a codification of the principles which the National Independence Party adopted during the independence struggle: an independent republic, unitary government, universal franchise, a welfare state, economic development for the benefit of the masses, and rejection of racism and colonialism. The third view, of course, is that Zambian Humanism is the thoughts of President Kaunda. The truth, I suggest, lies somewhere between these three points of view. Humanism preserves selected values from the past, embodies convictions which grew up during the nationalist struggle, and adapts these principles to the problems of the present in order to give direction for the future.

Ideology and the contemporary Zambian scenario

Ideology plays an important role in determining a country's development mission. Tordoff (1993:254) whilst looking at different strands of regimes in Africa: Afro-Marxist, Populist Socialist or African Capitalist, comments that ideology is helpful if it enables the leadership to instil a sense of direction and purpose in its followers, but that it can become an economic straitjacket if it is too rigidly applied and makes changes of direction difficult. In Tanzania, for example, Julius Nyerere implored his countrymen and women to adhere to communal production via a populist ideology of African Socialism or ujamaa vijijini, for development to accrue to every Tanzanian. Ujamaa was more ingrained in the minds of the local people than Humanism was in Zambia, where only the president and his lackeys really saw (or thought they did see) its practical application. Since Levy Mwanawasa came to power, there has been talk of a 'new deal' administration that seeks to fight poverty and corruption in the country. However, this new deal, in apparent aping of the New Deal concept of the American President Franklin D. Roosevelt,[6] seems not to be underpinned by any ideological orientation and therefore does not clearly articulate Zambia's development programmes from an ideological position.

Pronouncements about fighting poverty and corruption may all be well-intentioned, but the crucial question remains: from which ideological orientation? Is Zambia a neo-liberal state? Is it Leftist? Is it Centre-Right or Centre-Left? Once such ideological fogs are clarified by Zambian politicians, from both the ruling party and the opposition, then their supporters or the electorate could be better informed as to what ideals and aspirations political parties espouse for a better Zambia. They will also be inspired to join party A or B because its ideology spells out clear programmes for advancing the nation. Having a party manifesto is not enough. It can be reduced to a wish-list, if the party has no clear vision that is guided by a specific ideology. It is crucial that the practice of politics, the conduct of the politicians and the conceptualisation of party programmes should all be buttressed by an ideological tradition in countries like Zambia. In this way, ideology will serve as an important launch-pad for the realisation of human wellbeing in the country.

At present, Zambia's poverty reduction strategies have indelible imprints of the IMF and the World Bank. In order to qualify for debt forgiveness under what is referred to as the Heavily Indebted Poor Countries or HIPC initiative, Zambia had to follow the rules laid down by these multilateral donor agencies to the letter. The country did not, and still does not have the luxury of adhering to some form of home-grown initiative in this area or even applying unorthodox means to fight poverty. Furthermore, the existing social policy is still a throw back to the misguided Chiluba-led liberal policies of the 1990s. The government is still denying its responsibility in certain life-sustaining sectors, for example, employment creation. Recent utterances from the country's Minister of Finance, that it is not the government's duty to 'create employment', are simply regrettable. This understanding (or confusion) on the part of government ministers boils down to the fact that they are not being guided by any ideology in this matter. Despite catch-phrases like 'new culture' under Chiluba and 'new deal administration' in Mwanawasa's reign, the ruling party and, for that matter, the opposition parties seem to have no clear ideological position, when it comes to issues of national development.

All political parties refer to some manifesto about fighting poverty and generating economic growth in Zambia, but they do not enlighten people as to what their philosophical standing or value-base really is, or how their ideology will effect or guide development programmes in the country. For this discussion, a strong and inclusive state (with a clear ideology) that propels human development via multi-faceted programmes, in concert with civil society, is seen as the best option for a country like Zambia. In a context where there are few working institutions and where many people are weighed down by poverty, a resolute state is the preferred motor of development. In sum, the developmental state is advocated. Indeed, both the contemporary normative discourse and the emerging consensus on development insist on putting in place social institutions (including the state) that are developmental (in that they sustain high rates of growth and the structural transformation of economies), socially inclusive, and sanctioned by democratic processes that fully respect the human rights of all citizens (Mkandawire, 2004). After defining social policy, it is imperative to conceptualise human development and then establish how the two may be conjoined.

What is human development?

The idea of human development may be seen as emanating primarily from the misgivings of certain scholars in the light of the failure of development economics to help developing countries out of poverty, after the Second World War. The arrival of the Human Development Approach (HDA) on the development theory scene can be attributed to the work of, among others, Amartya Sen and Mahbub ul Haq, who looked for a theory that could bring people to the centre of development. Sen, through his extensive work on capabilities, has been very instrumental in laying the theoretical bedrock of the Human Development Approach (Fakuda-Parr, 2002). The *Human Development Report* (HDR) published annually by the United Nations Development Programme (UNDP) since 1990 has used Sen's capability approach as a conceptual framework in its analysis of contemporary development challenges, and developed the HDA paradigm. The reports have a much broader ambition of setting out a whole approach to development, with an agenda of policy priorities, tools of analysis and measurements, and a coherent framework (Fakuda-Parr, 2002). In order to launch the HDR, Haq brought together a group of fellow economists and friends to develop this paradigm, among them Paul Streeten and Frances Stewart who had worked with him on the Basic Needs Approach, Gus Ranis and Keith Griffin, as well as others who shared his vision (Fakuda-Parr, 2002).

The first *Human Development Report* of 1990 started by recalling that the purpose of development is the full flowering of human beings and that human development returns to the end of economic development (Streeten, 1995). There are at least six reasons for human development and the eradication of poverty:

First, it is an end in itself; indeed it is the whole purpose of development. Second, it contributes to higher productivity. Third, it lowers reproductivity and therefore population growth. This may seem odd, for lowering infant mortality rates appear to accelerate population growth. But families try to over-insure against infant deaths. Reduced child mortality leads to the desire for smaller families. Fourth, poverty reduction reduces the degradation of the environment from soil erosion, deforestation and desertification. Fifth, the growth of a civil society and democracy leads to greater social stability. And sixth, its political appeal is that it reduces civil disturbances and increases political stability (Streeten, 1995:19-20).

Essentially, people are the real wealth of a nation and therefore, the basic objective of development is to create an enabling environment for them to enjoy long, healthy and creative lives (United Nations Development Programme, 1990). Human development then aims to enlarge people's choices. The ability of people to lead long and healthy lives, to be educated and to enjoy a decent standard of living remains central to the Human Development Approach. Additional choices include political freedom, guaranteed human rights and self-respect, what Adam Smith called the ability to mix with others without being ashamed to appear in public (United Nations Development Programme, 1990).

Therefore, this theoretical thrust puts forward a different view of development that does not exclusively equate development with economic growth. It sees economic growth and higher consumption not as ends in themselves, but as means to achieve human development (United Nations Development Programme, 1998). The human development paradigm embraces every development issue, including economic growth, social investment, and people's empowerment. The Human Development Approach is based on the principles of *equity, sustainability, productivity* and *empowerment*. Equity highlights the enlargement of people's choices: if development aims to enlarge people's choices, they must surely enjoy equitable access to opportunities (Haq, 1995). Sustainability then follows as an essential element in this equation in the way it should nudge existing policies in the direction of future development efforts. This paradigm is neither paternalistic nor based on charity. Empowerment in this approach is therefore exemplified by a focus on development by people, who must participate in the activities, events and processes that shape their lives (Haq, 1995). In the Human Development Approach human resources become the fulcrum of development.

The human development perspective has two central theses about people and development, the *evaluative* and *agency* aspects. The first is concerned with improving human lives as an explicit development objective, with an understanding of how improvements are to be made. The second is concerned with what human beings can do to achieve such improvements, especially through policy and political changes. The human development approach is commonly associated with the evaluative aspect, but the agency aspect is less widely appreciated (Fakuda-Parr, 2002). In Zambia, when dovetailed with social policy, the HDA has the potential to lay the foundation for holistic, participatory and bottom-up development initiatives in the country (Noyoo, 2000). The Human Development Paradigm is extremely useful to a country that is plagued by poverty. Conscious public policy will be able to translate economic growth into better lives for people, and facilitate major restructuring of the economic and political power. Furthermore, links between economic growth and human choices may demand, among other things, far-reaching land reforms, progressive tax systems, new credit systems for poor people, a major expansion of basic social services to reach all deprived people, and the establishment of temporary social safety-nets for those who may be bypassed by the markets or public action (Haq, 1995).

This text further argues that human development requires more than health, education, a decent standard of living and political freedom. People's cultural identities must also be recognised and accommodated by the state, and people must be free to express these identities without being discriminated against in other aspects of their lives. In short, cultural liberty is a human right and an important aspect of human development, and thus worthy of state action and attention (United Nations Development Programme, 2004). This issue is of critical importance to countries like Zambia where there is a multiplicity of ethnic groups and a kaleidoscope of cultures that have been harmoniously existing side by side since independence, but which can easily be hijacked by unscrupulous politicians, bent on fomenting ethnic strife in order to gain political mileage. For Zambia and Africa generally, cultural liberty is crucial as the African people's cultures were deliberately retarded and then derided by outside forces that made them into spectacles for ridicule. *Cultural imperialism*, an offshoot of colonial subjugation, worked tirelessly to strip away African people's cultures and left them with no sense of 'rootedness' and belonging. In this sense, Africans were denied their indigenous knowledge systems, which could have provided them relevant and localised solutions to the countless problems affecting the continent. Cultural imperialism also went further to make Africans even hate themselves and anything that was indigenous; their over-reliance on foreign analyses (mostly, if not all being Western) to solve local problems is therefore not surprising. This is not to ignore that there are some retrogressive aspects in many cultures in Zambia and other parts of Africa.

Human development in Zambia

For almost three decades human development performances in Zambia have not been encouraging. The economic downturn and high poverty levels, among other things, can be linked with the deplorable human development statistics in the country. Zambia's Human Development Index (HDI)[7] stood at 164 in 2004, according to the UNDP's Human Development Report. On the other hand the Human Poverty Index (HPI)[8] value for Zambia was 50.4 per cent, ranking 90th among 95 developing countries for which the index was calculated. The long-term trends in human development in the country point to marked differences between Zambia and eight other countries. These countries' Human Development Indices were similar to Zambia's in 1975 and fell within the range of 0.4 and 0.5. All the nine countries, including Zambia, increased their HDI value between 1975 and 1985. However, it is noted that in the case of Zambia, the rate at which the HDI value rose was slower than those of the eight countries (United Nations Development Programme, 2003). The HDI has risen steadily in three countries: Papua New Guinea (the only non-African country included), Morocco and Ghana. Among these countries, Zambia and Cameroon were the first to show a decline after 1985, with the other countries joining the trend between 1990 and 1995.

The decline in HDI for Zambia has been so sharp that by 1995 it was lower than it was in 1975 (United Nations Development Programme, 2003). Nevertheless there have been some positive signs with short-term trends, indicating that there is cause for optimism. The HDI has been rising modestly since 1994. Zambia's HDI rose marginally from -0.424 in 1998 to 0.453 in 2000. The improvement suggests that the decline has bottomed out, and there is reason to believe that this may be the case (United Nations Development Programme, 2003).

Human development is inextricably linked to social policy responses. Similarly, social policy's concerns with health, education and social security are all important benchmarks of human development. Human development and social policy converge around the elevation of people's wellbeing, and in this sense they should be seen as aiding each other and not in competition. Social policy and human development also extend into the sphere of social welfare. However, conceptual muddles may arise if the scope of intervention is not clearly spelt out by the practitioners or policy-makers, when social welfare is brought into play. In many instances, the terms 'social policy' and 'social welfare' are used interchangeably. This is not surprising given the fact that there is a lot of overlap between social policy and social welfare. What is important, though, is that the two are separate in focus and application, and an endeavour will be made to make this distinction for conceptual clarity. It is suggested here that social policy subsumes social welfare, making social welfare one of its sub-categories. Social policy broadly covers social welfare, health, housing, employment, and education (Popple and Leighninger, 1998). Thus, social welfare is taken here as falling under the aegis of social policy. There may be no deviation between the two as they could for instance be underpinned by the same ideological and philosophical understandings, in the light of human wellbeing. However, differences may arise from the scope and coverage, as social policy could be broader in outlook than social welfare, and not from the content.

Defining social welfare

Before defining the concept of social welfare, it is important to locate it in an LDC and Zambian context. The view taken in this book is that the most important aspect of social welfare, especially in LDCs like Zambia, is the centrality of human beings' inclusion in initiatives aimed at uplifting their living standards. In contrast to conceptual definitions that perceive men and women as victims of social problems or as objects of charity, social welfare in LDCs must stress the importance of developing human resources, for example the strengthening of family life and preparing people, especially children and youths, to improve their own lives, as an integral part of national development (United Nations, 1986). This concept encompasses the fortifying of institutions such as the family and the community, enabling individuals and groups in society to participate actively in all spheres of the development process, and in general helping people to become partners in development, instead of being passive recipients of dole and charity (United Nations, 1986). The United Nations (1986:6-7) also observes that:

> Social welfare in LDCs must also be viewed in the context of pervasive poverty and lack of most of the basic amenities of life that are taken for granted elsewhere. Social justice, as an essential component of national development, is of particular significance to LDCs. Development *per se* is

not valued highly unless its fruits can be shared equitably by all segments of the population. The search for appropriate instruments to promote social justice covers all sectors of development, including social welfare. Another basic concern in LDCs is linked to building firmly upon existing social and cultural foundations, even as new efforts are made to reorient traditional institutions in a developmental direction. LDCs must adapt their institutions to new tasks and challenges posed by rapid urbanisation and industrialisation. New forms of social welfare must be formulated in a positive and supportive framework, rather than stressing the weaknesses of the traditional institutions.

In this work, social welfare is used in its broadest sense as referring to a social condition, and not to the charity given by philanthropic individuals, charities or public assistance provided by the government. This wider connotation of social welfare hinges on the economic, social and political wellbeing of the nation (Midgley, 1995). Johnson *et al.* (1997) regard social welfare as a system of arrangements, programmes and mechanisms, formal or informal, governmental or non-governmental, that try to meet the needs of individuals and families who cannot fulfil such needs through their own resources. In this respect, human needs have to be met through some form of system (whether formal or informal) that guarantees protection when people become vulnerable. In the traditional past the extended family fulfilled this role. In this setting, the extended family acted as a social security system and was based on shared interests and reciprocity, involving obligations on members to support each other in times of need. However, in the modern era, such systems have been formalised and are quite impersonal. There have been two contending notions of social welfare that have predominated for a long time in social welfare discourse: the *residual* and *institutional* models of social welfare (again echoing those of social policy).

1. The Residual Model

Wilensky and Lebeaux in their ground-breaking 1958 work Industrial Society and Social Welfare pioneered understanding of welfare systems in an industrial society. For them, the residual formulation is based on the premise that there are two 'natural' channels through which an individual's needs are properly met, the family and the market economy. These, the authors say, are the preferred structures of supply, but sometimes they do not always function adequately. When this situation takes place, the idea is that a third mechanism of need fulfilment should be brought into play, which is the social welfare system. The notion behind the residual model is that, although society should help in emergencies, people in need are responsible for their own problems and should solve them with minimal societal intervention. The residual perspective prescribes short-term welfare measures that last only until the family or market economy can resume their functions. A major criterion is whether people earn more than a set level of income and possess assets valued above a certain amount. Therefore, in order to access a certain service they will be obliged to undertake a means test that will establish whether they are eligible or not, based on their income levels. The means test aims to ensure that applicants do not get more help than they should. The residual perspective is the basis for the medical model of social welfare and ultimately social work treatment, in which social services are intended to 'treat' and 'cure' people who deviate from 'healthy society' (Day, 1997:37). The residual model carries negative connotations as people in the system are usually perceived as 'abnormal' or 'inadequate'. The whole process of ascertaining eligibility for a service can at times be humiliating to some people.

2. The Institutional Model

According to this conception of social welfare, welfare services are seen as the normal, 'first line' functions of modern industrial society (Wilensky and Lebeaux, 1958). This perspective is at the opposite end of the continuum from the residual viewpoint. Its criterion is membership of society: every person has a right to its services, without means testing or stigma. Programmes are universal, that is, they cover every person within their designated mandate, whereas residual programmes are selective in nature and apply only to a select few or a select group (Day, 1997). The institutional perspective is akin to the structural or social model of social work, whereby social problems are believed to come from oppressive or inegalitarian structures in society. Social problems are not based on personal fault, so solutions do not lie in controlling, punishing, or stigmatising the individual. Rather, they lie in root problems, such as classism, racism, and sexism, and their elimination (Day, 1997). From the institutional perspective also flowed other derivatives such as the institutional-redistributive model proposed and presented by Richard Titmuss in 1972.

Titmuss in Madison (1980:50) 'sees social welfare as a basic integrated institution in society providing both universal and selective services outside the market on the principle of need. Universal services, available without distinction of class, colour, sex, or religion, can perform functions which foster and promote attitudes, and behaviour towards the values of social solidarity, altruism, toleration and accountability.' For Titmuss, the key assumption underlying the model is that 'social welfare is not simply an adjunct of the economy or an ameliorative system providing services for poor people (while accepting a compensatory role), it also accepts a positive role through the development of social manpower policies, corrective regional and area economic policies, retraining and further education services, and other instrumentalities designed to bring about an improvement in the standards and quality of life of the individuals concerned' (Titmuss, 1972, cited in Madison, 1980:51).

3. *The New World Order Model*

The new world order model shows that the most serious problems confronting humanity are rooted in the fundamental inequalities that exist in the world order, that is, in the system of international social, political and economic institutions that govern relationships between nations and within nations, and between groups of people (Estes, 1995).

4. *The Developmental Social Welfare Model*

This model must be examined against the background of the United Nations Development Decade (1960-70), which called for progress towards self-sustaining economic growth and development. Developmental social welfare is a 'brain-child' of the United Nations. In 1968, the first International Conference of Ministers Responsible for Social Welfare was held under the auspices of the United Nations in order to: (a) reach across national boundaries and assess the status of social welfare in the countries of the world, (b) gain a new understanding of the potential of social welfare, and (c) chart its new course in the broad movement towards the fuller realisation of human potential. Among the most significant accomplishments of the conference were the recognition and emphasis it gave to the concept of 'developmental social welfare' (United Nations, 1986). According to this model, social welfare shares equal status with other sectors of the economy in the march towards social progress and development. It is predicated on the maximisation of human potential and based on the mobilisation of all segments of the population for the resolution of social problems and attainment of social progress (United Nations, 1986). Developmental social welfare generally emphasises change, partnership, justice, and the development of human potential in place of condescension, passive provision, segregation and negative labelling of needy individuals and groups.

The social claims of vulnerable groups continue to have an important place in developmental social welfare, as do remedial and custodial perspectives, where appropriate, but within this general orientation. One of the basic premises of developmental social welfare is that anticipatory and preventive measures should constitute a major aspect of all development planning and that the preservation and enhancement of the quality of life should be the foremost criterion of development (United Nations, 1986). The United Nations (1986:3) also observes that through the preventive function, social problems are anticipated and provision made to deal with them, thereby reducing the need for remedial investment. In times of rapid change, for example, developmental social welfare is effective in preventing or lessening the strains and dislocations of abrupt transition on those affected by consequences of development such as industrialisation, urbanisation or the move to a money economy, as well as on those migrating from rural to urban areas, and those who find their children acquiring customs and values unknown to their generation.

Furthermore, developmental social welfare presents many opportunities for close and equal collaboration in many sectors towards the attainment of common goals. This relationship signifies the fuller involvement of the social welfare sector in the mainstream of national and international struggles for progress. Also, enhancement of the social functioning of all people (including the marginal and vulnerable groups) is an important objective of developmental social welfare. Social functioning is meant to include the optimum utilisation of available individual and institutional resources. It is for this reason that developmental social welfare envisages a partnership between social welfare personnel and the population, as well as a strong emphasis on the maximum involvement of the population in resolving their own problems (United Nations, 1986:16).

Conclusion

The purpose of this chapter was to unpack the main concepts in the study in order to arrive at appropriate working definitions. This attempt was meant to allow the reader have a clearer understanding of the workings of social policy and human development in both an LDC and a particularly Zambian context. Taking into account, *inter alia,* the high poverty levels and a sense of powerlessness in poor communities in the country, it becomes extremely important to interrogate the effectiveness of social policy in reducing the foregoing societal challenges. Social problems currently strangling Zambia require not only innovation but a strong political will on the part of the government. Also, it is important to clearly delineate the role of informal or traditional structures in the social policy process as well. Afterwards, it would then be appropriate to interweave these efforts with the Human Development Approach. While executing these tasks, it is important to ask the following question: how can Zambia engender a visionary approach to social policy and human development that cuts across various sections in the country and harmoniously directs their efforts towards the improvement of people's livelihoods? Indeed, for a country like Zambia, social policy's transformative capacities should be accorded more attention, rather than having an over-reliance on the 'safety-net' route. It was only in the 1960s and 70s that this transformative role was appreciated and put to effective use.

In concluding this section, it needs to be re-emphasised that social policy should not be championed by government alone (even though a proactive state is advocated here) but by other sectors in the country as well. Therefore, a vibrant and critical civil society has to take a stance on this matter and also create enough space to undermine retrogressive government policies and advocate the cause of the poor and inarticulate. People can only be brought onto the development platform if there is an existing passion in both government and civil society for forward-looking innovations. Slowly, this is gaining ground in the country and one can only hope that a broad coalition or social movement – including progressive academics, researchers, grassroots movements, the media, the labour movement, artists, women's groups and the youth – emerges to lead the crusade against poverty, social exclusion, squalor and mal-governance in Zambia. There is also a need for concerted efforts from Zambian society, aimed at challenging the assumptions about development held by those who 'dispense' it, whether donors or the government. It is encouraging to note that this has begun to take place in Zambia, albeit not in a coherent and co-ordinated manner. The work of organisations such as Jubilee Zambia, various churches, the Catholic Commission for Justice and Peace, the women's movement, the Non-Governmental Organisations Co-ordinating Committee, and the media, among others, should be commended for acting as a voice of the poor and marginalised in Zambia.

Notes

[1] Chapter 2 closely examines social change and how it influences social policy.

2   In England the origins of parochial poor relief extend back at least as far as the 14th century. With the decline of the monasteries, and their dissolution in 1536, together with the breakdown of the medieval social structure, charity for the poor gradually moved from its traditional voluntary framework to become an official task administered at the parish level. Legislation prior to this point largely dealt with beggars and vagabonds. In the aftermath of the Black Death (1348-49) labour was in short supply and wages rose steeply. To try and keep this in check, several Acts were passed aimed at forcing all able-bodied men to work and keep wages at their old levels. These measures led to labourers roaming around the country looking for an area where the wages were high and where the labour laws were not too strictly enforced. Some took to begging under the pretence of being ill or crippled. In 1349, the Ordinance of Labourers (36 Edw. III c.8) prohibited private individuals from giving relief to able-bodied beggars. In 1388, the Statute of Cambridge (12 Rich. II c.7) introduced regulations restricting the movements of all labourers and beggars. Each county 'Hundred' became responsible for relieving its own 'impotent poor': those who, because of age or infirmity, were incapable of work. Servants wishing to move out of their own Hundred needed a letter of authority from the 'good man of the Hundred' – the local Justice of the Peace – or risked being put in the stocks. Following this Act, beggars could pretend neither to be labourers (who needed permission to wander) nor to be invalids (who were also forbidden to wander). The 1388 Act is often regarded as the first English Poor Law. However, lack of enforcement limited its impact and effect.

Further British legislation followed over the next two centuries. In 1494, the Vagabonds and Beggars Act (11 Henry VII c.2) determined that 'Vagabonds, idle and suspected persons shall be set in the stocks for three days and three nights and have none other sustenance but bread and water and then shall be put out of Town. Every beggar suitable to work shall resort to the Hundred where he last dwelled, is best known, or was born and there remain upon the pain aforesaid.' Worse was to come: the Statute of Legal Settlement (1 Edw. VI. c.3) enacted that a sturdy beggar could be branded or made a slave for two years (or for life if he absconded). The Act condemned '...foolish pity and mercy' for vagrants. On a more positive note, cottages were to be erected for the impotent poor, and they were to be relieved or cured. An Act of 1564 aimed to suppress the 'roaming beggar' by empowering parish officers to 'appoint, meet and convenient places for the habitations and abidings' of such classes – one of the first references to what was subsequently to evolve into the workhouse. In 1597, an Act For the Relief of the Poor (39 Eliz. c.3) required every parish to appoint *Overseers of the Poor* whose responsibility it was to find work for the unemployed and to set up parish-houses for those incapable of supporting themselves. (Retrieved, 12/07/2006 and adapted from: www.workhouses.org.uk/index.html?poorlaws/poorlaws.shtml).

3. The main objective of the growth-oriented approach is to increase the rate of output within a country over a period of time by increasing the rate of capital formation. In this case growth is a function of increase in capital stock, and emphasis is placed on the mobilisation of savings. Rapid growth in GNP and its components are seen as the sole objectives of development. The basic thinking is that increases in GNP would result in higher standards of living through its positive impacts on other economic and social parameters (Chukuwka, 2000).

4. See Chapter 3 for details.

5. Many philosophers and historians of ideas insist that fascism is, first and foremost, an ideology. It grew up in the third quarter of the nineteenth century and particularly in the 1890s, its 'incubatory period'. Its component parts included: (1) an extreme form of nationalism which insisted that human beings were sub-divisions of a larger national whole which alone could give meaning to their lives; (2) social Darwinism, which insisted that struggle between nations was natural and inevitable; (3) the 'science' of racism, which constructed a hierarchy of races and branded some, including the Jews, as inferior; and (4) anti-positivism, the idea that human beings are motivated not by logic and reason (as the philosophers of the Enlightenment had said) but by myths, intuition and emotion (as Romantic thinkers had believed). Yet several criticisms must be made. First, perhaps the ideas associated with fascism were little more than half-baked clichés and prejudices which do not deserve to be dignified as a political ideology. Certainly, it must be admitted, that if fascism was an ideology, then it was one of the vaguest and least coherent. Second, no two supporters of this school of thought seem to agree on the exact ingredients of the lowest common denominator. For instance, some - but not all - include the corporate state or anti-Semitism or an aggressive foreign policy or the 'leadership principle' (Führerprinzip). However, what should be grasped, above all, is that those who adopt this

method of defining generic fascism are not describing any particular regime or creating any complete model to which regimes must conform before they can be called fascist. Nor are they pointing to the most historically important aspects of these groups. They are simply arguing that the ideas which certain groups had in common allow them to be called 'fascist'. Hence, generic fascism is a means of classification - or, to use the jargon, a 'taxonomic device'. It is not an all-inclusive definition of any regime or the only label that can be used. (Retrieved 8/05/2005 and adapted from www.users.globalnet.co.uk/~semp/facism.htm).

6 The *New Deal* was the name President Franklin D. Roosevelt gave to the series of programmes between 1933 and 1937 with the goal of relief, recovery and reform of the economy of the United Sates during the Great Depression. Several alphabet agencies were created as a result. Historians distinguish the 'First New Deal' of 1933 that had something for every group, and the 'Second New Deal' (1935-37) that introduced an element of class conflict. The opponents of the New Deal, complaining of the cost and the shift of power to Washington, stopped its expansion after 1937, and abolished many of the programmes by 1943. The National Recovery Administration was ruled unconstitutional by the Supreme Court. The main programmes still important today are Social Security and the Securities and Exchange Commission, the Federal Deposit Insurance Corporation (FDIC) as well as the Tennessee Valley Authority (TVA). The New Deal had three components: direct relief, economic recovery and financial reform; these were also called 'the three Rs'. (Adapted from Wikipedia, 20/06/2006, http://en.wikipedia.org/wiki/New_Deal).

7 The Human Development Index (HDI) focuses on three measurable dimensions of human development: living a long and healthy life, being educated and having a decent standard of living. Thus it combines measures of life expectancy, school enrolment, literacy and income to allow a broader view of a country's development than does income alone. Although the HDI is a useful starting point, it is important to remember that the concept of human development is much broader and more complex than any summary measure can capture, even when supplemented by other indices. The HDI is not a comprehensive measure. It does not include important aspects of human development, notably the ability to participate in the decisions that affect one's life and to enjoy the respect of others in the community. It

is also important to note that the HDI is constructed using data from international sources. Sometimes more up-to-date data are available nationally, and sometimes there are slight differences in definitions between international and national data. For these and other reasons, discrepancies with national sources may occur. The HDI measures the average progress of a country in human development (UNDP, 2004).

8. The *Human Development Report* of 1997 introduced the Human Poverty Index (HPI), which focuses on the proportion of people below a threshold level in basic dimensions of human development - living a long and healthy life, having access to education, and a decent standard of living, much as the poverty headcount measures the proportion of people below a certain income level. The HPI-1 measures human poverty in developing countries (UNDP, 2004).

Chapter 2

SOCIAL CHANGE AND DEVELOPMENT IN ZAMBIA

Introduction

Social change has been a powerful force throughout history that has helped to transform the world in profound ways. The last two hundred years have exhibited cutting-edge technological changes that have also resulted in new ways of harnessing natural resources for the betterment of human society. Changes in the social and political organisation of countries have also led to novel ways of meeting people's needs. This chapter explores the phenomenon of social change and how it has been impacting on the Zambian society in different historical periods: prior to colonial rule, under colonialism and in the post-colonial era. Thereafter, the chapter attempts to weave social change, social policy, and human development processes into a single tapestry.

The meaning of social change

Social change has been contributing towards global transformation for centuries and remains dynamic even to this day. Social change is associated with unique transformative forces specific to certain historical periods, for societies are never static. In Zambia, the changes that took place in the past have not stalled but are continuous. Indeed, past changes in Zambia and what is currently transpiring in the country must be perceived as part of a wider process of social change that has characterised modern societies in different parts of the globe, notably Europe. The Industrial and French Revolutions of 18th and 19th century Europe, as well as the Russian Revolution of 1917, are all important events that helped to shape the world. The rise of nationalism in Latin America in the early 19th century, the emergence of the Eastern bloc after the Second World War, and the anti-colonial struggles in Asia and Africa in the latter part of the 20th century all added to the changes. Social change is inevitable in human society and it must be stressed that social policy and human development should be taken as processes that are in sync with social change, in that they all require deliberate human action (Midgley, 1995). The notions of change and intervention are all central to social policy and human development.

Interpretations of social change are as old as human society. The Greek philosophers wrote extensively about social change and the Chinese had well developed theories about it. The idea that human beings can intentionally improve society and even create ideal societies was first advocated by a group of social thinkers known as Utopians (Midgley, 1995). They made blueprints for what they thought would be perfect societies. Although often ridiculed, they were the first advocates of intervention and the modern idea of planning. Utopian thought has a long history. Plato was one of the first Utopians. He developed an elaborate plan for an ideal society (Midgley, 1995). This society would be ruled by philosophers who would govern wisely and maintain social harmony. To ensure that they were incorruptible and fully committed to promoting social wellbeing, the philosopher kings, as he called them, would not be permitted to marry or have property.

Many theories of social change were formulated by European philosophers during and after the Enlightenment era. Most of these theories are optimistic, believing that societies evolve in a progressive, linear fashion. Another common element was the identification of different stages in the process of social change (Midgley, 1995). Scientific explanations for social change can be traced back to the birth of Sociology, with classical theorists like Auguste Comte and Herbert Spencer. Sztompka (1993:3) notes that initial investigations of human society fall under the bracket of the organic metaphor or classical approach to social change. These are characterised by an analogy between a society and a biological organism. For instance, Comte divided his system of theory into separate parts: *social statics* and *social dynamics*. This distinction was explicitly described by Herbert Spencer in that *social statics* was conceived as the study of the anatomy of human society, the composite parts and their arrangement, just like the anatomy of the body (with its organs, skeleton and tissues), whereas *social dynamics* was assumed to focus on physiology, the processes running inside society, just like bodily functions (respiration, metabolism, circulation of the blood), and producing as their ultimate result the development of society, again comparable to organic growth (from the embryo to maturity). The understanding then was that there existed something like a steady state of society, which could be perceived and analysed prior to, or independent of, its motion. This thinking then led to theories aimed at interpreting human society: e*arly evolutionary theories* and *functionalist theories*.

Early evolutionary theories assumed that social change took place along a single path with societies evolving from simple homogeneous entities to progressively heterogeneous, interdependent, and complex entities. Functionalist theories became a sub-category of this strand of thought. Functionalism reigned as the dominant paradigm in sociology from the early 1950s to the late 1960s. Through the works of Talcott Parsons and Robert Merton, among others, the earlier insights of Comte, Spencer, and Emile Durkheim were refined and developed further (Farganis, 1996). Functionalist theorists also compared society to the human body existing in a state of equilibrium through use of self-regulating mechanisms. Society, via a complex of beliefs, values, and norms that are functionally interrelated, maintained social harmony. In general, the major distinctive contribution of functionalism has been its view of social order as a consensual agreement reflecting shared values and norms that bind a community together (Farganis, 1996:227). In summing up this line of thought, Bailey (1975) sees the functionalist theory as attempting to explain social phenomena in terms of parts they play in the existence and survival of the wider society. More broadly, functionalism is concerned with the inter-relationships and interdependence of parts of a social system. Some theorists from the neo-Marxist school of thought have regarded this theory as authenticating and entrenching the status quo, because of its over-emphasis on equilibrium and consensus in society.

Another way of interpreting social change in society is through conflict. At the centre of this perception is conflict theory, which, as opposed to consensus theory that elevates integration, stability and functionalism, puts emphasis on change, dissent, and deviation. A commitment to conflict as the basic theoretical principle can be based on more than just a perverse distrust of consensus theory. It may be that conflict is endemic in society owing to simultaneous desires for inevitable scarce resources and to the existence of incompatible interests (Bailey, 1975). The roots of conflict theory are to be found in the works of Marx and Weber, both of whom recognised that coercion rather than consensus maintains social order. While Marx and Weber envisioned different forms and degrees of social stratification, both argued that conflict was the fundamental dynamic that operated between these strata (Farganis, 1996). Marx saw capitalist society dichotomised into two major economic classes, the *proletariat* and the *bourgeoisie*, who were pitted in inexorable opposition, while Weber acknowledged that the economy was one of the determinant forces in society, but asserted that political power and status were also important (Farganis, 1996:268). It must be noted that from the Marxist perspective, conflict is seen as basic to society and comes to the fore as various interest groups based on race, sex, nationalities, classes, and religion compete for power and resources.

Mufune *et al.* (1990:17-18), assert that the exact form of social change will differ depending on situation, place, and time. They identify a number of critical factors and variables, which interact to produce social change:

a) The Physical Environment: Human societies must adapt their cultures and institutions to the physical environment. People in different physical and climatic environments, for example Eskimos and Desert Nomads, Aborigines vs. Central Europeans, and Swazis vs. Swiss, differ in terms of the social life they have created. Should the environment change then those who have created particular ways of social life must change them in order to respond to the environmental change.

b) Population: Alterations in population sizes and density also affect the forms of social life, i.e. culture and social structure. Too great a population exerts pressure on resources, goods and services, which may in turn lead to migration, social disorganisation, or starvation.

c) Innovation: Innovations are discoveries, inventions, and diffusions that represent additions to 'societal knowledge'. Discoveries and inventions contribute to social change by adding elements to society. Diffusions, by making societies and communities borrow ideas and artefacts from others, contribute to social change.

d) Human Action: Human action happens in the form of various movements and counter movements in society. These may be in the form of actions by powerful individuals or groups of people, e.g. the actions of Shaka Zulu, Mahatma Gandhi, the Women's Movement, poor people's movements, etc.

e) Values and Norms: Societal values and norms can stimulate change by allowing for acceptability of what is new, increasing tolerance of elements from other people's cultures, and encouraging those of its members with the imagination to do things.

Social change may be viewed as taking on various forms: *evolution,* implying a natural process without intervention, or *revolution,* implying crisis and upheaval, or *development,* which implies change in a positive direction assisted by planned intervention (Elliot, 1993).

Evolutionary change or evolutionism

The theories of evolutionary change maintain that major social and political changes are to be understood as forms of 'evolution', whereby social structures gradually adapt themselves to material conditions, and steady improvements in institutions emerge from failed attempts at change. This theory of change, as earlier highlighted, has a long history and versions were common in the 18th century, expounded, for example by Montesquieu and Kant (Scruton, 1982).

Radical or revolutionary change

Radical change can also be referred to as revolutionary or discontinuous change, as theories focus not only on the scale of the change involved, but also on a decisive break with the past for the entire system. It involves the overturning of old ways and ideas, and their replacement with new and unique ones. Radical change is characterised by its speed, scale and break with the past through wholesale changes to structures and systems (Burnes, 1992).

Planned change or development

Ideas of planned change or development rest on the notion that there must be a need for creating an awareness of the rationale for change. One can achieve this by contrasting an actual state with a more desired one (Burke, 1987). The distinguishing mark in this respect is that attempts are made at a balanced ordering of feasible objectives and the utilisation of analytical tools to relate means to ends, and to overcome problems in the process of change (Osie-Hwedie, et al., 1990).

Organisational change

Organisational change is based on the unanticipated consequence of ordinary action, solution-driven problems, the tendency for innovations and organisations to be transformed during the process of innovation, the endogenous nature of created environments, and the interactions among the three systems of individuals, organisations, and environments (March, 1988). In the study of changes in organisations, various models emerge, but the organisation development model appears to be one of the more feasible ones, probably because this model is about changing the organisation from one situation, which is regarded as unsatisfactory, to another by means of social science techniques for change. The philosophy of organisation development is one of long-term change. It is very much a strategic mechanism for initiating change that places emphasis on the process of attaining change (McCalman and Paton, 1992).

In order to understand the basis of organisation change one has to place it within the context of the organisation itself. There are four principles for understanding organisational change, and McCalman and Paton (1992:130) use Pugh's (1978) principles in discussing these points:

a) Organisations as organisms: the organisation is not a machine and change must be approached carefully and rationally.

b) Organisations as occupational and political systems: the reaction to change relates to what is best for the agency, how it affects individuals and groups, and how it affects the power, prestige and status of individuals and groups.

c) Members of an organisation operate in occupational, political, and rational systems at the same time: arguments for and against change will be presented using rational arguments as well as occupational and political considerations.

d) Change occurs most effectively where success and tension combine: two factors are important here, namely confidence and motivation to change. Successful individuals or groups will have the confidence to change aspects of their work, which are creating problems. Unsuccessful members of the organisation are difficult to change because they adhere to the status quo in order to protect themselves.

After looking at the different forms of change, an examination of one of the most used theories in analysing society is imperative at this juncture. This is the social systems theory.

The social systems perspective

Considering society as a social system allows a view of social change that includes an understanding of how change in one part of a system calls for change in other parts. A social systems approach provides a framework for analysing the manner in which social change affects both society as a whole and individuals within society. In other words, as change takes place in one part of society, mechanisms developed to maintain that society must also change (Johnson et al., 1997). The systems theory can be used to grapple with an enormous range of individual, group, and wider environmental variables by acknowledging the mutual interconnectedness of social systems and asserting the dialectical relationship between a range of variables, including the fact that the superstructure of political and social institutions, and the ideologies which justify them, interact with the infrastructure of economic production (Leonard, 1975). Furthermore, the systems theory may be interwoven with the ecological approach where transactions between people and their environment are highlighted. In this approach it is taken that the environment influences, and also is influenced by, the specific extent to which people use the space as well as the available natural resources.

Robbins (1990:11-19) provides insights into the workings of organisations by using the social systems framework. He differentiates between open and closed systems, and demonstrates how an open systems approach can be helpful in conceptualising better what it is that organisations do. A perfect closed system would be one that receives no energy from an outside source and from which no energy is released to its surroundings, whilst an open system recognises the dynamic interaction of the system with its environment. The underlying assumption of an open system approach is that all systems have inputs, transformation processes, and outputs. It recognises the interdependence between the system and its environment, and notes that changes in the environment affect one or more attributes of the system, and conversely, changes in the system affect its environment. Robbins (1990) concludes that the systems perspective encourages all managers to identify and understand the environment in which their system operates, by helping them to see the organisations as stable patterns and actions within boundaries and to gain understanding of why organisations are resistant to change. Robbins

(1990) is also aware that the systems perspective should not be viewed as a panacea in that it has its limitations, the most telling being its abstractness.

Social change is often precipitated by economic, political, technological, ideological, and environmental changes, events, and developments. Changes or new developments in any of the above may in turn call for change in the way human needs are met (Johnson et al., 1997). New challenges emerge with change, especially when it comes to meeting human needs. In some instances, change in fact disrupts the functioning of a society's subsystems, its institutions, families, and individuals. Therefore, change and adaptation must continue if the needs that exist in the contemporary societal system, those of individuals and families that are negatively affected by the change process, are to be met (Johnson et al., 1997). Such change can be likened to the period when Zambia abolished Socialism for the free market system. Zambians experienced drastic changes in their lives, and indeed the country faced major social upheavals because of this occurrence. Hence the changes in Zambia can be seen as catalysts that, among other things, heightened uncertainties in the country's social policy. Without doubt, social policy is not immune to either positive or negative influences of social change.

Pre-colonial Zambia

Zambia's earliest inhabitants were the San people who had been living a nomadic type of existence for thousands of years. It was only around the 16th century that some tribes started arriving from the north and disrupted the lives of these indigenous inhabitants. The new arrivals were part of the Luba-Lunda migrations in the area of the present-day Democratic Republic of the Congo (DRC), which were triggered by many factors such as dwindling natural resources coupled with population growth. The dispersions led to many tribes migrating southwards and occupying huge areas in Zambia. Many of these tribes were pastoralists or farmers, whilst the San were hunter-gatherers. Therefore, the new tribes were able to establish permanent settlements where the San had not. These tribes were Bantu and also had higher forms of social and political organisation, and therefore easily displaced the San people. The Tonga are thought to be the earliest Bantu-speaking people to inhabit Zambia.

These migrations from the Luba-Lunda Kingdom and the establishment of new societies in pre-colonial Zambia can be categorised as part of larger processes of social change in the country prior to colonial encroachment. The new tribes also introduced other ways of harnessing natural resources, for instance iron ore for tool-making, and agriculture for the cultivation of crops. Thus, early forces of social change in pre-colonial Zambia can be said to have come in the form of the Luba-Lunda dispersions. After a period of almost a hundred years, outside influences began to be discernable in this area. The first incursions were by Portuguese explorers and traders who tried to establish links with the east coast of Africa. The Arab slave raiders were next in line. With the slave traders and explorers came guns, beads and other European artefacts that the local people had never been exposed to. Further, there were new tribes that arrived in the area, escaping the *mfecane* of Shaka Zulu in the south.[1]

All these forces, converging on pre-colonial Zambia, acted as catalysts for social change (there are numerous works that have been written on the history of Zambia and Central Africa; see for instance Mainga, 1973; Colson and Gluckman, 1951; Gann, 1958). Also, Dr David Livingstone's explorations and his anti-slavery and philanthropic work in Central Africa inadvertently opened up the area for British colonial rule. By the end of the 19th century, the area now known as Zambia had attracted a host of missionaries, traders, farmers and colonial administrators from Europe. Never again would the local people have a say over their lives in a long time.

Colonial rule

There are two distinct periods in Zambia's colonial period. There were first the Charter years when Zambia was administered by the British South Africa Company (BSAC) of Cecil Rhodes from the 1890s to 1924. Then Zambia was first ruled as two territories, North-Eastern and North-Western Rhodesia, then as the single territory of Northern Rhodesia from 1911. The second period was from 1924 to 1964, when Northern Rhodesia was governed by the British government. Zambia was occupied by Britain in a roundabout manner. Lewanika, king of the Lozi of Barotseland had signed a treaty with agents of the BSAC, with the aid of the French Missionary François Coillard.[2] Unfortunately, Lewanika was beguiled into believing that he was signing a pact with Queen Victoria of Britain for 'protection'. After this devious act, the Charter secured mineral rights in the territory and the BSAC started exploring for minerals in the area as well as exploiting the natural resources for its own benefit. There was a steady in-flow of white settlers into Zambia in search of new wealth. Many came to the territory after the Anglo-Boer War and were attracted by new opportunities for farming, mining, trading and hunting. As part of Rhodes' grand design for the extension of British imperialism, the construction of the railway from the south to the north had begun towards the end of the 19th century. By 1902 it had reached Livingstone, and it was extended to Kabwe in 1906 and Ndola in 1909 (Mwanakatwe, 1994).

British rule

On 1 April 1924, the BSAC after 34 years of Royal Charter handed over Zambia to the British Colonial Office after it had effectively subdued and subjugated the African populace. Prior to occupation, the country was inhabited by different tribes with varying degrees of political organisation. For the better part of the pre-colonial period, many Zambian communities were self-sufficient and able to meet their needs, although at rudimentary levels. Therefore, social distress was quite minimal and many social problems could be contained. It was only in times of war and when natural calamities struck that social problems were manifold. However, with the advent of colonial rule, this situation changed for the worse as indigenous populations were forcefully alienated from their productive processes by the colonialists, and had to abandon their crops and livestock. They were also coerced to work for menial wages in the colonial economy through instruments like the hut and poll taxes. For the whole colonial period, Zambians lived the lives of serfs on their own lands. In spite of some spin-offs of modernity such as education and health care, which were insignificant anyway, colonialism did not have the plight of Zambians at heart, but merely saw them as tools for propping up the colonising country's economy. Colonial rule was highly exploitative.

In the 1950s, white settlers began flirting with the idea of a Federation of three colonial territories. In effect, the Federation of Rhodesia and Nyasaland was created to pursue only settlers' interests. This arrangement lasted for ten years from 1953 to 1963. In this period, there was also talk of settler self-determination from the British Crown. However, this move was vehemently opposed by the African liberation movements in the three countries of Malawi, Zambia and Zimbabwe. In fact, the Federation was one issue that galvanised Africans around the call for self-rule. For Zambia, the Federation was a double blow: first, the rights of Zambians were usurped by a white settler population and secondly, and more important, all its wealth was siphoned off to Salisbury in Southern Rhodesia (the Capital of the Federation) to build the latter country's infrastructure. The Federation of Rhodesia and Nyasaland had only benefited Zimbabwe (then Southern Rhodesia, with the largest settler population, fully self-governing since 1923) at the expense of Zambia, as Mwanakatwe (1994:45) records:

> Zambia's own birthright had been whittled away for the benefit of Southern Rhodesia. Money from the mines was being spent for the benefit of Southern Rhodesia. It was there that the roads were built; it was in Salisbury and Bulawayo that buildings were constructed in an unprecedented economic boom. In fact, it was in Southern Rhodesia that the defence forces were based, that the Federal airline had its headquarters and from which the Rhodesia railway system was controlled. Although the copper mines were 1 000 kilometres away in Northern Rhodesia, the owners of the giant mining groups established head offices in Salisbury far away from the scene of operations.

The main political movement against colonial rule in Zambia was the United National Independence Party (UNIP) headed by Kenneth David Kaunda. UNIP's firebrand type of politics endeared it to the mass of the people who were in most cases poor and extremely disadvantaged by the racist policies of the colonial government of Northern Rhodesia. UNIP had split from the Northern Rhodesia African National Congress (NRANC), which was later renamed the African National Congress (ANC). It was Zambia's first politically organised group fighting colonial rule; its President General was Godwin Mbikusita-Lewanika. Later, Harry Mwaanga Nkumbula became president with Kaunda as Secretary General. Kaunda then split from the ANC in 1958 to form the Zambia African National Congress (ZANC), later known as UNIP (see Mwanakatwe, 1994; Noyoo, 2000). UNIP and Kenneth Kaunda would eventually lead Zambia to independence. Nevertheless, it was not plain sailing for UNIP at the polls during the elections of 1962, which were aimed at setting the stage for African self-rule and also to prepare the country for independence two years later, through another round of general elections.

The making of a post-colonial society

The post-colonial period can be better understood if divided into several historical eras that the Zambian nation traversed: the First, Second, and Third Republics. The First Republic Zambia was the first period of the country as an independent sovereign state, while in the Second Republic Zambia was declared a one-party state. In the Third Republic multi-party politics were re-introduced in the country and Zambians began to imbibe the values of democracy.

It is important to bear in mind that even though UNIP was popular with the masses, it did not win an outright majority in the polls of 1962. Prior to the elections of 1964, a coalition government ruled for two years, after the elections that had allowed African participation for the first time (see Mwanakatwe, 1994 for details). In the 1962 elections the United Federal Party and the Liberal Party (which were in fact settler parties) obtained 17,000 and 1,500 votes respectively, while Nkumbula's ANC managed to win 21,000 votes. Kaunda and UNIP could not form an African government as the elections were a stalemate with no outright winner, and only a coalition government could be mandated to rule Northern Rhodesia as it prepared for independence. Thus, Kaunda convinced Nkumbula to form a coalition government with him, which then made it possible for Zambia to move on to the next stage, the 1964 elections. All these initiatives were preconditions set by the colonialists for Zambia to attain independence.

The point to note from these assertions is despite a unanimous desire to end colonialism, Zambian society was not politically homogeneous as UNIP and Kaunda had attempted to make it, but a plural society that had a wide array of political interests. Also, Kaunda was not the saviour of Zambia from colonialism, as UNIP's propaganda machine wanted people to believe when the country's history was distorted by the one-party state. Indeed, other segments of Zambian society that were not in UNIP had also fought for Zambia's independence. If Nkumbula had been selfish, power-hungry or unpatriotic, he would have formed a coalition government with the settler parties and this would have truly stalled Zambia's quest for independence.

Ironically, immediately after Zambia became independent, Kaunda and UNIP worked quite vigorously to undermine and ostracise Nkumbula and the ANC. There were already calls then for a one-party state and for nationalisation of Zambia's key industries. Kaunda and UNIP also made sure that they reneged on certain commitments that they had made with certain sections in the colony prior to liberation. These agreements were pivotal to Zambia's eventual freedom. One outstanding issue that was not honoured by the Zambian government after independence was the Barotseland Agreement of 1964.[3] Just like Nkumbula, if the Barotse Royalists or the Lozi nation had been selfish, they could have formed a pact with the settlers, or better still seceded from Northern Rhodesia, and in the process thrown the whole independence initiative into disarray.[4]

The institutionalisation of the one-party system in Zambia was not justified at all. It was selfish and uncalled for and cost Zambia tremendously as it retarded the country's development.

The First Republic

Zambia became independent on 24 October 1964 and its first president was Kenneth Kaunda, the son of an evangelist/missionary sent by the Church of Scotland in present-day Malawi for church work in the Northern Province of Zambia. Kaunda was born in this area in 1924. During colonial rule, UNIP was forceful in advocating an egalitarian and non-racial society premised on African values. This call would later be refined into a working ideology of UNIP known as Humanism. As a condition for granting Zambia's independence, nationalist leaders had to accept a multi-party system and a politically neutral civil service on metropolitan lines. In consequence, civil servants were instructed to adhere to universalistic criteria and to insist on the separation of powers, and on the distinction between politics and administration (Chikulo, 1985). At the time, there existed a lot of international goodwill in terms of advice to the new Zambian government, for example, from the United Nations and other international organisations. These agencies were in the forefront of sending advisers and personnel to help the new nation. The country was also privileged to have the advice of renowned development experts like Dudley Seers and many more at its disposal.

For the better part of the 1960s and early 1970s, Zambia experienced positive growth in the economy, enabling people to easily access free quality health care, education and social welfare services. All these things were made possible by soaring copper prices that earned the country substantial foreign exchange. Copper was and still continues to be Zambia's economic mainstay. Nevertheless, this glowing picture would diminish when copper prices plummeted on international markets, leading to also an implosion of the country's economy. Other factors, for example political misrule and maladministration, also hastened the economy's downfall. As poverty levels began to spiral out of control in the 1980s and the 1990s the writing was on the wall that the country was headed for tougher times. By the end of the 20th century, Zambia was categorised as one of the poorest countries in the world, having been one of the richest countries in Africa after South Africa in the 1960s.

One may wonder what went wrong. Indeed, this section is an attempt at shedding some light on what could have been the contributing factors towards Zambia's dismal performances in the political and economic arenas that in turn negatively affected the country's human development standing.

Zambia had inherited a lopsided economy that dogged development efforts at the outset. The economy had inherent structural weaknesses; first, it was primarily and extremely dependent on the copper mining industry which accounted for about 40 per cent of Gross National Product (GNP), 92 per cent of total export earnings, 71 per cent of government revenue and about one third of employment in the directly productive sectors. Secondly, there was lack of internal sectoral linkages: the mining sector was developed with minimal backward or forward linkages to the rest of the economy. Thirdly, the economy manifested regional dualism and racial inequality (Maipose, 1989). Hence the industrial-manufacturing and agricultural sectors, accounting for 6.1 per cent and 11.5 per cent respectively of GNP, were largely undeveloped and remained unintegrated into the economy with the aforementioned sectors. Human resource development and use were below par as was shown in the general chronic shortage of qualified and experienced manpower and to some extent in the inappropriate attitudes associated with elitism and amateurism inherited from the old British system (Maipose, 1989). Mwanakatwe (1994) points out that the colonial administration's legacy in many areas of development was poor. The network of good roads and effective telecommunication systems existed mainly in urban centres for use by the white settlers.

Although there were these obstacles, immediate post-independence development surpassed by far what the colonial administration had achieved in seventy years. Mwanakatwe (1994) considers that Kenneth Kaunda will be remembered for many years for building sound economic and social infrastructure following independence. He notes that it is the vision and vigour with which development programmes were implemented during the first ten years of Kaunda's term of office as president of Zambia that will endure with the passing of time. This discussion contends, though, that it was not accidental that Zambia's development rapidly expanded in this period. The expansion was due not just to the economic boom, but also to the fact that Zambia from 1964 to 1972 was a plural society with functioning opposition politics. Parliamentary politics were essential in seeing to it that the ruling party fulfilled the dreams and aspirations of the Zambian people, through checks and balances. Furthermore, Kenneth Kaunda's first cabinet has been described as the most professional and educated of his 27-year rule. Many of these individuals had sat in the 'trenches' with Kaunda as they fought colonial rule together. For instance, the late Nalumino Mundia and Simon Kapwepwe were men of high stature and calibre who would not allow Kaunda to get away with misrule.[5] They were not 'yes-men', nor did they feel that they owed him anything as they all had strong struggle credentials. Kaunda was merely a colleague and a brother, and not a demi-god.

Therefore, most of the positive strides made by UNIP during the First Republic should also be attributed to the multi-party system that kept the ruling party in check and denied it carte blanche in matters relating to Zambia's development. Even though Kaunda and UNIP accused the opposition of practising tribal politics, at least this burgeoning democratic system demanded transparency and accountability. It was opposed to the one-party philosophy that UNIP espoused and which Kaunda explicitly sought immediately after independence.

In the 1960s and early 70s the agricultural sector also received considerable attention from the government. Co-operatives were set-up around the country, among other initiatives. The Credit Organisation of Zambia (COZ) was also created in order to enable poor farmers to access loans to help them purchase agricultural implements. In this sense, Zambia was aspiring to become a developmental state in this era. The development strategy pursued in the 1960s and 70s was import-substitution industrialisation which emphasised the expansion of public ownership and central planning within the framework of administrative controls over prices, imports, and foreign exchange allocation. Price signals and incentives were accorded only a minor role in policy-making. However, such controls imposed a severe burden on a country which had extremely limited human resources in management and the economy. Public sector enterprises were typically either inefficient or hamstrung by the centrally imposed pricing policies which threatened their financial viability (Pearce, 1994a).

During the First Republic (1964-72), Zambia had what was referred to as a mixed economy. Private enterprise was encouraged to flourish, although the government was also very active in the economy, especially in the areas of infrastructure development and agriculture. Having inherited a backward and mono-commodity type of economy, the state was compelled to try to diversify the economy, but with little success as Ndulo (1985:18) observes:

> This has been the prime objective, of not only the post-colonial government, but also of the colonial government. They all espoused the diversification of the economy away from copper – both in terms of the share of copper exports in total exports and the domination of the

copper industry in the economy. The implementation of this policy has however proved elusive. Partly because both governments have used copper resources in their efforts to diversify away from the dependence on copper. This policy is likely to be a contradiction in itself. It is similar to the old problem of trying to cure a drug addict with drugs. Inevitably, it has had the tendency to lock the economy into more copper investments, so as to generate more revenue and foreign exchange to expand the other sectors of the economy.

In the same period, the government also invested heavily in human development, with schools, hospitals, roads and houses being built for the benefit of the Zambian people. During this era, it can be said that the government indeed scored very high marks as it elevated the living standards of Zambians, and it was a truly caring one.

Zambia had already embroiled itself in regional politics even before the independence gains were consolidated. Liberation movements in the region were given sanctuary as they fought colonial rule. Despite remonstrations from the opposition when it advised the government to tread carefully on this issue given Zambia's fragile economy and precarious geographic location, Kaunda and UNIP nonetheless went ahead and courted the wrath of minority white regimes in the region, with devastating results for Zambia's economic development.

The Second Republic

In December 1972 Zambia was officially proclaimed a one-party state, and a year later the consolidation of this system started in earnest. All opposition political parties and activities were effectively banned. The country's political landscape was now dominated and controlled by one party, UNIP. In the same vein, the economy also quickly changed into a command type with the state now assuming direct control of the country's industries. Therefore, public enterprises predominated in this period after the Mulungushi and Matero Reforms of 1968 and 1969, which paved the way for government's involvement in and almost total control of Zambia's economy.

The one-party state can be referred to as one of the darkest times in Zambian history. In this era, dissent and alternative views from those of the ruling party were thwarted. All spaces for political contestation were closed down and Zambia slowly became a regimented society. There were arbitrary and mass detentions of Zambians who were perceived as enemies of UNIP and Kaunda. Innovation and talent were treated with suspicion and perceived as potential threats to single-party rule.

Businesspersons or wealthy individuals were also targets of the one-party state, and they in turn felt insecure. The country began to 'mark time' in this period. Indeed, the room for competition and an adherence to the merit system were virtually wiped out during this era. Kaunda became highly unpredictable and autocratic during this form of governance.

In many respects, the one-party state stalled the forces of social change in Zambia. For instance, brakes were put on Zambia's political evolution and for 17 years the country was bogged down in the politics of one party, UNIP. This arrangement did not augur well for the growth of democracy, political maturity and an appreciation of competition and diversity in the political arena. It was the one-party state that effectively snuffed out the plurality of Zambian society and a spirit of open dialogue, transparency and constructive criticism. That is why the Third Republic proved to be a political circus, primarily because of the leadership void created by the one-party state. This also had a knock-on effect on associational life and the vibrancy of civil society. The state of emergency that was put in place by the colonial government just prior to independence and inherited by the UNIP government became an effective tool in quelling political opposition by the Kaunda regime (including students) for twenty-seven years. Up to the demise of the single-party regime, Kenneth Kaunda continuously refused to lift the state of emergency.

Political intimidation, harassment, threats and innuendos were part and parcel of the one-party system's daily lexicon. Certain areas that were considered opposition strongholds, like the North-Western and Western Provinces, were left to wallow in poverty despite their rich natural resource bases. The one-party state also bred laziness in the manner that people expected hand-outs from the government, and this situation suited Kaunda as it created a passive populace. That is why patronage was at an extremely high level during this era. The one-party state was top-heavy, wasteful and mostly less innovative. It subsidised urban consumption at the expense of agricultural production in the rural areas. Free-loading also meant that people were no longer willing to pay for services and expected everything free of charge. This ingrained culture proved extremely detrimental to Zambian families and communities when the economy was liberalised, as they could not immediately move away from this dependent mind-set to one of self-reliance.

Because of all this, the economy went into deep recession. In fact it was already facing a crisis in its external account, around 1975, before the start of the Third National Development Plan. In 1978 the IMF was, as the then Minister of Finance put it, 'invited' to Zambia to help the country resolve its balance of payment crisis. This introduced an external factor into the formulation of economic policy (Ndulo, 1985). By the 1980s, attempts were made by the Zambian government to stabilise the economy, while its external position was also becoming critical, with the shocks to world interest rates and oil prices compounding the problem of debt and low copper prices. The pressure on the government to carry out significant reforms, and the bargaining power of the IMF and the World Bank, increased significantly as the external position weakened (Pearce, 1994a).[6] After the external economic jolts suffered in the early 1970s and the decline of the economy's performance in the 1980s and 90s, Zambia's total external debt had risen to unimaginable levels by the new millennium. The country's total stock of external debt amounted to US$7.1 billion by the end of 2004 (Jubilee Zambia, 2005).

It must be stated that Kenneth Kaunda and his colleagues, with all their shortcomings, can be said to have initially had Zambia's best interests at heart. This was before they were corrupted by power. Indeed, this characteristic was clearly exhibited when Kaunda lost power in the 1991 elections. After all the elections results were counted and showed that the MMD was in the lead, Kenneth Kaunda immediately held a news conference over the airwaves of Zambia's State Broadcaster, the Zambia National Broadcasting Co-operation (ZNBC), informing the nation that he had accepted the will of the people and graciously conceded defeat. He went on to thank the incoming president Frederick Chiluba and began waiting for him at State House so that he could hand over the reins of power. The former president had to wait for more than four hours while the MMD and Chiluba were busy celebrating. Kaunda's magnanimous attitude in defeat has remained imprinted in the minds of Zambians, and left a soft spot in their hearts for the 'father of the nation'.

These days the old man or bamudala, as he is fondly called by many Zambians, is involved in many causes of social justice such as HIV/AIDS advocacy (having himself lost a son to the scourge in 1996 and being the first leader in the world to come out publicly on a personal tragedy relating to AIDS), debt cancellation, environmental and poverty related issues. From time to time he is also called upon by African leaders to offer advice on certain issues of critical concern. He also plays an advisory role to both the ruling party and the opposition, especially when the country reaches a political impasse. The end of Kaunda's and UNIP's rule was to usher into power a breed of selfish and amoral leaders who further plunged Zambia into the abyss of despair. However, many Zambians were at the time simply euphoric with the 'change'.

The Third Republic

Frederick Titus Jacob Chiluba swept to power in 1991, riding on a crest of popularity that had only been witnessed in Zambian politics in the early post-colonial years. There were distinct shifts that emerged with the Third Republic. The return to a multiparty political system entailed changes in the operations of, among other institutions, the legislature, the judiciary, the cabinet, and the public service (Mukwena and Lolojih, 2002). To reorient some of these institutions to the new political dispensation, the government embarked on governance and institutional reforms, launching the Public Service Reform Programme (PSRP) in November 1993, to improve the quality, delivery, efficiency and cost-effectiveness of public services to the people of Zambia. The three main components of the PSRP were restructuring of public services, management and human resources improvement, and decentralisation and strengthening of local government (Mukwena and Lolojih, 2002:215).

On the economic front, deregulation and liberalisation of institutions were set into motion. Public enterprises were unbundled with many state-owned industries either being privatised or simply shut down. Instead of following prudent and well thought-out policies of stabilisation, the new Movement for Multiparty Democracy (MMD) literally mortgaged the country. The privatisation programme was ill-conceived and all caution was thrown to the wind. In certain instances, companies were simply stripped of assets by unscrupulous individuals posing as 'foreign investors'. Frederick Chiluba, a former trade union leader, was at the helm of the new MMD government when the decision to liberalise Zambia's economy was made. It was thus ironic that this individual was to profoundly betray Zambian workers when the MMD government began to strictly adhere to the IMF/World Bank-led Structural Adjustment Programme (SAP). And, as in the past, the implementation of the SAP by the Zambian government, in collusion with its donor 'masters', was shrouded in secrecy and was neither transparent nor consultative in approach.

The effects of the SAP were immediate and drastic: the Zambian currency, the kwacha, was devalued by 120 per cent. Prices and bank interest rates were freed, while trade and foreign exchange controls were liberalised. The privatisation programme saw 19 state companies sold and 70,000 public sector workers losing their jobs. Living standards declined rapidly with malnutrition affecting nearly 50 per cent of the under-15 age group and at least 30 per cent of the adult population. In the same period

(18 months to be exact), the erosion of the manufacturing industry had effectively commenced (Nyakutemba, 1993). As a result, Zambia witnessed an unprecedented 56 strikes by workers in the first nine months of MMD's rule, who demanded the government's resignation. But Frederick Chiluba and his government were resolute and did not relent.

Zambia became a 'dumping ground' for all sorts of goods that further undermined the local manufacturing base. There were no stringent measures to counteract the influx of such goods as the economy was supposedly liberalised. The liberalisation of the economy also meant that certain ridiculous concessions were made to some 'investors'. Tax free incentives to business entities like Shoprite effectively meant that they could import everything from South Africa for the Zambian consumer without paying any tax for a period of over five years. Thus, there were imports of agricultural products such as vegetables, tomatoes, onions, etc., from South Africa that undermined Zambia's agricultural base. These products could have been easily sourced in Zambia. Such was the farce of Chiluba's privatisation programme. Some companies that took over the operations of former state enterprises were no better or even produced products which were of low quality. Many did not engage in infrastructure development, but merely took over the buildings of the former state-owned businesses and painted them. For example, the former state shops of Mwaiseni or the National Import and Export Corporation (NIEC) stores were simply bought by Shoprite. Shoprite did not even build one shop, but simply renovated these old dilapidated buildings and commenced trade.

The policy framework that was put in place by the MMD did not deliver any new impetus to economic growth and social progress in the 1990s. In 1991-98 average growth was negative, annual growth rates being positive in only three out of the eight years; GDP per capita declined from US$305 in 1990 to US$257 in 1995. In 1998 the economy contracted by 2 per cent, lowering income per capita by around 5 per cent. Even though real GDP grew by 2.4 per cent and 3.6 per cent in 1999 and 2000, the economy did not perform well. Zambian consumers also suffered high levels of inflation throughout the 1990s, with the rate peaking at 188 per cent in 1993, before falling to an annual average of 26 per cent at the end of the decade (International Labour Organisation, 2005).

The privatisation programme under the ten-year rule of Chiluba and the MMD had devastating effects on the social fabric of Zambia. The government's approach can be said to have been callous in some ways. Many workers who were retrenched from the various state-owned enterprises were never paid their dues. Many of the employees of such organisations lived in poverty and even died whilst waiting for their retrenchment packages. Even today there are some retrenched workers who are still waiting for their severance packages. The plight of the former employees of the defunct United Bus Company of Zambia (UBZ) is a case in point; at the time of writing, these workers had not been paid their money although the dissolution of the company occurred in the early 1990s. When a spokesperson for the surviving UBZ workers made representation to government, its response was that the issue was before a liquidator and therefore nothing could be done. To take another example: when the wives and widows of former workers of the Nitrogen Chemicals of Zambia (NCZ) marched to State House to petition the president over non-payment of retrenchment packages, they were simply met by riot police.

Should the liberalisation of an economy result in unnecessary deaths due to lack of income on the part of retrenched workers who are genuinely owed by so-called liquidators? One wonders how the families of these workers have been able to maintain their livelihoods all these years. This is one area where the government should have boldly stepped in and dealt with the problem in a humane way. After all these years, these poor workers' packages have been eroded by inflation and a highly volatile currency. This is one issue on which Chiluba will be harshly judged in years to come. There was no compassion on the part of the government when it came to dealing with the question of retrenched workers. The privatisation of almost all state-owned companies was not diligently mapped out.

In 2002, Levy Mwanawasa was sworn into office as Zambia's third president after narrowly winning the elections the previous year. His accession to power rekindled a sense of sanity in Zambian politics and the country in general. Insanity – which in this book means not purely clinical insanity, but actions resembling those of mad people, even by those who are 'normal' in the true sense of the word – had been exhibited in the way political hoodlums held the country to ransom during Chiluba's ten-year rule. Zambians witnessed ludicrous situations whereby professionals were relegated to being street vendors; street vendors even had their own minister and a vendors' desk was set up at the president's official residence, State House. There is nothing wrong with street vendors, but when a country reaches a stage where there is actually a president for vendors, then, there is really a problem at hand. Owing to the president's 'policy', major towns began to be choked with informal traders as they partook in 'free trade' on the streets. Chiluba firmly believed that street trading would be Zambia's 'engine for growth'.

Also, the rule of law and professionalism on the part of politicians were severely eroded. Thugs, idle youths, petty criminals etc., were all lured to Chiluba's party and became quite powerful in intimidating Chiluba's opponents (this was evident during Chiluba's Third Term campaign).[7] Even Mwanawasa was at the receiving end of this type of harassment when he challenged Chiluba for the presidency of the MMD in the run-up to the general elections of 1996, on an anti-corruption platform. After this episode, Mwanawasa almost became a relic of history. In this environment, tribalism, corruption and nepotism were blatantly encouraged. It paid to speak the president's mother tongue as positions in the civil service, diplomatic corps, the military and remaining parastatals were distributed to Chiluba's cohorts. Chiluba was also renowned for carrying around suitcases full of money, which he distributed to those he favoured. This money, appropriately called a 'slush fund', was never accounted for or audited.

Mwanawasa was to become Zambia's first intellectual president. He had studied law at the University of Zambia and risen to the position of State Counsel. His predecessors were of humble education. Kaunda was a teacher who had studied up to Form Two. Nevertheless, in those days, these were strong credentials for an African. Kaunda also strove to perfect himself and was passionate about education, probably because of his teaching background. The government of Zambia invested heavily in education after independence. On the other hand Chiluba, who was once a bus conductor and had risen to the position of Chairman General of the most powerful trade union organisation in Zambia, the Zambia Congress of Trade Unions (ZCTU), was simply clueless as to what governance entailed. Immediately after taking over, Mwanawasa began cracking down on corruption, and Chiluba and some of his ex-officials were indicted. At the time of writing, these individuals were still being tried.

Having an intellectual in State House also brought forth certain sober and logical decisions in the political arena. For instance, the question of investors and liberalisation of the economy, which had in effect become a free-for-all in Chiluba's time, began to be regulated to some extent. When Mwanawasa became president, the biggest private mining group in the country, the Anglo American Corporation of South Africa, pulled out of Zambia under mysterious circumstances. The country was left in the lurch, with no foreseeable compensation and no prospects for future mining activities. As explained earlier, mining (especially of copper) remains the backbone of the country's economy. Mwanawasa personally flew down to South Africa to renegotiate favourable terms for Anglo's exit. In the same vein, Mwanawasa and colleagues began to look for other investors in this sector. At present, Zambia has quite a diversified investor profile in the mining sector with Australian, Canadian, Indian and Chinese companies all operating.

However, there are still some disturbing continuities from the one-party state and the Third Republic that are discernable in the present political dispensation. The vestiges of these past political dispensations are still well entrenched in the political arena. Meritocracy is still lagging behind in the political sphere and the country as a whole. Government officials are still appointed for other reasons than ability, the aim, it seems, being still to reward the loyal. Thus a professional cadre of technocrats is yet to gain a firm footing in this present political environment. The Zambian citizens have also not changed. They still expect the politicians, 'the big men', to 'feed' them. Thus they remain gullible, especially during elections. The hungry masses are bribed with bags of maize meal, beer, and clothes (usually women's wrappers) so as to influence their votes. Women still go to the airport to dance for the president and his entourage every time he flies out of Zambia or returns from a trip abroad. It will take time to erase this culture of servitude that was created by the one-party state and the culture of sycophancy and piracy crafted in the Third Republic. Probably, as Zambian society continues to evolve and the forces of social change envelop the country, a new psyche will emerge.

Social change and notions of development

This discussion not only assumes the importance of grasping the quintessential linkages between social policy and human development, but also finds it essential to establish how the two relate to the overall development process. Therefore, an elucidation of the term 'development' is imperative. The term is subject to many interpretations. Turock (1999:6) writes that 'development and its importance, remains highly controversial. Many policy-makers pay lip-service to development. Many government programmes around the world refer to development in positive terms, yet millions of people remain excluded and marginalised from the advances of economics.' Development theories and strategies are also subjected to various applications. Amartya Sen (1999) describes development in terms of *human capabilities* and sees it as a bundle of *freedoms*. He distinguishes five types of freedoms: (i) political freedoms, (ii) economic facilities, (iii) social opportunities, (iv) transparency guarantees, and (v) protective security. It is also important that public policy fosters human capabilities and substantive freedoms in general, as well as working through the promotion of these distinct, but interrelated instrumental freedoms. Development is then achieved through the removal of poverty, tyranny, lack of economic opportunities, social deprivation, and neglect of public services and the machinery of repression (Sen, 1999).

The enhancement of human freedom is regarded as both the main objective and the primary means of development. The objective of development relates to the valuation of the actual freedoms enjoyed by the involved. Individual capabilities crucially depend on, among other things, economic, social and political freedoms (Sen, 1999). This thesis' basic proposition is that we should evaluate development in terms of the expansion of people's capabilities to lead the kind of lives they value and have reason to value. Unlike increases in income, the expansion of people's capabilities depends both on the elimination of oppression and on the provision of facilities like basic education, health care, and social safety-nets (Evans, 2002). At the same time, growth in real output per head is also likely to expand people's capabilities.

W. Arthur (Sir Arthur) Lewis, the celebrated development scholar, observed that LDCs had all the resources required for their own development, in his seminal 1954 article on *Economic Development with Unlimited Supplies of Labour*. He argued that developing countries have within themselves all that is required for growth and should not be producing primarily for developed markets. He observed that international trade could not substitute for technical change, and that those who depended on it as a major of hope were doomed to frustration. The most important issue in developing countries, according to Lewis, was to transform the food sector, create agricultural surpluses to feed the urban populations and thereby create the domestic basis for industry and modern services (Lewis, 1954). Surprisingly enough, what Lewis was opposing was being championed by the World Bank and the IMF in their SAPs; they consider trade to be the engine for growth without considering its embedded unequal terms or the possibility that SAPs' prescriptions will create a glut in the market due to overproduction. Indeed, as SAPs were applied across the board in the developing world, it meant that primary producers in one commodity, for example coffee, would step up their production and increase tonnages for export. The end result is straightforward: depressed prices due to over-supply.

Development is also about economic growth, but should not be viewed as its sole criterion. The relevant question to ask then is: what produces economic growth? Román-Zozaya (2005) observes that behind growth we find the establishment and consolidation of a particular context of interaction which involves citizens, government, legislation and territory: the state. Without the state, there are no institutions to back economic relations or a functioning pro-growth social policy, which are again important for economic expansion and development. However, his main thesis is premised on the notion that societies which are *capitalism-capable* are the ones most likely to produce economic growth and, in that way, generate the wealth necessary for development. In this sense, development is seen as a social context or network which involves a particular set of institutions, the capitalism-capable society. The state, social policy and economic growth are all critical. In making his case, this author expresses the view that developing countries are not capitalism-capable and that this in fact remains their main problem: 'Whether we like it or not, capitalism, i.e., the system of production in which economic decisions are made mostly by private agents who seek profit in free or at least, relatively free markets, has proven to work; it produces wealth in amounts vast enough for humans to meet their needs, specifically to meet those of mass societies' (Román-Zozaya, 2005:4).

The present work does not entirely agree with Román-Zozaya's views, as he seems to treat only superficially the deleterious effects of international capitalist systems on the progress of developing countries. It is international capitalism that cemented the perpetual dependency of LDCs on the West and crystallised the unequal terms of international trade vis-à-vis LDCs' economic growth. The stark inequalities and inequities entrenched by the capitalist economic order between the West and LDCs are simply glossed over by Román-Zozaya. Despite this, he makes interesting points in terms of how growth could be viewed as a motor of development, or how a holistic social policy is important in the construction and preservation of economic growth and development. In this case, social policy should play a role in creating or consolidating technological innovation or adaptation capabilities; compensating those who lose when society changes owing to economic growth; redistributing income through education and health services, as well as support for entrepreneurial projects; and civic education to strengthen the state (Román-Zozaya, 2005).

The first *United Nations Development Decade* launched in the 1960s, followed a decade later by the *Second Development Decade*, and later on the *Copenhagen Summit on Social Development* in 1995, are important landmarks in development thought, signifying countries' commitments in the fight against poverty and social exclusion. In the first decade of development it was envisaged that countries could at least attain 5 per cent annual growth. But the poor economic growth and unimproved living conditions of most of the people in many parts of the world dimmed these hopes. This initiative was undertaken at the time when development was seen as being exclusively fostered by economic growth. Hence, growth-led theories of development were to predominate in this era. Nonetheless, this growth did not 'trickle down' to the poor, and a change of strategies had to take place over the decades.

In this text, development is taken as a holistic and ever-evolving process that is context-specific. The ultimate goal of development is the realisation of human progress and the eventual eradication of human suffering. Therefore, it should not come as a surprise that this grand vision elicits so many theories, strategies and political solutions. For this study, Rodney's (1972:9-10) definition of development seems appropriate, especially for contexts such as Zambia:

> Development in human society is a many-sided process. At the level of the individual, it implies increased skill and capacity, greater freedom, creativity, self-discipline, responsibility and material wellbeing. Some of these are virtually moral categories and are difficult to evaluate, depending as they do on the age in which one lives, one's class origins, and one's personal code of what is right and what is wrong. However, what is indisputable is that the achievement of any of those aspects of personal development is very much tied in with the state of the society as a whole. From earliest times, man found it convenient and necessary to come together in groups to hunt and for the sake of survival. The relations which develop within any given social group are crucial to an understanding of the society as a whole: freedom, responsibility, skill, etc. have real meaning only in terms of the relations of men in society.

In this definition there is less stress on economic indicators such as the GDP, or interest and inflation rates. Although these indices are important, a fixation on them tends to result in skewed development strategies. Rodney's definition seems more suited to a holistic and cross-cutting appraisal of the human condition that is also closer to the Human Development Perspective. For instance, if the issue of individuals being catalysts of development is closely examined, the above-cited attributes, even if they are moral categories, do play significant roles in charting the course of a country's development process. It goes without saying that a nation that has a significant number of free-loading, ill-disciplined and criminally inclined individuals will not be able to develop in the same way as a nation that is devoid of such elements. Therefore, even if these issues seem pronounced at the micro level, they significantly influence macro development imperatives. This text proposes that there ought to be a balance between the 'social' and the 'economic' dimensions of development if it is to be implemented in totality.

Selected theories of development

Different interpretations of development abound, and in the period after the end of the Second World War there was a particular increase in development theories that aimed at interpreting and providing solutions to mainly emerging problems of the developing world. Many of these theories hinged on Western-liberal paradigms, with the modernisation theory initially taking an upper hand. This section will cast some light on some selected development theories; it does not make pretensions at exhausting all of them. The intention is to allow the reader to appreciate the diversity in development thinking.

Modernisation theory

In the 1940s and 50s, there were widespread conceptions of development as a process of modernisation: a structural change process whereby the traditional and 'backward' 'Third World' countries needed to develop towards greater similarity with the Western, or rather, the North-Western world (Martinussen, 1997). Modernisation theory and its successors in neo-liberalism have their beginnings in structural-functionalist social and neo-classical economic theory (Graaff, 2001). This theory is bipolar, positing two contexts, the traditional society and a modern one. Modernisation theory presupposes that 'backward' or 'traditional' societies have to follow the same trajectories as Western nations in order to become developed. Traditional traits were said to hamper development in these 'backward' nations. Among the features of modern societies worthy of imitation were an extensive division of labour, a well-functioning and active state apparatus, a democratic form of government and equality before the law (Martinusen, 1997). Modernisation theorists saw development as an evolutionary process going through various stages and transforming all societies from traditional to modern. The number of stages varied from one writer to another: Hoselitz referred to two, traditional and modern; Lerner added an intermediary third, transitional stage. Parsons extended the number of stages to five, and so did Rostow with his well-publicised stages of traditional, pre-take-off, take-off, the road to maturity and the society of mass consumption (George, 1988:5).

The main weakness of this theory lies in its Eurocentric appraisal of social phenomena. It fails to capture the realities of the developing world such as the neo-colonial relations that still bind countries of the South in a bondage-kind of existence, where they cannot for instance define the terms of international trade, even though they are major producers of raw materials for the developed North. Modernisation theory merely assumes that by aping the West, LDCs will extricate themselves from their underdeveloped state that was in many ways created by Europe and America in the first place, through slavery, colonialism, and later on neo-colonialism. Modernisation theory seems to have little practical application in developing countries, as it perceives other cultures as not being in line with the notion of development. It also assumes that societies can only evolve along a single path, that is, the Western path. But even European countries did not have similar evolutionary patterns. They had and still have different political and economic histories. In a nutshell the theory is too simplistic and smacks of paternalism.

Dependency theory

This is one of the best-known neo-Marxist development theories. As with most social science theories, this theory was a child of its time (the end of the 1960s). Its major elements were: (a) the failure of the import substitution strategy, (b) the Cuban revolution, (c) the military coup in Brazil and (d) the United States' invasion of the Dominican Republic (Shuurman, 1993:3-4). Dependency theory was for a long time associated mainly with Andre Gunder Frank, though its origins are to be found in Marxist writings of Paul Baran in the late 1950s and the structuralist writings of a group of Latin American economists working with the United Nations Economic Commission for Latin America (ECLA) in Santiago in the early 1960s (George, 1988). Unlike Marx, who saw all countries going through a series of stages until they reached the Socialist stage, Baran saw Third World countries as being stuck in their stage of underdevelopment as a result of their structural exploitation by the industrialised countries. The Third World provided the rich countries with both raw materials and export markets at very favourable trade terms (George, 1988). On the one hand, Frank asserted that the spread of capitalism from the First World countries had a destructive influence on Third World countries. Also, he saw capitalism in the wealthier or core countries actively underdeveloping poorer or periphery countries. According to Frank, development in the core countries and underdevelopment in peripheral countries were two sides of the same coin (Graaff and Venter, 2001). This theory was criticised for its neglect of class analysis and the diversity of the Third World, and the assumption of non-workable political options such as self-reliance and a Socialist world government (Schuurman, 1993).

Structuralist theories and industrial development

Structuralist theories were originally launched in parallel in Latin America and Western Europe. Classical economic structuralism was in many ways affected by Keynes' perspective and method. Among other things, it shared with Keynes a great interest in unemployment. The structuralists paid particular attention to the barriers that obstructed structural changes (Martinusen, 1997). Their theory tended to be interventionist, albeit with strong differences between individual writers in the emphasis given to market failure. There was, however, some evolution as regards attitudes towards the desirability of a stronger role for the state. This change happened particularly during the 1970s, when structuralist writers, having concentrated heavily on the analysis of constraints on economic growth in developing countries, shifted their attention increasingly towards questions of income distribution and poverty alleviation (Colclough, 1991). The structuralist approach and the neo-Marxist perspective both agree that the dominance of advanced industrial societies is of crucial importance to the prospects of development in Third World countries. They disagree somewhat on the degree to which the former group of countries dominate and exploit the other (George, 1988).

Neo-liberalism

Neo-liberalism is more of an ideology than a theory. From the mid-1970s this development perspective enjoyed increasing popularity. The oil crisis at the beginning of that decade and the subsequent restructuring of international capitalism led to a redefinition of the role of the state. This development also meant the end of Keynesianism and the idea of the welfare state (Schuurman, 1993). The basis of the neo-liberal perspective revolves around limiting the role of the state, a liberal economy, and a strict monetary policy according to the guidelines of the IMF and the World Bank (Schuurman, 1993). Neo-liberals deny many of the main ideas of structuralist orthodoxy. They have been revisionists in reasserting the primacy of economic growth amongst policy objectives, believing that poverty will thereby be most effectively reduced (Colclough, 1991).

This slant of development thought eventually reached greater heights in later years, through the IMF and World Bank packages such as the Structural Adjustment Programmes.

The basic needs approach

The famous pronouncement in 1972 by the then president of the World Bank, Robert McNamara, that old economic development models had failed unleashed a flurry of theories that moved away from the conventional thought of the time. The International Labour Organisation (ILO) took its cue from this change in attitudes to broaden its earlier emphasis upon unemployment to encompass a commitment to the fulfilment of the 'basic needs' of the poor, whether employed or unemployed (Sandbrook, 1982). The ILO cited in Sandbrook (1982:16) referred to this approach in this way:

> A focus on meeting the basic needs of the people should imply a lessening of the dependence of the Third World on the markets, capital and technologies of the industrialised world; a greater potential for trade expansion among developing countries; an improvement in their terms of trade *vis-à-vis* the industrialised countries; a reduced dependence on and role for multinationals and sophisticated technologies; re-orientation of development assistance.

The shift towards an understanding of basic needs had a monumental effect on development thinking. The impact of this strategy redefined the aims of development towards fostering fairer distributions of income and resources, encouraging local participation and promoting small-scale projects employing socially and environmentally appropriate technologies (Brohman, 1996:204). The basic needs and equity with growth strategies were short-lived, however. Their demise was linked to the economic crisis of the 1970s and the ideological ascendancy of neo-liberalism in the leading developed countries and the international financial institutions (Mkandawire, 2001). After this, the stage was then set for alternative approaches to development in direct opposition to the prevailing economic dogma.

Sustainable development

Defined in 1987 by the Brundtland Report as 'development which meets the needs of the present without compromising the ability of future generations to meet their own needs', sustainable development is centred on the belief that social, economic and environmental objectives should be complementary and interdependent in the development process (Organisation for Economic Co-operation and Development, 2002:12). Elevated by the Earth Summit of 1992 at Rio de Janeiro and the Johannesburg World Summit on Sustainable Development (WSSD) in 2002, sustainable development includes taking into account the impact of present decisions on future generations. Sustainable development contains two key concepts around which balance must be sought: the 'needs' among the world's population, and the limitations associated with current states of technology and social organisation and their relationship to the capacity of the ecosphere to satisfy present and future demands (Singh and Strickland, 1994). The transition to sustainable development requires:

(i) full and true valuation of the natural, built and cultural environments;

(ii) longer term horizons reflecting both medium and long-term interests;

(iii) greater equity among members of present societies in terms of access to economic, social and political rights and resources; and

(iv) greater intergenerational equity across time, promoting fair treatment of future generations in their access to the means of sustainable development (Singh and Strickland, 1994).

Sustainable development has often been mistakenly interpreted in a narrow sense as an environmental issue. This understanding ignores the power and utility of the concept in its integration of economic and social development in the context of high quality environmental management. Approaches to sustainable development have been varied, reflecting the diversity of challenges faced by individual countries (Organisation for Economic Co-operation and Development, 2002).

Social development

Social development is another perspective that emerged out of the disquiet relating *inter alia* to the dominance of neo-classical economic theories in interpreting human wellbeing or their failure to provide solutions to pervasive poverty in LDCs. The United Nations was quite instrumental in bringing this alternative development slant to the fore, first in its 1968 International Conference of Ministers Responsible for Social Welfare and during the Copenhagen Summit for Social Development in 1995. Social development approaches have moved from strength to strength since these events. This human focused approach to development has as its starting point the recognition of people's roles in the overall development of their specific countries. Social development's focus is on productive capacity, participatory skills, cultural experience and enhancing the capacity and opportunity of everyone (Osei-Hwedie, 1990). Its main goal is to improve the social and material wellbeing of human beings and, in so doing, promote the possible level of human development. The more specific objectives of social development include (a) the realisation of more balanced approaches to social and economic development; (b) the elimination of the various barriers to development; (c) the realisation of new social arrangements that accelerate the pace of development and guarantee the satisfaction of people's basic needs; and (d) the transformation of societies towards more humanistic values based on social justice and human development (Chukwuka, 2000:53).

Social development must also be conceived as an agent of a larger process of development. The indicators of social development, therefore, should include improved economic productivity, improved efficiency, and stable and mutually supportive interactions among units of social systems. Defined in this way, social development encompasses community development and other specific-focused or directed development processes (Osei-Hwedie, 1990). It follows that the personnel, or agents of social development, must be able to understand the nature of development, have the capacity to tackle questions of cause and effect, and the implications and ramifications of present and future actions. Their focus should also transcend the symptoms of individual, group or community malaise (Osei-Hwedie, 1990).

Furthermore, different professionals can play various roles in the realm of social development so as to enhance human capacities and people's coping strategies, for example: change agent - to effect positive change in society against structural barriers; explorer - venturing into new social terrains and identifying novel interventions; innovator - to arrive at new ideas to reduce social distress and human deprivation; motivator - to encourage people to change their deplorable circumstances for the better; and initiator - effecting something new in communities in order to arrest social decay (Noyoo, 2000).

These development perspectives have been selected because of their dominance in development discourse in different epochs. It must be noted that there have been many derivatives of these theories, which have also come and gone with different ages. One cannot but agree with Streeten (1995:17-18) when he asserts: 'Sometimes one gains the impression that the development debate is just a succession of fads and fashions. But the evolution from economic growth, via employment, jobs and justice, redistribution with growth, to basic needs and human development represents a genuine evolution of thinking and is not a comedy of errors, lurching from one slogan to the next.'

Conclusion

This chapter was preoccupied with the task of developing an understanding of social change and how it influences societal processes such as development. In the same way, there were attempts to link social change to social policy and the idea of human development in the context of Zambia. For this purpose, the country's evolution from the pre-colonial period to the present time was illuminated. The next chapter focuses on the development and evolution of social policy in Zambia.

Notes

1   A Sotho-speaking tribe from present-day South Africa led by their king, Sebitwane, trekked from the south via Botswana to western Zambia and conquered the Lozi people. The Sotho, or Kololo as they are known by the Lozi, assimilated into the tribe and to this date the language used, Silozi, is a mixture of Sotho and Luyi (the old language of the Lozi). The Ngoni people were a tribe of Nguni origin from present-day Kwazulu-Natal in South Africa. Led by their king, Zwangendaba, they moved from the area fleeing Shaka up to the eastern part of Zambia. Their language has almost been lost through intermarriages with various local tribes, but they still maintain distinct customs from the south.

2   Coillard was a French missionary who had led the Paris Missionary Society (PMS) into Barotseland or Bulozi Kingdom of Lewanika. He had persuaded the Lozi king to seek British protection after several skirmishes with the Ndebele in Zimbabwe who were bent on annexing Barotseland. With further advice from Lewanika's allies: King Khama of the Tswana and King Moshoeshoe of the Sotho, he signed the infamous *Lochner Concession* that gave exclusive rights to the

Chartered Company of Cecil Rhodes to mine, prospect and exploit minerals in the area. The company could also exploit other natural resources in Barotseland and adjacent areas that came to be known as North-Western Rhodesia. However, Lewanika was only prudent in trying to safeguard his kingdom by seeking British 'protection' after witnessing the brutal suppression of King Lobengula of the Ndebele at the hands of the BSAC. The reality was that white people had arrived to conquer Africa and not to be partners in its development, and as a leader with foresight, he thought that he could honourably get into an agreement with the British Crown. However, he was tricked by the BSAC. This treaty enabled the Chartered Company to gain a foothold into Zambia. On the other hand, North-Eastern Rhodesia was annexed by the company through brute force. The Ngoni suffered huge losses in terms of both the death of thousands of their warriors and livestock that was confiscated by the BSAC after their defeat.

3. Barotseland was always treated differently by the British colonial authorities because of the treaties that Lewanika had signed with the BSAC. Barotseland would at times be seen as a 'Protectorate within a Protectorate'. It had its own Native Government and Treasury. Most of the money in the Treasury came in the form of taxes from its subjects who worked as migrant labourers in the mines of South Africa and royalties from the BSAC and other commercial entities. Even though Lewanika had been tricked by the Company, these treaties would serve a very critical role decades later. Indeed, they were extremely important in the whole equation of Zambia's independence as they were used as 'bargaining chips' during the negotiations for Zambia's self-rule at Lancaster House in London. The Barotseland Agreement was a sign of goodwill on the part of the Zambian government that it would guarantee some form of autonomous government for Barotseland. However, after independence, Kaunda and UNIP went on to strip Barotseland of all its rights and privileges and 'commandeered' its Treasury to the new Ministry of Finance. It has been speculated that this Treasury was worth at least £70 million. Despite the problems that emerged in the new Zambian state, ironically it was the British government that had started undermining Barotseland's sovereignty.

4. After the abrogation of the Barotseland Agreement of 1964, Kaunda and UNIP then systematically demonised and ostracised the Lozi

people, besides severely undermining the political processes in Barotseland. In response, Barotseland has for the better part of Zambia's independence been an opposition enclave. Kaunda's and UNIP's stance towards Barotseland has had far-reaching repercussions for the area as it is one of the most impoverished provinces in the country. To this day the Barotseland Agreement remains a contentious issue.

5   It is therefore not surprising that these gentlemen later fell out favour with Kaunda. Kaunda imprisoned and harassed Nalumino Mundia and Simon Mwansa Kapwepwe, who went on to form their own political parties, the United Party (UP) and the United Progressive Party (UPP) respectively.

6   A chronology of major economic policy agreements between the Zambian government and the international institutions from 1983 is given below:

1981-85 - Attempted stabilisation and limited liberalisation, initially under an IMF Extended Fund Facility, and then under a stand-by agreement;

1985-86 - An intensive reform effort during which the foreign-exchange auction operated and the abolition of food subsidies was attempted;

1986-87 - A period of disintegration of the IMF and the World Bank programme, culminating in a break in May 1987;

1987-89 - An attempt to go it alone under the Interim National Development Plan from May 1987 to June 1989;

1989-91 - Rapprochement with the Bretton Woods institutions, a phase beginning formally in June 1989 and lasting up to September 1991 when the programme broke down as food subsidies were increased following drought and the collapse of the marketing system in the run-up to elections (Pearce, 1994a:27).

7   The Zambian Constitution stipulates that a president can only serve two five-year terms of office. However, towards the end of Chiluba's ten-year rule, which was effectively two terms, he instigated certain segments of his party (MMD) to begin campaigning for his continued presidency. Chiluba had gambled that Zambians would be passive without putting up any form of resistance. In his quest to amend the Constitution so that he could run for office for another term, he

recruited all sorts of party thugs to drive his message home. A lot of money was also spread around to any would-be third term advocate. However, he had not anticipated a determined Zambian populace. Firstly, some members of his own cabinet resigned and formed an opposition party. Secondly, all sectors of the Zambian society including children rose up in a resounding No! Almost all Zambians (except those blinded by Chiluba's kleptocracy) rose to the occasion and effectively thwarted moves to sanction Chiluba's third term manoeuvres. This is one struggle that was waged by the Zambian people alone. While the Commonwealth was busy putting sanctions on Zimbabwe, no one in the international community was in the least interested in what was happening in Zambia as Chiluba audaciously flouted the rule of law. It was up to the Zambian people to fight despotism, and in the end, democracy won this tussle. The joke doing the rounds of Lusaka was that there were not many whites in Zambia to warrant any intervention from the Commonwealth, or for the international community to even bother with the unfolding political shenanigans in the country.

Chapter 3

THE DEVELOPMENT AND EVOLUTION OF SOCIAL POLICY IN ZAMBIA

Introduction

This chapter charts the development and evolution of social policy in Zambia from the colonial era to the present. Social policy in Zambia was firstly articulated by the colonial government just before the end of the Second World War and further elaborated upon after 1945. Later, social policy was dramatically transformed by the new Zambian government when the country gained independence. There are various forces that shaped the development and evolution of social policy in Zambia, which will be given some thought in this chapter, bearing in mind that both political and economic factors have been key determinants in its formulation and implementation.

Colonial society and social policy

As stated in the last chapter, Zambia was a British colony, part of the British Empire, from 1924 to 1964. The prevailing logic then was that the priorities of the colonial powers took precedence over those of the colonies. However, the end of the Second World War also signalled a new period when colonialism was no longer regarded as a viable venture by the imperialists. With the rise of nationalist politics in the colonies and the need for social and economic reconstruction in most of Europe, changes in the official colonial policy began to unfold. It was also felt in some quarters of British society that certain colonies needed to be prepared for self-rule. Therefore, Britain was willing to begin unbundling its colonies after the Second World War purely from a pragmatic point of view. This thinking also led to an understanding that colonial subjects needed to be engaged in some form of productive activities that could allow them develop their respective countries. Mass education or literacy campaigns that later on took the form of community development projects were spearheaded by colonial officers. This changed approach also brought forth a different way of handling the welfare of colonial subjects. To this end, social intervention in the colonies would be given scope by the formulation of the *Juvenile Welfare Policy in the Colonies of 1943* and the *Colonial Welfare Policy of 1945* (Colonial Office 1943; Colonial Office 1945).

The Zambian colonial setting was racially polarised and guaranteed better opportunities to Europeans, followed by Coloureds (people of mixed race descent) and Asians, or more specifically Indians, while Africans were at the bottom of this social ladder. The highly stratified colonial society clamped down on the African populace and did not allow them to maximise their potential. The colonial system was crafted in such a way that all the profit and wealth of the colony went into the hands of the Europeans, while Africans were exploited and gained nothing. On the whole, it was an extremely exploitative system with ownership of property restricted, and employment only available at the lowest levels in administration to Africans. In the mining industry, skilled and semi-skilled work was reserved for white labour, whilst management jobs were wholly out of the reach of Africans. There were no black army or police officers, judges, or senior managers. Commercial farming and the best land were monopolised by settler farmers (Turock, 1991).

With no tangible socio-economic opportunities available to Africans, poverty and squalor in their designated areas of abode were quite manifest. Therefore, colonial social policy primarily emerged to deal with African urban problems and make sure that they did not spill over into the Europeans' quarters. In the then Northern Rhodesia, unlike many other African colonies, a strongly knit European working class core grew rapidly as a result of the copper mining industry. This was founded on a small scale at the beginning of the 20th century but expanded quickly in the 1920s (Turock, 1991). The mining industry was extremely influential in shaping social policy in colonial Zambia via the provision of social welfare services. From the time the mines were established, the link between their activities and other sectors of the economy was for long recognised. For example, it was anticipated that the 'native labour' requirements of the railways, the farms, the Department of Public Works, and in fact every modern employment in the country would increase as mining expanded (Rhodesian Anglo-American in Lungu and Mulenga, 2005).

As early as 1929, the mines became responsible for provision of housing and hygiene. This form of patronage also extended to wages and food, and various other social services. It was the duty of the mine management to provide well-arranged sanitary and orderly compounds to house the employees (Lungu and Mulenga, 2005). Adequate hospitals for black workers were provided along with European medical staff. The mine management also gave minimum scale rations to their employees. They distributed maize-meal, millet, rice, beans, meat, fresh vegetables, and groundnuts on a weekly basis. Cinema shows were also periodic treats for the miners (Lungu and Mulenga, 2005). These services were extended to Europeans, but for them were qualitatively superior in all respects:

> Adequate and comfortable hospitals with competent medical personnel were provided in all mining settlements. However, European quarters had added facilities, such as electric light and water and generally they presented attractive appearance. The mining companies also provided recreation clubs for employees; cinema shows for European workers were provided once or by-weekly. Tennis, golf, cricket and football were encouraged and sponsored by the mine managements. Inter-mine contests were encouraged and competitions were arranged between teams of the Northern Rhodesian side and those from the Belgian Congo. During this phase, the mines provided many facilities to their employees (Lungu and Mulenga, 2005:35).

The mining sector was an enclave of prosperity and its employees duly benefited from its profits. To attain these profits, it needed a healthy and functioning workforce; hence the mining management's social investment plan. The mining companies were engaged in direct social welfare service provision which was at variance, in some instances, with the overall thrust of the colony's social policy. The services were more targeted and well-resourced. Only employees of the mining companies were catered for, but it can be argued that there was a 'spread effect' from the mining sector as miners would go back to their home areas with earnings from their work, which would help in meeting the needs of members of their extended families. In the wider colonial setting there were more needs as well as diverse recipients, while provision was from a discriminatory perspective.

Arguably, social policy was also used as a tool of social control in the colonial era. It was not only employed for the purpose of arresting urban decay and squalor that were emerging in the African quarters, but to control the colonial subjects through a 'carrot and stick' mechanism. Indeed, the colonial administration was always preoccupied with maintaining law and order, and keeping the subjugated Africans passive in order to safeguard the maximum exploitation of the resources of the colony by private enterprise.

Thus there was already a social policy framework existing before independence, but it was tilted towards the needs of the settler population and not those of indigenous Zambians. Colonial social policy was driven by racial discrimination, social exclusion and elitism. Like most African countries, colonial social policy was largely determined by the colonial mission, and adhered to a residualist approach. In different parts of Africa, the colonial mission was shaped and interpreted through the pressures of dominant interest groups such as missionaries, settlers, traders, mining groups, colonial officials (military and administrative) and privileged local groups such as kings and chiefs and some ethnic and racial middlemen like Coloureds, Asian, and Levantine businessmen. It was restrictive both socially and spatially (Aina, 2004:11).

The development of social policy in Zambia clearly testifies to the importance of path dependence and initial conditions in determining appropriate policies and their effectiveness. Zambia emerged at independence as a monocultural dualistic economy in which the 'modern' sector was only tenuously linked to the 'traditional sector', largely through the importation of labour for the mines. Superimposed on this dualistic model was a racialised formal labour market in which, over the years, the white working class had won for itself a fairly extensive set of welfare rights (Mkandawire, 2004:28). In the initial years, the colonial government treated the African workers as essentially 'target workers' on a brief sojourn through the urban areas. Consequently, no provisions were made for social welfare. Growing militancy of the black labour force also drew attention to the plight of black labour and to their disruptive potential. In addition, stabilisation of the labour force required improved living conditions in the urban areas. 'Native welfare' therefore entered the policy agenda of the colonialists (Mkandawire, 2004).

Social policy in post-colonial Zambia

Social policy formulation in post-colonial Zambia changed markedly after independence as it brought to centre-stage the plight of indigenous Zambians. Primarily, social policy attempted to solve social problems by making the economic system more equal. The economy had to be transformed as it was based on inequalities between the races and also between the rural and urban areas. Furthermore, the formulation of social policy in Zambia was based on incremental responses to social needs. When Zambia gained independence in 1964 the ruling party, UNIP, designed a number of policy and programmatic responses which used public expenditure to extend service provision to those areas which were believed to have been neglected by the colonial administration. Gradual increases in budgetary allocations were made during the 1960s and 1970s towards the expansion of basic education and health services; the replacement of expatriate labour through *Zambianisation*, and the promotion of social equity between the rich and poor were also main features of policy efforts (Siamwiza *et al.*, 1993). Policy under the UNIP government was influenced by the ideology of *Humanism*, the political philosophy of the party, which stressed communal responses to social issues and a commitment to the equitable distribution of resources to the population. Between 1964 and the early 1970s, the government's commitment to financing the provision of social services to the population intensified as it began to invest heavily in the social infrastructural sectors (Siamwiza *et al.*, 1993). All these efforts had to be translated into a better life for all Zambians by the new African government, because Zambia inherited an economy in which great mineral wealth was not used to develop human capacities but was siphoned off overseas.

The post-colonial government was faced with a number of challenges: de-racialising the labour market, creating more employment opportunities and bridging the urban-rural divide. For a while, high copper prices gave the state the resources to address some of these problems. The policies eventually ran into a fiscal crunch (Mkandawire, 2004), but important strides in social protection were made:

> During this period, a relatively significant amount of resources were invested in the development of the country's education and health infrastructure. The Government's role in the provision of the educational services expanded as it took over church-run schools and expanded primary and secondary schools across the country. Clinics, hospitals, and health centres, particularly within the rural areas were also constructed by Government in its efforts to extend health services towards the disadvantaged areas. In addition to its efforts in these sectors, it also implemented various other initiatives aimed at facilitating equitable distribution of resources including controlling and subsidising prices for agricultural products and basic food stuffs to ensure cheap food for the poor (Siamwiza *et al.*, 1993:10).

The UNIP government had started out as a nationalist liberation movement and fought colonial rule so as to institute an egalitarian society in Zambia. The party's ideology, Humanism, permeated social policy planning. Nevertheless this planning, though purporting to be 'people-centred', was 'top-down' and did not solicit people's views for the planning and policy process. Despite this, it is of critical importance that all the above-mentioned social services were provided free of charge to the Zambian people. Furthermore, the government did not only guarantee Zambians a better life through an expanded and inclusive social welfare system, but also abolished a lot of oppressive laws of the colonialists. For instance, the much hated hut and poll taxes that had negatively affected the lives of rural dwellers were discontinued by the African government. Thanks to huge investments made by the Zambian government in the social sector, by 1970 the country had one of the highest levels of per capita income in sub-Saharan Africa. Also, the country's investment was concentrated largely on import substituting industrialisation, in part to reduce dependence on the white-supremacy regimes in the south (Jones, 1994).

The development strategy followed by Zambia after independence relied too much on copper export earnings and tax revenues to provide resources for expanding public sector employment and government services (World Bank, 1994). For some time the picture seemed rosy enough as Zambians enjoyed decent standards of living and upward social mobility secured through free education and universal employment. However, by the end of the 1970s social and economic conditions had stalled, and then began to slide backwards. By the second oil crisis in 1979 and 1980 there was another sharp decline in the prices of copper. As a consequence, the trade balance turned negative. Treating the crisis only as temporary, the government of Zambia did not properly respond to the economic changes. It continued to run a budget deficit, resulting from the unexpected low revenue in 1975 and the need to pay for increased imports. Rising import prices, due to import licensing, all contributed to rising inflation rates (Nokkala, 2001). The increased public expenditure on consumption had also adversely affected domestic savings and this, in turn, reduced domestic investment considerably. Thus, although Zambia's capital formation during the 1971-76 period averaged 13 per cent of GDP, this had declined to 10 per cent of GDP at the time the Structural Adjustment Programme was introduced in 1985 (Saasa, 2001).

Social policy in the 1980s and 1990s

A country that was in the ranks of the richest on the continent and fared remarkably well with other countries in the world was to plummet to become one of the poorest in just two decades. By the 1980s, Zambia's economic situation had worsened so much that citizens could barely meet their basic needs. During this period, Zambia's educated cadres – technocrats, scientists, academics, doctors, teachers, nurses, pilots, engineers, accountants and a host of other professionals – left the country in droves for greener pastures. The country was depleted of valuable human resources and the results were and still are devastating. For those that remained, life was a struggle for survival. This was a time when the Zambian government's development strategies were defined by IMF/World Bank led economic reforms. These measures effectively hastened social dislocation in the country.

Government responses to the IMF and World Bank-led economic reforms

Rationalising the economy resulted in cutbacks in the social sector that in turn led to drastic changes in certain features of Zambia's social policy. As a response, the government also undertook counteractive measures that it thought would lessen the harsh effects of such reforms on the poor. For instance, the food subsidy, which was one of the pillars of Zambia's social policy, dramatically changed after the economic downturn. The government's ability to shore up the country's food subsidy had been severely curtailed by the IMF and World Bank interventions. Zambia's first food riots, in 1986, were a direct result of the removal of the food subsidy on the country's staple food, maize meal, by the government, on the insistence of the Bretton Woods institutions. The general food or maize subsidy which had been a major component of food policy, and ultimately social policy, for many years could not be maintained in a constrained economic environment:

> Before 1989 food policy in Zambia was focussed on the potentially contradictory objectives of achieving a high degree of self-sufficiency in food production while supplying the urban population with cheap staples. The principal mechanism for achieving this was a system of controlled producer and consumer prices. The controls were implemented by the state food marketing system and were widely spread (Pearce, 1994b:85).

The government introduced the *coupon system* in 1989 to cushion the shocks from rising food prices due to the removal of the food subsidy and the related price controls, which together had helped Zambians to have at least guaranteed access to cheap food. The coupons were exchangeable for maize meal at a certain value. The coverage of the food-coupon system was limited and restricted to urban households, and registration closed after two months. Limits were also imposed on the total number of coupons issued and the maximum number in a household for whom coupons could be claimed. In July 1989, modifications were made to the system in an attempt to make targeting more effective (Pearce, 1994b). The coupon system was meant to be a safety-net, and in this case it was a short-term palliative to stave off political groups, especially in the urban communities. The problem with safety-nets is that their implementation is not free of political constraints, and there are distinct trade-offs involved in directing benefits to the politically vocal versus the truly needy. They are not necessarily cost-effective, from either a political or poverty reduction perspective (Graham, 1997).

The second mechanism that was instituted by the UNIP government, shortly before losing power, to counteract the harsh effects of economic restructuring on the poor, was known as the Social Action Programme (SAP). Guided by Humanism, the programme was launched in 1990 and aimed to cover a three-year period, as part of the government's overall adjustment programme. The SAP included interventions in the areas of health, education and training, food security and nutrition, women in development and transport infrastructure. In the short term, the SAP aimed to improve the availability of social services and employment opportunities for the poor. In the long term, it was supposed to initiate policy analysis and reform that would then enable improved and sustained delivery (Government of the Republic of Zambia/Swedish International Development Agency, 1990). All in all, the economic difficulties Zambia was experiencing in the 1980s and 1990s created an unfavourable environment for social policy. The Structural Adjustment Programme had undermined the capacity of the government to deliver social services. This situation was manifested in the reduction of government expenditure in the social sector in real terms (Masiye *et al.*, 1998).

When Frederick Chiluba took over the presidency in 1991, the economy had virtually collapsed. Even though the Structural Adjustment Programme had been started in 1985, its implementation was only deepened after 1991. The SAP was identified with the notions of stabilisation and adjustment. It may be argued that adjustment is a necessary but sufficient condition for poverty reduction. However, there are many unanswered questions on this, first of all one concerning the relationship between poverty and inequality: undoubtedly, it is very difficult either to reduce inequality or to implement institutional reform in the absence of growth (Graham, 1997).

Social policy in the 1990s strove to create 'safety-nets' while being guided by economic austerity measures in the process. To this end, the government designed the Social Safety Net Scheme, which aimed to 'cushion' those who had lost employment and were unable to meet their basic needs. Additionally, women, children and the aged (vulnerable groups adversely affected by SAP) were targeted. A number of women both in urban and rural areas were engaged under various programmes in order to help them sustain their livelihoods, for instance the Programme Against Malnutrition (PAM), the Project Urban Self Help

(PUSH) and food for work (which did not only earn food for the families, but also enabled women to contribute to economic and social public sector ventures such as the rehabilitation and construction of feeder roads, streets in townships and rural water facilities) (Government of the Republic of Zambia, 1994).

Zambia went through different political phases that also defined the way social wellbeing was approached. From independence in 1964 to 1991, the Socialist approach to social policy was favoured; from 1991 to 2001, social policy was at the mercy of the IMF and World Bank and bilateral donors that dictated its scope and content, and was also reactive and short-term in perspective. Thereafter, there were moves to strengthen social policy's application. However, the better performance of the economy remains a key determinant in this equation.

Social policy trends in the new millennium

Social policy formulation and implementation in the new millennium continued at almost the same pace as in the late 1990s. There were no drastic changes made in the light of its philosophical underpinnings. Safety-net types of intervention typified social policy engagements in the new century. In the same year, 2000, the government of Zambia introduced the Targeted Food Security Pack (TFSP) that focused on what were referred to as vulnerable but viable farmers, as a poverty reduction strategy. This intervention focused on agriculture, since the majority of the rural poor lived by farming. This was a welfare mechanism aimed at empowering the beneficiaries as opposed to making them dependent on the welfare system. Small scale farmers cultivating less than one hectare, households headed by terminally-ill individuals and those looking after orphans, the aged and disabled, and child-headed households affected by drought were included in the TFSP.

The overarching regulatory framework that guides all policy and legislation in Zambia, as well as enabling the government to meet the needs of citizens, is the Constitution of the Republic of Zambia. It is recognised in the Constitution that the state shall endeavour to provide clean and safe water, adequate medical and health facilities and decent shelter for all persons and take measures to constantly improve such facilities and amenities. It also commits the state to provide equal and adequate opportunities in all fields and at all levels for all (Government of the Republic of Zambia, 2002). Therefore, even if there is no clear-cut way of enforcing these constitutional aspirations, the state does commit itself to provide for the wellbeing of Zambians.

The Ministry of Community Development and Social Services oversees the implementation of social policy in Zambia as it conceptualises and guides both policy and programmatic interventions in the welfare sector. These are also backed up by relevant legislation. The Ministry encompasses three sections: the Department of Culture, the Department of Community Development and the Department of Social Welfare. Each of these departments has a policy that aids in their operations. It was only after 1991 that the Ministry was constituted in this manner. At the time of writing, it was discovered that the policy on social welfare was still in draft form and had been delayed owing to certain contentious issues regarding children. The Department for Social Welfare needed to confer with the Ministry of Sport, Youth and Child Development over certain questions in order to arrive at some common understanding (Mulenga, 2006). The Ministry of Community Development and Social Services deals with cross-cutting issues that overlap with the functions of other ministries, such as HIV/AIDS, children, women and people with disabilities. That is why it is important that all government line ministries work in tandem as an integrated and coherent system, partly so as to minimise duplication of effort.

According to the Draft Policy on Social Welfare, social welfare services are provided by mainly the government and complemented by Non-Governmental Organisations (NGOs), Faith-Based Organisations (FBOs), Community-Based Organisations (CBOs), communities and individuals. These services take cognisance of the family's central role in matters of social welfare. Hence, specific social welfare programmes strive to strengthen individuals, families and communities, besides aiming to develop interventions that are practical, effective and sustainable both socially and economically (Government of the Republic of Zambia, 2002:2).

The scope of social welfare policy in Zambia includes juvenile welfare; care for older persons and for Orphans and Vulnerable Children (OVCs), welfare assistance and family welfare. Family welfare is classified into two categories: *statutory* and *non-statutory services*. Statutory services are governed by certain legislation so as to carry out specific duties, whereas non-statutory ones are not (Government of the Republic of Zambia, 2002). These services focus on the protection, custody, correction, rights, and responsibilities of children. All statutes emphasise the best interest of the child. The law allows only gazetted officers to carry out these statutory functions. Non-statutory services refer to welfare services that are provided by the government without reference to any Act of

Parliament and may be provided by private individuals or NGOs. These services are aimed at alleviating poverty through programmes designed to assist vulnerable groups, which include orphans, street children and the unsupported elderly. Such services encompass counselling, public assistance, and services focusing on street children and care for the aged, among others (Government of the Republic of Zambia, 2002). The services include juvenile justice, children's homes, care for the aged, medical social work and prison welfare, and counselling, which is taken as a cross-cutting issue.

The government's vision relating to social welfare hinges on the 'improved wellbeing of individuals, families and communities through effective, efficient, well-targeted and co-ordinated social welfare services by the year 2010' (Government of the Republic of Zambia, 2002). The rationale for social welfare policy rests on the need to regulate and guide the implementation of social welfare services, which then ensures their improved provision, on an equitable basis, so as to increase vulnerable persons' access to services for improved quality of life (Government of the Republic of Zambia, 2002).

According to the government, the following guiding principles undergird Zambian social welfare policy (Government of the Republic of Zambia 2002:4-5):

1. *Partnership* - The provision of social welfare services is a huge task, and requires the concerted efforts of all stakeholders. The delivery of effective services will be achieved through close collaboration among government departments, NGOs, CBOs, churches, civil society, co-operating partners, and others;

2. *Participation* - Participation of all stakeholders is vital for social welfare service delivery and for improved access and increased sustainability;

3. *Accountability and Transparency* - Accountability and transparency are crucial in social welfare service delivery as they facilitate public confidence, acceptability and promote wide participation in programmes. All services must ensure the best use of available resources and account for their utilisation;

4. *Human dignity* - Matters of social welfare are private and confidential, and individuals concerned should be treated with respect and professionalism. They should not be made to lose their dignity through the nature of service design or implementation. All social service providers should respect the rights of persons in accordance with international, regional, and national conventions and protocols. Social welfare recognises the dignity of clients and strives to ensure that their rights are respected;

5. *Equity* - The provision of social welfare must recognise or take into account the actual needs and abilities of different individuals, with attention, for example, to gender, disability and HIV/AIDS status;

6. *Tradition* - Social welfare must complement and promote the good and unifying Zambian traditions and culture of helping the vulnerable;

7. *Co-ordination* – As social welfare is a cross-cutting discipline with several players, there is need for co-ordination of all programmes to avoid duplication and overlap of responsibilities;

8. *Professionalism* - Social welfare services, being sensitive and ethical, should be implemented in a manner that ensures professional standards and promotes high quality services.

The welfare policy also covers social safety-nets. These are part of government intervention aimed at lessening the impact of the social and economic recovery programmes such as privatisation and retrenchments, as well as the effects of natural calamities, such as drought, on the poor. In the new millennium, the government has implemented the following safety-nets: the Food Security Programme (FSP), Project Urban Self Help (PUSH), the Public Welfare Assistance Scheme (PWAS) and the National Social Safety Net (NSSN) (Government of the Republic of Zambia, 2004). The overall objective of the FSP is to increase food productivity and household security; it targets viable farmers including female-headed households, households headed by the terminally ill, the aged and the disabled. The PUSH aims to improve the standards of living of vulnerable households among disadvantaged communities with particular focus on women.

Major interventions include the erection and rehabilitation of infrastructure, and also including skills training through community participation. The PWAS focuses on providing assistance to the vulnerable in society to meet their basic needs of health, education, food and shelter. The overall objective of the NSSN is to design and implement social mitigation programmes, co-ordinate other safety nets and mobilise resources from a broad base to finance programmes as they relate to displaced workers and the vulnerable in Zambia (Government of the Republic of Zambia, 2004).

The National Policy on Community Development focuses on poverty eradication through the empowerment of communities for sustainable human development. Its rationale is to eradicate poverty, whilst enabling people to take charge of the development programmes in their community. In pursuit of this aim, the policy concentrates on self-help initiatives, non-formal education and skills training, and gender and development (Government of the Republic of Zambia, 2002). The Department of Community Development also spearheads an adult literacy and non-formal education programme aimed at the peri-urban and rural communities. In 2003, there were 238 centres around the country where officers and volunteer instructors were responsible for the organisation and teaching of literacy classes. In the same period, there were 1,216 classes with a total enrolment of 19,282 students – 6,140 men and 13,142 women – and 456 instructors.

This programme also has a poverty reduction component, being aimed at provision of literacy, entrepreneurship, skills training and the empowerment of women's groups (Government of the Republic of Zambia, 2003) to assist poverty reduction. The Department of Culture provides guidelines on culture-related issues in accordance with the aspirations of Zambians and the development of the country. These departments are reliant on culture for their programmes to have relevance in Zambia.

The Department of Social Welfare

This is the oldest component of the ministry, dating back to the colonial times, and oversees the implementation of Zambia's social welfare policy. The following areas fall under its ambit:

I. CORRECTIONAL SERVICES

These are services provided to juveniles in conflict with the law and include:

(a) Investigations for courts

Social workers in their capacity as Probation Officers carry out investigations on behalf of the courts to determine and advise the courts on the best forms of punishment to mete out to young people in conflict with the law. An officer interviews the juvenile, his or her parents and other persons or institutions with a bearing on the case(s) and then prepares a report relating to the problem, with an analysis of the case giving recommendations for the best judgment to be carried out in the best interest of the juvenile.

(b) Probation Services

Probation services are institutional or community-based rehabilitation processes in which a juvenile in conflict with the law is placed under the supervision of a Probation Officer in accordance with the Probation of Offenders Act, Cap 93 of the Laws of Zambia. Officers provide counselling, guidance and support to the probationers that will ensure they do not commit any more offences during their probationary period.

(c) Community-based Probation

This is a process of rehabilitating juveniles in conflict with the law within their families and community set-up. The juvenile reports to the District Social Welfare Officer and is monitored on the process of reformation by the Probation Officer (Social Welfare Officer) for a period of one to three years depending on the court order.

(d) Institutional Probation

This is where the juvenile in conflict with the law is placed in an institution for one year. Currently there is only one such institution, the Insakwe Probation Hostel in Ndola for boys, while girls continue to receive community rehabilitation (Department of Social Welfare, 2005:1-2).

(e) Correctional Institutions

These are institutions meant to provide for the reception, care and rehabilitation of male juveniles in conflict with the law and children with disruptive behaviour, as ordered by the courts. At present there are two such institutions in the country, the Nakambala Approved School in Mazabuka and the Katombora Reformatory in Kazungula. The Department also runs the Nakambala Approved School in Mazabuka for reformation of delinquent juveniles, while the Katombora Reformatory in Kazungula is run by the Prisons Department. The Prisons Department assists by seconding an officer to the institution.

(f) After-Care Services

These are services offered to juveniles in conflict with the law who are discharged from the two aforementioned correctional institutions. These juveniles are assisted in preparing for eventual reintegration into the community through supervision. Social Welfare Officers in their roles as Probation Officers and Juveniles' Inspectors execute this undertaking.

(g) Persons in correctional institutions in respect of whom home contacts are made

Through this service, Social Welfare Officers provide counselling to juveniles' parents/guardians on the need to maintain contact with their children or dependants in institutions, in order to help in the preparation for their eventual reintegration into the community (Department of Social Welfare, 2005:1-2).

II. CHILDREN

The Ministry of Community Development and Social Services regulates the care of children in distress through the following avenues:

(a) Children's Homes

These are institutions providing care to children in need of care or who are orphaned, abandoned, or whose parents or guardians are unfit to provide them with proper care and guardianship. Government policy, however, is to encourage community participation in the care of such children, and institutional care is regarded as a measure of last resort. The ministry does not run these institutions, but networks with and provides guidelines to NGOs and individuals permitted to operate children's homes. The Department of Social Welfare supervises these homes to ensure their suitability and also provides grants to some of these homes.

(b) Child Care and Upgrading Programme (CCUP)

This is another child welfare programme that was established as a response to address the proliferation of children's homes, in order to regulate service delivery and provide guidelines to all the child care service providers for better, effective and quality services in line with national obligations to orphans and other vulnerable children, as enshrined in international conventions, national policies and laws. The programme is partly funded by the United Nations Children's Fund (UNICEF).

(c) Foster care service

This service provides a temporary home to children in need of care in accordance with provisions of the Juvenile Act, Cap 53 of the Laws of Zambia. The Department of Social Welfare provides, on request, a monthly token of appreciation to foster parents through the Adoption Act, Cap 54 of the Laws of Zambia.

(d) Adoption service

This service provides a permanent home, legal protection and security to children in need of care, in accordance with the Adoption Act, Cap 54 of the Laws of Zambia (Department of Social Welfare, 2005:2-3).

Social security/protection

Social security or protection is an integral part of social policy and human development. Social protection refers to actions taken in response to levels of vulnerability, risk and deprivation which are deemed socially unacceptable within a given polity or society. It thus deals with both the deprivation and vulnerabilities of the poorest and the needs of the existing non-poor, for security in the face of shocks and life-cycle events. The 'public' character of this response may be governmental or non-governmental, or a combination of both. Rights to elements of social protection are contained in the Universal Declaration of Human Rights (Norton *et al.*, 2001). Generally, social security benefits may be divided into (a) *non-contributory* benefits and grants (which recipients qualify for on grounds of need or because they fall into a particular category, such as parents/children); and (b) *contributory benefits*, which are based on the principle of insurance and the recipient being eligible by having paid into the system (or by having credits paid on his or her behalf by the government or employer). Non-contributory benefits are either *non-income-related* (that is, they are paid irrespective of the recipient's income) or *income-related* and dependent on a means-test of some kind (Blakemore, 1998).

In the last decade, there has been a global shift towards social protection/poverty-reduction policies. They now have a broader mandate incorporating risk prevention and mitigation strategies, as well as the perennially necessary safety-nets. Despite such advances, in practice, social protection still tends to focus on income/consumption protection of the poor through the provision of cash transfers and other safety net provisions (Moser, 2005). A shift in the scope of coverage is important in this regard. For instance, the concept of Sustainable Livelihoods (SL), while linked to issues of social protection, alters the focus from income and consumption to directly address the critical role that assets and capabilities play in improving individuals' and households' social and economic wellbeing (and associated poverty reduction). Yet the emphasis on livelihood *per se* means that the importance of Asset Building (AB), the accumulation and longer-term consolidation of assets, is often not given sufficient emphasis (Moser, 2005). In addition, both sustainable livelihoods and asset building have been primarily identified as frameworks or approaches to poverty reduction, rather than as specific components of 'social policy'. It must be noted that a framework based on an asset-institutions-opportunities nexus has the potential to locate social policy in the centre of mainstream poverty reduction development debates, rather than as a residual concern for the 'other' who is 'excluded', important though this is (Moser, 2005).

Social protection has long been a domestic concern of wealthy nations, which have developed sophisticated institutional arrangements to protect against risks to their citizens and provide assistance to the destitute. Social protection has however been largely neglected, or addressed only with inappropriate tools, in the majority of poor countries (Norton *et al.*, 2001). For instance, despite an apparent political commitment to developing a comprehensive social security system in Zambia, policy outcomes have entrenched a strict separation between employment-based social insurance and tax financed social assistance. The impact of the economic decline, structural adjustment, and the decline in formal employment has been felt in both branches of social security. The contributor base of the social insurance system has shrunk and this, together with financial underperformance of the pension funds, has generated large deficits (Barrientos et al., 2005).

Overall, Zambia presents something of a paradox with regard to the politics of social protection; although the underlying political context seems to be largely inimical to generating a nationally-owned social protection scheme, the narrower sphere of development policy-making may nonetheless offer more fertile ground within which such an agenda can initially be promoted. Arguably, the absence of government leadership on social protection reflects the priorities of the political elites in a residual non-developmental state (Barrientos et al., 2005).

The dearth of social protection related initiatives in Zambia also extends beyond the parameters of the state:

> Few civil society organisations have prioritised social protection to date, in terms of either advocacy campaigns or service delivery. Although a few international NGOs have expressed an interest in social protection in Zambia (e.g. CARE, OXFAM), they have little experience of policy influence themselves. Social protection was only belatedly included as a subject area for civil society shadow thematic group NDP process. Few policy researchers, academics or journalists comment regularly on social protection issues. There are glaring weaknesses in poverty research capacity in Zambia, with no more than a handful of researchers working in this area. However, there is genuine potential for civil society actors to become key members of a political constituency for social protection (Barrientos et al., 2005:44).

According to Mukuka et al. (2002), Zambia has two social security systems existing side by side. The first is one that is offered by the state while the second is the traditional system. For traditional social security, the extended family and semi-formal schemes such as reciprocal urban networks, the church, *chilimba* (informal banking systems) and market associations are pivotal in providing social protection to Zambians. The authors also point out that traditional social security arrangements were destroyed by a series of governments, starting with the colonial state and continuing through to the late 1990s under post-colonial authorities.

Social security in Zambia has been defined as the:

> protection which society provides for its members through a series of measures, against the economic and social distress that otherwise would be caused by the stoppage of substantial reduction of earnings resulting from sickness, maternity, employment injury, unemployment, invalidity,

old age and death; the provision of medical care and the provision for families with children (National Pensions Scheme Authority, 2005).

Currently, there are several types of social security schemes existing in Zambia. They are the following:

(a) Social Assistance Schemes

These are typified by Social Welfare Programmes under the Ministry of Community Development and Social Services.

(b) Occupational Pension Schemes

These are schemes set up for specific groups of people usually within a certain industry. An example is the Mukuba Pension Scheme for mine workers.

(c) Employer Liability Schemes

These schemes cover work-injury related benefits such as those under the Workers' Compensation Fund.

(d) Provident Funds

These are savings schemes for all employees, which guarantee a lump sum payment at retirement with total contributions and interest earned.

(e) Social Insurance Schemes

These arrangements are designed on the principle of risk sharing by all members of the scheme and the benefits paid relate to a number of factors, not just a member's total contributions (National Pensions Scheme Authority, 2005).

Box 1: The Public Welfare Assistance Scheme (PWAS)

This is one form of state assisted type of social protection that falls under the aegis of the Ministry of Community Development and Social Service's Social Assistance Schemes. PWAS can be regarded as a decentralised, participatory and sustainable scheme and should be seen as a major achievement of the government in the framework of its Poverty Reduction Strategy. It is funded through the annual budget. When the new guidelines for PWAS were approved in 1997 by the cabinet, a plan was drawn up to launch the new programme through a 'phased introduction' process with the scheme being introduced gradually throughout the country over a four-year period.

The introduction of PWAS in each district of Zambia (there are 72 districts in all) involved an 'initial visit', informing the local authorities and potential partners of the new scheme. On this visit, the District Social Welfare Officer (DSWO) was guided in making an institutional and human capacity assessment of the district. Having noted which organisations were the strongest in each area, the DSWO then identified the location and possible partnerships for each Area Co-ordinating Committee (ACC). PWAS provide clients with help to meet basic needs through *social support* - food, shelter, blankets and other basic welfare needs - and *health care*, covering the costs of accessing health services, plus assistance towards meeting the costs of transport and drugs as well as fees and levies at the health centre or hospital, and *education costs* - support for accessing primary and secondary education.

This programme provides social protection to vulnerable households in the informal sector (Social Safety Net Project, 2007). PWAS addresses all the key aspects of destitution, that is, shortage of food, health, clothing, education; all the other safety-nets tackle only one or two aspects (Ministry of Community Development and Social Services/GTZ, 2004). Ninety per cent of households in Zambia depend on the informal sector for their livelihood, and therefore the task of PWAS is enormous. The importance of PWAS is also underlined by the fact that social protection schemes like the extended family networks, urban reciprocal social networks, etc., have been weakened by a combination of rural urban migration, poverty and AIDS.

In order to be able to fulfil its roles of alleviating poverty, the Ministry of Community Development and Social Services has been assisted by the European Union in reorganising the PWAS since 1999. The first phase of the reorganisation was concentrated around nine districts of which three are in Southern Province (Kalomo, Monze, Siavonga). In the second half of 2002 another 27 districts were included. This means that the schemes now cover more than 50 per cent of all districts in Zambia. The remaining districts will be included in the forthcoming third phase. Some of the merits of the PWAS are that it integrates NGOs and CBOs and is self-help oriented. Some of its constraints are that it only targets 2 per cent of the population while, because of a

> combination of extreme poverty and AIDS, at least 10 per cent are in urgent need of social welfare intervention; it reaches only 0.5 per cent of the population, mainly in and near urban centres; it is supply-oriented; and, compared to its task, its budget is small. Mainly because of extreme under-funding, PWAS so far has no significant impact on the welfare of households (Adapted from Schubert, 2003).

The National Pensions Scheme

The National Pensions Scheme Authority (NAPSA) was established by a statute in 1996 but only came into operation in 2000. It succeeded the Zambia National Provident Fund (NPF) that had been in existence since 1966. The agency has statutory responsibilities for collecting mandatory contributions from workers and employers as well as disbursing pensions and other social security benefits to contributing members. The pensions scheme covers the following categories of workers:

(i)   all private sector workers;

(ii) workers in the public sector who are not covered by public service pension schemes;

(iii) all public service workers recruited after the commencement of the scheme (Fashoyin, 2002).

The following categories of benefits are provided by the national pensions scheme to members:

(i)   pensions at the age of fifty-five years, with a minimum qualification of fifteen years' contributions.

(ii) lump sum benefits for those who have not qualified for pension;

(iii) death benefits, including funeral grants; and

(iv) injury benefits.

Mandatory contributions are set at 5 per cent of salary by both the participating workers and the employer. The scheme had about 300,000 members as at December 2000. Although the scheme covers 80 per cent of those in wage employment in the formal sector, this only translates into about 10 per cent of the total population (Fashoyin, 2002). Furthermore, the fund was established with the following understanding:

> Pension benefits to be determined on a defined basis, related to both earnings and length of services (as measured by contributions paid). Contributions to be shared between employees (members) and their employers (with no subvention by Government) determined on the basis of a percentage of those earnings taken into account for the calculation of benefits. Existing members of NPF to join NAPSA from outset; future new employees to join as and when qualifying, including all new employees of the civil service and local authorities. Normal retirement (men and women) at age 55. Retirement benefits paid on the basis of a minimum contributory period of 180 months (i.e. 15 years). Existing members of NPF to have an option (but not an obligation) to exchange their rights to lump sum benefits under NPF for enhanced pension benefits under NAPSA. Retirement benefits payable up to 5 years early, but subject to reduction to actuarially equivalent value to the benefit at age 55. Pension benefits to be paid on invalidity subject to members with contribution records of 60 months or above, with 12 months paid in the last 36 months. Survivors' benefits payable where deceased members had either qualified for a pension benefit, or would have qualified for invalidity benefit if not deceased, also a funeral grant to be paid in lump sum form. Benefits to be protected against inflation by indexing to a measure of National Average Earnings (National Pensions Scheme Authority, 2005:1).

The pension system is currently based on two pillars: the NAPSA is the largest fund in the country, while the second Occupational Pension Scheme (OPS) consists of the public schemes, the Local Annuities Superannuation Fund (LASF), and the Public Service Pension Fund (PSPF). The financial status of the two pillar pension schemes is mixed. The two public sector schemes, the PSPF and LASF, are insolvent although both have some assets and are owed considerable amounts in contributions (Government of the Republic of Zambia, 2006). According to the Fifth National Development Plan, the financial insolvency of the public pension scheme poses a serious risk to fiscal sustainability and macro-economic stability. The financial distress of the PSPF has impacted negatively on its operations, resulting in poor service delivery. The major reasons for the poor performance of the public pension include lack of harmony in legislation relating to pensions; inadequacies in the Pension Scheme Regulations Act, 1966; deficits in the statutory pension funds as a result of non-remittance of pension contribution by the state; lack of a supervisory agent at NAPSA; and absence of local actuaries (Government of the Republic of Zambia, 2006).

Undoubtedly the most significant shortcoming of the NAPSA, so far as the social protection of workers is concerned, is limited coverage. While it is true that there are several private occupational schemes in the private sector in Zambia, the fact that these schemes are limited to wage earners in the modern sector underscores the need for a scheme, such as NAPSA, to cover the majority of workers in Zambia. This poses a serious challenge to NAPSA and indeed the government to find a practical way of extending social protection to a wider cross-section of society (Fashoyin, 2002:26). For these reasons, several reforms by government are envisaged in this area. The key legal reforms in the sector will revolve around the amendment of Article 124 of the Constitution. This should allow for (a) changes to be made in the Public Pensions Act No. 35 of 1996 in terms of the sustenance of the pensioners' and members' benefits, and (b) protection of only accrued pension benefits via amendments of Public Service Act No. 35 of 1996. The other important legislative reforms should be to: (i) allow for changes to be made to the benefits formula variable to suit the changing circumstances, and (ii) promote transparency, accountability and incorporate good corporate governance in the management of the PSPF (Government of the Republic of Zambia, 2006). Apart from these reforms, the liquidation of the government's indebtedness to the PSPF, through the increase of pension allocations, shall be pursued by the state.

Another important reform in the arrangement of pensions is to be the creation of a supervisory authority for NAPSA. Also, the government hopes to establish the Pensions and Insurance Authority (PIA) to enhance Pensions and Insurance regulation. Besides amending the Pension Scheme Regulation Act, certain pension reforms aimed at addressing the structural problems facing the pension system in Zambia are going to be carried out within the framework of the Fifth National Development Plan (Government of the Republic of Zambia, 2006).

Although its policies are not well articulated, the government now seems to regard social protection as an important tool for poverty reduction as well as economic growth. To this end, it drafted the *Social Protection Strategy* with the aim of contributing towards the social security of all Zambians, by ensuring that incapacitated and low capacity households and people have sufficient income security to meet their basic needs, and protection from the worst risks and shocks (Government of the Republic of Zambia, 2005). Moreover, the implementation of an effective national

Social Security Protection Scheme in Zambia will require a wide constituency of support. To provide guidance on and support to this endeavour, the British Department for International Development (DFID) commissioned a study in Zambia: *'Drivers for Change' for a National Protection Scheme in Zambia,* to gather more information relating to the issue (Department for International Development, 2006). This study arrived at certain key findings and recommendations and identified certain barriers to the creation of an effective social security system. Its main findings are:

(a) Strengthening demand for social protection

Restructuring of the Ministry of Community Development and Social Services is an opportunity for policy, planning and implementation of social protection schemes.

(b) Strengthening policy design, monitoring and evaluation

Policy design should be informed by lessons from pilot schemes and ongoing programmes. This will be facilitated by the monitoring and evaluation of pilot schemes and by briefings on the effectiveness of alternative instruments and policy options.

(c) Strengthening civic and political spheres

Research and advocacy are needed to generate understanding of, and demand for, social protection. This can be supported through capacity building among trade unions and faith-based and civil society organisations (Barrientos *et al.*, 2005).

The data in Table 3 show that the bulk of pensions' mechanisms cater for public service workers. Nevertheless, the record of pension disbursement under successive Zambian governments has been poor. Many pensioners have retired without being given their dues for long periods, some even for more than ten years. Many have died without seeing any disbursement of their money while a good number have remained destitute. This is unacceptable and inhumane as well as also promoting elder abuse, as many retirees are senior citizens who require adequate protection. Many of them worked tirelessly and faithfully for the country and their only reward now is penury. The past pension mechanism was riddled with inefficiency and fraud for a long time and it is only hoped that the proposals in the FNDP regarding this matter will be duly implemented. Furthermore, some of the interventions made in the sector by the government in order to remedy the situation are not backdated or applied retrospectively, but only help present retirees, as the case study in Box 2 on page 109 explains.

Table 3: Key findings and recommendations of the 'drivers for change' study

Barriers	*Opportunities*
1. Limited understanding of poverty and vulnerability.	1. Growing consensus around the need for social protection amongst government, donors and civil society.
2. Few opportunities available to influence key individuals within the political system.	2. Increasing political focus on social issues through elections, constitutional debate, policy, and budget cycle.
3. Relative newness and technical nature of social protection agenda and cash transfers in particular.	3. Effectiveness of pilot projects.
4. Absence of government leadership on social protection.	4. Increasing opportunities for longer term, multi-donor, on-budget financial commitments.
5. Limited scope and poor targeting of existing social protection. Concerns related to dependency and 'hand-outs'.	5. Existence of public welfare schemes over a long period of time.
6. Lack of institutional policy-making, and implementation capacity.	6. Inclusion of Social Security chapter in National Development Plan.
7. Social protection is assumed to be costly and unaffordable.	

(Adapted from: Barrientos *et al.*, 2005)

Box 2: Case study

It is early evening and Fred Wallace Phiri is sitting in his chair thinking of where he will get the money to pay his bills and feed his family. Outside, the young orphans he is looking after, oblivious to the economic hardships their grandfather is going through, are playing noisily and enjoying the nocturnal breeze. The sound of their voices sends him into a deeper silence because he is constantly reminded that although the economic problems are biting, he just has to find a way of ensuring that the young children have the basic necessities of life. Phiri, one of the unsung heroes who served mother Zambia for 35 years, gives an account of his life after retirement. 'I worked from 1961 to 3rd January 1997 in the Ministry of Education as an acting head, deputy head and teacher,' he reminisces. 'I worked at Kabwata Basic School, St. Patricks Basic School, Mumuni Basic School and Lusakasa Basic School.' He expresses grief that after working for 35 years he was given only K12 million. 'It was not enough to sustain me because I am keeping ten orphans, have to pay for electricity, water and this house,' Phiri laments. 'Those who retired in the Kaunda era got very little and when I look at them today I do not know what to call them.' He expresses concern at the stark contrast between what his contemporaries get as pensions and what some sections of society are getting. 'Government has got to help us. What do we do with the little that they give us?' Phiri muses. 'Some people who worked for only five years are getting K500 million. Can you compare five years to 35 years?' He appeals to the government to listen to the cries of the retirees if their suffering is to be reduced. 'We as retirees are suffering. You go to Zambia National Commercial Bank (ZNCB) at Findeco House and you will see that people queue up as early as 08:30 hours up to maybe 14:30 just to get a K50, 000 or even less,' complains Phiri.

His wife Paulina echoes his assertions, saying that the poverty they are enduring is more like a bitter pill they have to swallow every day. 'We have suffered and there are many orphans to look after,' moans Paulina. 'We have to beg to survive, it is painful.' She further says she cannot go to the village because she is sick. Paulina had a tumour on her neck which was operated on, and this makes it difficult for her to breathe. The problems of retirees play themselves over and over in all the nine provinces of Zambia. As the number of the aged in the Zambian population is rapidly rising, the issue of pensions is becoming big and it needs to be placed high on the government's agenda. It is however, disheartening to look at the way the issue is ignored. The old often remain unprotected by formal systems as policy-makers grapple with the difficult question of how to reform the social security system. As the World Bank points out, considerations of risk and vulnerability are key to understanding the dynamics leading to the perpetuation of poverty. Poverty is more than inadequate consumption or inadequate education and health; it is also fear for the future. Vulnerability affects everyone but it is greater for the poor who face large risks from shocks to their income earnings, due to natural and man-made disasters such as crime, violence, exclusion and discrimination. The poor need to feel empowered with skills and values to overcome poverty.

It is unfortunate that critical programmes such as the social safety nets continue to be grossly underfunded. The government as the custodian of social policy must play a leading role in demonstrating unwavering commitment to the achievement and sustenance of social security objectives. In the recent past, pensioners across the country planned to stage a demonstration to protest over the meagre monthly pensions, which stand at a paltry K50,000 at the moment. In a statement, the Zambia National Pensioners Association Chingola Branch Chairman Augustine Mbewe accuses the government of contributing to the pensioners' destitution. Mbewe bemoans the fact that the government's failure to honour its debt to the PSPF has negatively affected the pensioners. 'We the pensioners as senior citizens of Zambia who have diligently offered meritorious service in our various fields to the development of this country have been neglected by the government,' he declares. 'The government has failed to liquidate its debt to the PSPF to enable the fund to pay pensioners meaningful monthly pensions.' Mbewe calls for the upward adjustment of the monthly pensions, as the current sums are too little. 'It was hoped that government would address the plight of pensioners upon the attainment of the HIPC completion point but to no avail,' says Mbewe.

According to the World Bank Manager for Central Africa and Poverty Reduction and Economic Management, Luca Babone, and consultant Luis Alvaro Sanchez, in a paper presented to the XIII International Social Security Association's African Regional Conference in Accra, improving governance is the first step for improving formal social security institutions. 'It is the first order of business for existing formal social security institutions, which have too often failed to deliver on promises to their members due to mismanagement and sometimes outright pillage of assets.' The two experts note that the main task involves increasing transparency, curtailing apparatus for corruption and most importantly protecting beneficiary rights.

Babone and Sanchez explain that an important component of improving governance is the creation of protective barriers around the social security organisations to prevent undue interference from outside interests and facilitate precise allocation of responsibilities and their oversight and enforcement. They reason that regulation is important whether management of these institutions remains in public or private hands; within the context of a strong regulatory framework, they say, it will then be possible to grant social security institutions administrative and legal autonomy with clearly defined objectives. Further, unbundling institutions according to the different services and activities they provide helps to fine-tune the relationship between objectives, responsibilities and incentives, thus improving governance. They express

> pessimism about pensions' coverage being extended to the informal sector which represents the majority in the country. At present, the social security system in Zambia and Africa at large is a perquisite of the middle class. It is important to note that social security schemes designed for the stronger economic agents who can contribute more end up penalising those at the margin of small and medium economic concerns. African populations on average are younger compared to other countries. The ratio of the population over sixty stood at 4.7 in 1995. Well-designed social security policies can contribute to a better environment for economic growth in Zambia. It would be erroneous to think that social security is a luxury to be afforded only when growth has taken place.

(Adapted from Laura Mushuakwa's article in *The Post*, 22 October 2006)

Another area that deserves attention in this chapter, although not always seen as a component of social protection and ultimately of social policy and human development, is disaster management.

Disaster Management

Disasters or natural calamities have the propensity to make people vulnerable in a short space of time, as their properties are destroyed or their capacities for self-sustenance are severely compromised. Natural disasters have negative impact on the economy as they will eventually disrupt productive activities such as agriculture and wealth creation. Transport systems, electricity power lines can also be completely destroyed, while the environment suffers significant setbacks. There are three broad categories of disasters that have afflicted and/or have the potential to afflict Zambians: *human induced disasters, natural disasters* and *complex humanitarian emergencies*. Examples of human induced disasters are epidemics, famines, influx of refugees and internally displaced persons, fires, deforestation, and accidents. Disasters associated with natural hazards include floods, droughts, plant pests and disease infestation, livestock diseases and plant parasite invasions. Disasters associated with complex humanitarian emergencies are human crises in a country or region or at an international level, where there is considerable breakdown of authority, resulting from internal or external conflict (Government of the Republic of Zambia, 2005). In the First and Second Republics, the coordination of responses to emergencies came under the *Contingency Planning Unit* located in the then Office of the Prime Minister. This Unit was established in 1966 and phased out in 1992 (Government of the Republic of Zambia, 2005).

Following the devastating drought of 1991/92 that affected most of the Southern African region, and the major relief operation that followed, four key ministries of Health, Agriculture, Energy and Water Development formed an *ad hoc* committee, which was responsible for managing different aspects of responses to the drought (Government of the Republic of Zambia, 2005). As a result of the fragmented disaster framework that existed, it became necessary to create a permanent unit within government structures to initiate and facilitate the implementation as well as co-ordination of disaster management policies and programmes. The mandate for overall disaster management and co-ordination has been overseen by the *Disaster Management and Mitigation Unit* within the Office of the Vice-President since 1994 (Government of the Republic of Zambia, 2005).

Conclusion

Social policy in Zambia has had a mixed impact on the citizens of the country. Some of the interventions have been highly successful, for instance, the free education of the 1960s, while a significant portion has been less successful. With the successes there was also the failure to achieve sustainability. Mhone (2004) argues that the failure of social policy in post-colonial Zambia rests on its inability to 'seize upon traditional systems as stepping stones for the developing of new support systems.' Indeed, such failure as well as the unfolding pattern of Zambia's social policy can be linked to what Aina (2004) refers to as the *legitimisation model*. Central to this model is a strong social policy initiative tied to the 'constructionist' approach to economic development, that is, the building of physical and social as well as human infrastructures. The trappings of this model can be summed up thus:

> However, the accumulation and legitimising models ran into trouble and soon reached the real limits of their capacity to incorporate more and more new elements both socially and economically, given finite resources, unfavourable global economic trends, increasing corruption and rapidly growing populations. From the late 1960s to the early 1970s, the core elements of the 'nationalist project' began to disintegrate politically. The struggle for legitimisation and incorporation gave way to increasing authoritarianism and monolithic politics. The emergence and consolidation of one-party states became a common feature, as identified with military regimes run increasingly clientelist and personal rule

mechanisms. With this decline of popular democratic politics and the collapse of the economies, the social policy frameworks became equally eroded and downplayed. Social services and social infrastructures decayed, from sheer neglect and mismanagement or, where they existed in rudimentary forms, were appropriated by local barons and misused for political patronage (Aina, 2004:13).

This is exactly what happened in Zambia, and to this date social policy remains in a state of disarray, punctuated by halting, inchoate responses from the state that are in themselves constrained by the agendas or warped visions of the so-called donor community. This chapter served as a central instruction to the characteristics of Zambia's social policy and how it dovetails with human development endeavours. An important element of this section was to delve into the country's past in order to highlight how human need was tackled by successive governments.

Chapter 4

SOCIAL POLICY AND HUMAN DEVELOPMENT IN A LEAST DEVELOPED COUNTRY (LDC): ZAMBIA

Introduction

Zambia can be described as a Least Developed Country (LDC), and the status so described implies various human development challenges. Like most African countries, Zambia was colonised by a foreign European power, in this case Britain. For a long time, indigenous Zambians did not have control over their destinies. As a result, even after independence, Zambia did not have command over its own resources or the manner in which they were exploited and exported to European markets. Furthermore, Zambia was bound in a dependent relationship to its former colonial 'master' which had to 'support' it via development aid. In essence, 'flag' independence did not liberate the country from the unequal global economic system that was also inimical to the development of the country.

This chapter begins to contextualise social policy and human development issues in the terrain of an LDC, Zambia, on the understanding that the efficacy of social policy or the realisation of human development in Zambia was not, and still is not, solely defined by endogenous factors such as the existing political economy among others, but by also exogenous factors such as the terms of international trade. Whenever prices of exports plummet on international markets, this immediately affects human wellbeing in Zambia. For Zambia, the lessons remain stark because of the country's experience in the early 1970s, when copper prices drastically dropped on the London Metal Exchange (LME). Because of this, Zambia began to experience extremely poor social conditions which the country is still trying to reduce. Therefore, international trade is treated in this discussion as a significant external factor, among others, that has direct bearing on the development of a particular country.

Characteristics of Least Developed Countries (LDCs)

Since 1971, the United Nations has described as 'Least Developed Countries' (LDCs) a category of low-income states that are deemed structurally disadvantaged in their development process and face more than other countries the risk of failing to come out of poverty. Because of this

LDCs are considered in need of the highest degree of attention on the part of the international community (United Nations Conference on Trade and Development, 2005). The following criteria are used to characterise LDCs:

(i) *low income*, based on a three-year average estimate of the gross national income per capita (under US$ 750 for cases of addition to the list, above US$ 900 for cases of graduation);

(ii) *weak human assets*, measured by a composite *Human Assets Index (HAI)*, based on indicators of: (a) nutrition; (b) health; (c) school enrolment; and (d) adult literacy;

(iii) *economic vulnerability*, measured by a composite *Economic Vulnerability Index (EVI)* based on indicators of: (a) instability of agricultural production; (b) instability of exports of goods and services; (c) diversification from traditional economic activities; (d) merchandise export concentration; and (e) economic small-ness (United Nations Conference on Trade and Development, 2005:6).

Because Zambia is an LDC, the country encounters a host of challenges which impact on its human development prospects. LDCs have unique characteristics that ultimately have a bearing on the way national governments and civil society formations respond to the question of human needs. These include persistently high levels of poverty, largely rural-based populations, heavy dependence on agriculture in terms of gross national income and export earnings (which are particularly dependent on primary commodity exports), and significant numbers of people who remain undernourished. For those LDCs that are landlocked, the problems of extreme poverty and reliance on agriculture are even more severe (Food and Agricultural Organisation, 2003). Zambia is a landlocked country, and has relied upon the goodwill of neighbours to transport its goods to ports for export. Such a precarious position means that the country was, is and will be at the mercy of its neighbours. In past epochs, when the decolonisation process was unfolding in Southern Africa, the country's development efforts were severely curtailed as its neighbours could stop letting it transport goods through their territories. Angola, Mozambique, Zimbabwe and South Africa (not Zambia's immediate neighbour but a major outlet for its trade) as white-ruled colonial states could at any time stop Zambian goods going to their ports, or imports for Zambia getting through. The consequences of such actions for Zambia were extremely dire for its socio-economic development.

Clearly, most landlocked developing countries are very poor, with low Gross National Incomes (GNI). For instance, in the year 2000 most of them had a GNI of US$ 356 per capita. Seventy-three per cent of the total population of these countries is based in rural areas, with 67 per cent of the economically active population involved in agriculture (Food and Agriculture Organisation, 2003). It is also instructive that:

> The most extreme poverty is evident for those sixteen Land-Locked Developing Countries (LLDCs) that are also considered LDCs, with the lowest GNI per capita of the various groups (US$ 186) and the highest proportion of the economically active population dependent on agriculture (82 per cent). These LLDCs continue to be amongst the poorest of all developing countries, with weak economic growth and heavy dependency on a very limited number of commodities for export earnings. The unique characteristic shared by the LLDCs is their extreme isolation from world markets due to territorial access to the sea. Transport distances for most of these countries are excessive, with difficult terrain and inefficient road and railway conditions. Kazakhstan is the most remote of this country group (3 750 kms from the nearest sea coast) followed by Afghanistan, Chad, Niger, Zambia and Zimbabwe, all with distances greater than 2, 000km from the nearest sea access. Landlocked developing countries in Africa face one of the highest freight-to-export ratios, spending 40 per cent of export earnings on transportation costs and insurance services (Food and Agriculture Organisation, 2003:4).

Thus the mere geographic location of a country becomes a crucial development imperative, which then has a direct bearing on its ability or inability to successfully participate in international trade. The country will also engage in such trade from a position of strength if it has its own ports to export or import goods. If it has none of these or is situated far away from major ports in the region, then it will have to contend with huge freight charges as well as being mindful of political considerations. As the landlocked country needs to maintain good relations with its neighbours at all costs, it needs, for instance, to have a pragmatic foreign policy. Therefore, the power of external factors in shaping local conditions cannot be ignored in this matter. Thus LDCs face numerous hurdles as regards their participation in international trade.

International trade and LDCs

For most LDCs, if not all, trade with the developed North is not free at all as prices of their main exports, which in this case are primary products, are determined by Western markets. Furthermore, the trade regimes of the West are extremely protectionist, while countries in the developing world are 'encouraged' by the IMF and World Bank to liberalise their trade, if they have to develop. Like that of most LDCs, Zambia's economy is dominated by primary activities such as mining and to a lesser extent agriculture. Even if LDCs can harness their natural resources for export to international markets, they are encumbered by the same unequal terms of trade that were initially sculpted by European nations from around the 15th century and then crystallised during colonial rule. In his seminal work, Walter Rodney (1972:84-5) asserts that Western Europe and Africa had a relationship which ensured the transfer of wealth from Africa to Europe. The transfer was possible only after trade became truly international. He further records that the strategy behind international trade and the production that supported it was in European hands, and specifically in the hands of the sea-going nations from the North Sea to the Mediterranean. They owned and directed the vast majority of the world's sea-going vessels and controlled the financing of the trade between the four continents, Europe, America, Asia, and Africa.

Undoubtedly, the underdevelopment of the LDCs or Africa and the existing lop-sided global trade regimes are all directly linked to colonialism. These days when one brings up the realities of slavery and colonialism in public debates, especially in the West, there is always a retort from the audience that the time for blaming colonialism is over. Some even go so far as to intimate that colonialism was in fact a blessing to Africa. It actually baffles the mind that many Europeans regard criticisms of colonialism as outmoded and genuinely believe that Africans should move on. This might be a prudent viewpoint if all African governments were depraved from the start and had not tried to improve the conditions of their people after independence, or if outsiders had not meddled in the affairs of the newly independent countries all over Africa, or if some of Africa's brightest leaders who were also shining examples of selfless leadership were not brutally murdered by the same Western powers, in collusion with local reactionary forces. One has only to think of Patrice Lumumba and the chaos that has dogged the Democratic Republic of the Congo (DRC) for decades to be reminded that the mayhem is actually a product of certain forces in Europe and America.

The denial of the harm done by both slavery and colonial rule to Africa's development would be valid if Africans had found themselves in this current scenario on their own accord and had not been oppressed for hundreds of years. Arguably, the African race is one of the few races on this planet that has been brutalised and oppressed beyond human comprehension (this discussion does not in any way downplay the fact that other non-Europeans have also been greatly oppressed, indeed to the point of near extermination, for example, Native Americans and Native Australians). It was sold into slavery and treated as a commercial product like rice, cotton or farm animals on a grand scale. It is the only race that has suffered the onslaught of a well-co-ordinated, systematic and relentless process of oppression, de-humanisation and eventual brainwashing, so that Africans hate themselves and believe that they are useless beings. (See the works of Marcus Garvey, Walter Rodney, Amilcar Cabral, Kwame Nkrumah and Frantz Fanon, among others.) Even though they are constantly demonised by a cruel and racist global sub-system, Africans and their kindred in the Diaspora have done a lot for this world via the natural sciences, social sciences and humanities and continue to add value to the growth of the global economy in many ways. People of African descent also add colour to this world through their various cultures expressed through music, sport, and a whole genre of the arts. Without Africans, the West would not be where it is today in terms of development. Therefore, it is this work's contention that slavery and colonialism should be brought to the fore by all Africans, until kingdom day. However, they should not be used as excuses for mediocrity or foolishness.

Zambia is still reeling from the inability to have a say over its export earnings, for the reasons mentioned, coupled with its landlocked status. Development becomes extremely difficult when such external vagaries predetermine the route that a country is going to follow in this matter. Social policy and human development concerns are not protected from these external shocks, for example, high oil prices or globalisation. International trade indeed has a direct correlation with the living standards of citizens of LDCs (for example in the way that profits accrued from this type of trade are deployed to critical areas of health, education and housing). This issue is quite emotive because the money earned from trade is in hard currency which can be used to import essential commodities such as medicines and machinery for the mining and agricultural sectors. LDCs are unable to compete favourably with the developed North as regards trade. This situation is even more pronounced in an ever changing and fast-paced global economic system.

Despite these shortcomings, it is important to nudge international trade in the direction of poverty reduction in LDCs if it is going to be effective at all. There is a need for better national development strategies that will outline the role of international trade in poverty reduction. LDCs have to formulate a methodology that focuses on the balance-of-payments constraints and the changes in the income elasticity of imports and exports which are necessary in order to achieve sustainable growth rates sufficient for meeting poverty reduction targets (United Nations Conference on Trade and Development, 2004). There should also be an examination of demand prospects of traditional exports and the criteria for identifying promising trade sectors that can help in achieving trade development goals. On this basis, alternative trade policy measures can be explored. This would be most effective within the context of a strong national trade policy in which a wide range of stakeholders, and particularly the private sector, are involved (United Nations Conference on Trade and Development, 2004).

UNCTAD examines how LDCs can promote development and poverty reduction in a newly liberalised open economy. Innovative strategies need to be explored, and certain key questions must be asked, for example: what is the nature of a post-liberal development strategy? What kinds of public action can facilitate development and poverty reduction in an economy without barriers to international trade? (United Nations Conference on Trade and Development, 2004). We need therefore to focus on another exogenous force impacting on LDCs and Zambia, which is interlinked with international trade: the phenomenon of globalisation.

Globalisation and LDCs

Globalisation may be seen as a multiple process involving the movement not only of capital, but also of people, technology, images and ideas. This produces tendencies not only towards homogenisation, but also towards the production of difference and conflict (Appadurai, 1990). Globalisation also leads to enhanced communications and greatly increased trade, and opens new opportunities for sustained economic growth as well as development of the world economy (United Nations, 1996). However, these attributes of globalisation favour the developed North and not LDCs. Thus globalisation must also be seen in the context of the domination of the world by the economic systems of the West, especially the United States. Therefore, any examination of globalisation must be undertaken against the background of capitalist development. The global web which was initially woven through trade links during the mercantile era must be taken as an antecedent to the present process commonly referred to as globalisation. The mercantile era should serve as a point of departure if an informed analysis of current trends vis-à-vis globalisation and capitalism is to be attained.

In the mercantile era the engine for capitalist expansion was international trade. During the same period the world was carved up into unequal enclaves and then interlinked for the benefit of Europe and America. It can be argued that the contemporary processes of globalisation are based on earlier factors such as mercantilism and colonialism, as well as the spread of nation-states and the transformation of rural communities that these produced (Appadurai, 1990). For Amin (1999), the process dates back to the 'old world' (Eurasia and Africa), and has now led to what he terms the new globalisation of capitalism. He observes that it is also a polarising process: in 'two centuries, from 1800 to the end of our century, it has been able to reduce the population of the centres of the system, whose frontiers have not changed much and which generally embrace the contemporary triad (the United States, Europe, Japan) to 20 per cent of the population of the planet' (Amin, 1999:32). The point to note here is that globalisation has not resulted in positive spin-offs, in most cases, for LDCs, while the developed world has benefited tremendously from this phenomenon. The reality is that globalisation has resulted in poverty for the bulk of the LDCs, again confirming that the process arose out of the unequal ties between the North and the South.

Globalisation has more often than not been detrimental to the development of LDCs. Furthermore, the main agents of globalisation, such as the World Bank and the IMF, have compounded human misery and despair in the developing world through so-called economic restructuring packages like the Structural Adjustment Programmes (SAPs), which negated the whole notion of human development for the sake of economic austerity measures (Noyoo, 1999). As regards international trade, an export-led growth strategy will be unlikely, in itself, to lead to a virtuous trade-poverty relationship in the LDCs or Zambia in particular, where there is mass poverty with most people living at or below income levels sufficient to meet their needs. Export-led growth is generally synonymous with an exclusionary growth trajectory with benefits concentrated in an enclave (United Nations Conference on Trade and Development, 2004). In Zambia for example, data for the country's 1991, 1996, and 1998, household surveys show that the proportion of the population living in poverty increased dramatically in the period 1991-96; this was the period during and immediately after a rapid and comprehensive trade liberalisation. Nevertheless, this situation improved somewhat after 1996, and in 1998 the national incidence of poverty was around the level it had been in 1991 (McCulloch *et al.*, cited in United Nations Conference on Trade and Development, 2004).

Therefore, it is important to bear in mind that export-led growth is not the only promising development strategy that can be pursued after trade liberalisation. Alternative routes can also be utilised, for instance:

(a) An export-led growth strategy with a human face, including increased linkages to diffuse benefits, and also a basic needs strategy.

(b) A balanced growth strategy based on agricultural productivity growth and export-accelerated industrialisation.

(c) An agricultural-development-led industrialisation (ADLI) strategy, which includes infrastructure investment and technological progress in agriculture together with forward linkages into processing activities, with an export component.

(d) Development and diversification through management of mineral revenues.

(e) Development of natural-resource-based production clusters.

(f) A triadic development strategy that includes the promotion of competitive tradables, employment-intensive non-tradables and technological change in subsistence-oriented activities to reduce constraints on household labour (United Nations Conference on Trade and Development, 2004:xi).

A highly important question is how globalisation interfaces with social policy and human development in LDCs and specifically in Zambia. Globalisation affects social policy both at the normative level and in a more practical way, by setting constraints that social policy must be attentive to. Adherence to international conventions, adjustment to fiscal pressures and responses to an international discourse on 'social rights' permeate domestic politics and affect social policy, or at least the thinking about it (Mkandawire, 2004). Any meaningful and relevant analysis of globalisation and social policy in LDCs, Africa, or Zambia must start with an understanding of the twin processes of poverty and development. It must investigate both process and context as they relate to the recent history and experiences of different countries. Such an analysis must revisit the 'development process', its promises and failures, and, in particular, the recent epoch of persistent crisis and adjustment (Aina, 2004). In Zambia, as in several African countries, globalisation and liberalisation of trade have created great insecurity in the labour force and in society at large. Loss of jobs, high unemployment, and skills mismatch are the main factors contributing to social exclusion and poverty (Fashoyin, 2002).

After this background discussion, a closer examination of the context in Zambia is now important. Attention will be paid to the existing sociopolitical landscape and the country's economy, and their effects on Zambia's social policy, as well as its human development efforts.

The setting and prevailing conditions

Zambia is situated in south-central Africa with Angola bordering its western boundary, while Botswana and Namibia occupy the south-west parts of the country. The Democratic Republic of the Congo (DRC) is on the northern stretch of Zambia's border and to the east is Malawi. On the south-east side of Zambia is Mozambique, and Tanzania lies on its north-eastern border. Zimbabwe is directly located to the south of the country. Zambia's total landmass is 752,614 square kilometres and its population was estimated at 11,798,678 in 2006 (Government of the Republic of Zambia, 2006).

Zambia has extremely high poverty rates as well as high unemployment levels. National statistics show that the poverty in the country in 2004 averaged 68 per cent, with the rural regions averaging higher percentages (Government of the Republic of Zambia, 2006). Urban employment and incomes are still decreasing in real terms. Formal sector employment has contracted to less than 10 per cent of the labour force, of which more than half consists of employment in the private sector. Besides the contraction of formal employment opportunities, demographic factors have also put pressure on Zambia's labour markets. This resulted in high unemployment in the 1990s, especially among the youth. In 1996, the youth unemployment rate of 32 per cent was more than double the overall rate of unemployment, sitting at 15 per cent (International Labour Organisation, 2005).

Underemployment and *casualisation* of labour are also quite rampant in Zambia. These phenomena are offshoots of the hasty liberalisation policies of the Third Republic. In many cases, Zambian workers are not protected from audacious exploitation by some of the so-called foreign investors. However, as earlier pointed out, Zambia's economy has shown signs of recovery. The country is experiencing its best economic growth rate in almost twenty years, boosted by increased investment in copper mines and rising output levels. Between 2000 and 2005, earnings from copper tripled, as output rose by 24 per cent. Favourable prices on international markets have resulted in the economic revival of the country. Improved fiscal policy can also explain some of Zambia's recent successes (*Zambia Daily Mail*, 2006).

Several positive and encouraging developments have also taken place in Zambia in the last six years. For instance, between 2001 and 2002 the Zambian government targeted investment, trade and export promotion towards the manufacturing sector, which had taken a hard knock in the 1990s because of the privatisation programme. It also undertook measures aimed at rural industrialisation and Micro, Small and Medium Enterprises (MSMEs) development. In the area of investment promotion, efforts were made to attract both local and foreign investors into the country. The Zambia Investment Advisory Council was launched to facilitate the design and implementation of investment programmes. The National Investment Plan was also finalised and the Zambia Export Processing Zone Authority (ZEPZA) was created to facilitate the promotion of investments in Export Processing Zones (EPZs) (Government of the Republic of Zambia, 2004). Credit to the private sector has been increased by 9 per cent in the last four years because of improved capital inflow, which is essential for the survival of the private sector. However, there were a number of obstacles such as lack of information, volatile commodity prices, underdeveloped finance and management on the part of MSMEs and high transaction costs. What is essential, though, is that access to innovative capital is critical to unlocking Zambia's vast economic potential (*Zambia Daily Mail*, 2006).

Levy Mwanawasa's first term of office (2001 6) exhibited some positive indicators in regard to Zambia's economic performance. Consistent economic growth was recorded, averaging 4.9 per cent per annum; macroeconomic stability strengthened with inflation falling to single digit levels, while budget management also improved. The country also succeeded in obtaining substantial debt relief through the Heavily Indebted Poor Countries (HIPC) mechanism and the multilateral debt relief initiative, relieving it of the previously high debt burden. Lower inflation increased stability in prices of goods and services as well as prevented the erosion of incomes. Fiscal discipline, through reduced government borrowing, now meant that the private sector could borrow more from the banks for further investment (Mwanawasa, 2006).

Other steps in the right direction included the creation of the Zambia Development Agency (ZDA). The ZDA is an amalgamation of various agencies that were created to bolster economic activities, such as the Zambia Investment Centre (ZIC), Zambia Privatisation Agency (ZPA), Zambia Export Processing Authority (ZEPA), Small Enterprise Development Board (SEDB) and Export Board of Zambia (EBZ). These measures were taken to help reduce duplication and overlapping, and time-consuming procedures in the issuance of investment permits. The government also began to blacklist contractors that did not honour their contractual obligations in the development of infrastructure in the country, such as roads. The government has committed itself to investing close to US$ 2 billion in the energy sector, specifically for the expansion of hydro-electricity. Already, there are signs that hydroelectric power stations will be built in certain provinces that have the potential and capacity to produce power for the country. The government released a 2007-9 Medium Term Expenditure Framework (MTEF) and the National Budget to stakeholders before their finalisation – the first time that the government has done this. This will help to ensure transparency and allow Zambians to have an insight into the workings of the country's macro economic strategy.

It is hoped that the political will shown in these measures will be consolidated and channelled into further development. Also, the establishment of the Road Development Agency (RDA) is commendable. The Public Roads Act No.12 of 2002 established the RDA which took over the role of the Roads Department in the Ministry of Works and Supply. The agency is responsible for the country's ten-year Road Sector Investment Programme with a projected total funding of US$ 1.65 billion. It is mandated to carry out all routine and emergency maintenance of public roads through its employees or independent contractors, as well as conducting studies that are necessary for the development, maintenance and improvement of the road network in Zambia (*Times of Zambia*, 2006).

The government has also published a proposed policy on Public-Private-Partnerships (PPPs), and called for comments from stakeholders and the public. The proposed draft is a co-operative venture, which will allow the private sector to invest in infrastructure development once implemented. The PPPs would be established within the Zambia Development Agency (ZDA) to promote technical support on infrastructure related issues (*Zambia Daily Mail*, 2006). Recently, the government raised from US$ 50,000 to US$ 500,000 the sum that the would-be investor needs to have upfront before the government can issue him or her with an investor's permit; it is hoped that this move will nip the problem of shoddy investors in the bud.

During his maiden speech to Parliament after re-election in October 2006, Levy Mwanawasa reaffirmed the social contract with the Zambian people (although he would pass away two years later). He also assured Zambians that the government was not going to be complacent with its electoral victory, but would ensure that the concerns raised by citizens before and during elections were seriously considered. He also pledged and hoped that he could leave behind a legacy of the rule of law, self-sufficiency in food production, increased employment and stability in Zambia's socio-economic policies. It is important to quote extensively from this speech as it serves as a platform for the government's plans for transformation of the country in the next five years.

(a) *Governance*

There was a pledge to continue the commitment to constitutionalism, human rights, transparency and accountability. The government would continue reforms in those areas as well as the administration of justice and democratisation.

(b) *Human rights*

The government, it was declared, will strive to domesticate international human rights treaties to which it is party and consider other appropriate protocols in order to enhance the rights of Zambians. Also, the following goals were going to be pursued so as to enhance human rights in the next five years: improving the justice delivery system and its efficiency through continuing rehabilitation of court infrastructure, particularly for subordinate courts and local courts; enhancing access to justice through, *inter alia,* decentralisation of the operations of the Legal Aid Board and the Director of Public Prosecutions' Chambers; the promotion and protection of human rights, especially for the vulnerable, for instance women and children, through strengthened legislation and specific social programmes to complement policy measures. The rehabilitation and improvement of reformatory schools will be undertaken, so that young people in conflict with the law are treated in the most befitting manner.

(c) Public accountability

It was stated that government's policy on the fight against corruption would undergo further review. Once finalised, the policy would provide guidelines in the reviewing and reforming of laws on corruption. The office of the Auditor-General would be further strengthened and have presence in all the districts.

(d) Media

The government also promises to continue providing the policy and legal as well as the institutional framework for the development of the media.

(e) Economic management and focus

The government aims to achieve higher and sustained economic growth of at least 7 per cent per annum, with agriculture, tourism, mining and manufacturing continuing to be the key focus. It will also seek to broaden and accelerate economic growth, and attempt to re-focus public resources and efforts towards implementation of programmes in order to have a quicker and more profound impact on the lives of the majority of Zambians. Job and wealth creation will be prioritised. However, it remains to be seen whether these pronouncements will be followed through, and Zambians may have to use them as yardsticks so as to gauge the performance of the President and the MMD after five years. It is important that Zambians revisit these pledges in the next general and parliamentary elections in 2011.

The Fifth National Development Plan also puts forward the following macroeconomic objectives for the plan period of 2006-10:

(i) to accelerate pro-poor economic growth;

(ii) to achieve financial and exchange rate stability; and

(iii) to sustain a viable balance of payments.

With respect to the acceleration of pro-poor growth, the primary focus remains reducing poverty through the implementation of policies that are both growth-oriented and pro-poor. Focusing on pro-poor growth will ensure that the poor participate in the development process. On the second point, Zambia has yet to attain full macroeconomic stability and still faces a number of challenges to its macroeconomic position. Fiscal stability is overshadowed by a high domestic debt estimated at 20 per cent of GDP, while budgetary interest payments take about 16 per cent of revenue (Government of the Republic of Zambia, 2006).

Even though there are healthy signs in the country, some negative forces are still retarding the country's progress. These are highlighted below.

Corruption

Corruption is a serious development impediment, because it impacts negatively on society by inappropriately deploying society's resources which are vital for social and economic development to undesignated or undesirable ends. It directly affects human development as it deprives individuals or communities of much needed assets. For instance, when Zambia experienced floods in one of the poorer areas of Lusaka, in Kanyama, in 1978, many houses and properties were destroyed. People were left homeless and destitute by this natural disaster. The government appealed for help and a Disaster Fund, the 'Kanyama Disaster Fund', was launched to collect either money or materials like blankets, clothes, shoes, etc., to help the victims of the floods. Voluntary organisations and charities as well as many individuals responded overwhelmingly to the call for help. Upon receipt of these items, a member of the UNIP Central Committee (these were high ranking officials in the UNIP government) misappropriated the donations for personal use. Despite overwhelming evidence, this UNIP official was never prosecuted. The flood victims suffered hunger, exposure and disease due to one corrupt official. Corruption is quite endemic in Zambia and did not flourish only under Frederick Chiluba's rule. However, it was amplified when that president and his lackeys led the corruption bandwagon for ten years. Zambia's score on the Corruption Perception Index (CPI) in 2006 was 2.6. This index measures the degree to which corruption is perceived to exist among public officials and politicians. It is a composite index drawing on different expert and business surveys. The scale is from 0 (highly corrupt) to 10 (highly clean) (Zambia Daily Mail, 2006:2).[1]

If left unchecked, corruption may lead to societal decay and an erosion of the moral fibre, while underhand methods will override virtue. Corruption also engenders poverty and inequality in that resources are unfairly apportioned to undeserving people. It also leads to inefficiency and wastage as it seriously corrodes and infringes upon meritocracy. Zambians do not need donors to tell them how to fight corruption or why fighting corruption is important. It only takes the right political will and conviction on the part of the leadership to turn things around; once the tone has been set by the government, the rest of the populace will follow. Corruption is rife in the public sector, for example, through the awarding of government tenders, employment recruitment and 'vote-buying' during elections by politicians. Corruption is a symptom that something has gone wrong in the management of the state. Institutions designed to govern the relations between the citizen and the state are used instead for personal enrichment and the provision of benefits for the corrupt (Rose-Ackerman, 1999). Indeed corruption has huge implications for a country's overall development. It has been established empirically that high levels of corruption are associated with lower levels of investment and growth. Furthermore, corruption reduces the effectiveness of industrial policies and encourages business to operate in the unofficial sector in violation of tax and regulatory laws. The price mechanism, so often a source of economic efficiency and a contributor to growth, can, in the form of bribery, undermine the legitimacy and effectiveness of government (Rose-Ackerman, 1999:2).

Infrastructure development

After decades of independence, Zambia's infrastructure remains really below international standards. At times it looks as if the country had experienced a time freeze (probably in the 1950s or 1960s) or has undergone a long protracted civil war. Neither has happened and it baffles the mind why there is such a high level of decay and dilapidation in the existing infrastructure. Whenever a traveller goes out of the country to developed parts of the world and returns to Zambia, he or she always gets the feeling that the erection of infrastructure is not a key policy issue in the country. One could be absent for a period of about ten years and return to find the same unfinished structures still standing in the middle of the city, which in this case are mere eyesores. Even though the Zambian end of the line built in the early colonial era to pursue Rhodes' 'Cape to Cairo' dream was supplemented after independence by the Tanzam (Tanzania-Zambia) railway from Kapiri Mposhi in Zambia to Dar es Salaam, within Zambia, in most rural areas, rail transport is non-existent. Even the existing railways operate below par. One would have thought that rail transport could have been prioritised by government as it is cheap, but this has not been the case in Zambia for decades. Trains cannot be used by Zambians, for instance, to commute to work. Zambia has not been proactive and serious enough in regard to development of the rail sector.

Infrastructure plays a critical role not only in the development of the economy, through Foreign Direct Investment (FDI) for instance, but also in enhancing the quality of life of people, as in the construction of new hospitals or houses. Infrastructure, including various modes of transport such as roads and rail networks, are essential for creating broad-based opportunities for income generation and thereby promote economic growth and the alleviation of poverty (United Nations Economic and Social Commission for Asia and the Pacific, 2001). The adequacy of infrastructure helps determine one country's success and another's failure in diversifying production, expanding trade, coping with population growth and urbanisation, or improving environmental conditions. Good infrastructure raises productivity and lowers production costs. Deficient infrastructure, along with weak management and poor economic organisation, accounts for a large share of low factor productivity in developing countries (World Bank, 2006).

So infrastructure is a critical development imperative that must not be taken lightly by governments in LDCs like Zambia. President Levy Mwanawasa recognised how undeveloped this sector remained and how it continued to pose a great challenge to national development efforts. To this end, he committed his administration to the enhancement of the construction, rehabilitation and maintenance of public infrastructure.

It is hoped that the setting of standards and regulations of construction and maintenance will be enhanced following the National Council for Construction Act and the subsequent establishment of statutory bodies to implement the provision of these Acts. The government has set the framework for the development and maintenance of quality socio-economic infrastructure for sustainable national development. Although the performance of the rail infrastructure in the country leaves much to be desired, at last some action is being considered by the government. Mwanawasa reported to Parliament that his government wishes to encourage both local and foreign investors to partner in the construction of the following rail lines: Chipata-Mpika, Nseluka-Mpulungu, Solwezi-Chingola, Solwezi-Lumwana-Benguela, Mulobezi-Namibia and Kafue-Lions Den (Mwanawasa, 2006).

Agriculture

After disastrous performance in the Second Republic, agriculture was poised to plunge further in the Third Republic. The misguided liberalisation of the sector also constrained its capacity to produce for the country, whilst marketing systems were characterised by grave anomalies. In the first year in power, overseeing the first agricultural season, Chiluba's MMD agreed to pay farmers promissory notes under the pretext that the government had no liquid cash. The promissory notes system was a recipe for disaster as it was plagued by inefficiencies and fraud. Many farmers were not remunerated for months and could not reinvest profits into other productive areas. Agriculture has exhibited moderate growth rates in small-scale farming and highly specialised cash commercial farming has shown very impressive growth rates, but from a low initial level. For small-scale farmers poor infrastructure, both in terms of roads as well as delivery mechanisms and marketing systems, is still a barrier to progress (International Labour Organisation, 2005).

In agriculture, a recurring headache is the amount of the country's harvested produce going to waste owing to rains. Year in year out, grain goes to waste after the onset of the first rains because it has not been collected. The main problem here is that there are, first, only very bad feeder roads that cannot easily facilitate the collection of produce from the hinterland, where most of the peasant farmers are located. Secondly, the storage of agricultural produce remains a challenge as there are not enough storage facilities. The few silos that were inherited from the colonial and Kaunda periods are not functioning at all. Many of these failures can be attributed to lack of planning.

Despite this, there were also successes for the country in agriculture after the devastating drought of 2001 when much of Southern Africa was gripped by famine. The sector that had been doing badly was able to feed the nation, in spite of the refusal of the government to distribute genetically enhanced food as aid. In the 2005/6 agricultural season, food and cash crops had significantly increased with a surplus of 160,000 tonnes of maize. Some of the well thought out policies in this sector had borne fruit. In this regard, government is convinced that the private sector can also do more and areas like agri-business will be supported in strengthening linkages with smallholder farmers through private sector participation in agricultural service delivery, equipment and produce marketing (Mwanawasa, 2006). Furthermore, the government has prioritised a number of programmes to be implemented in the next five years:

(a) Promotion of a well regulated and profitable irrigation sub-sector that is attractive to both the public and private sector.

(b) Promotion of agricultural infrastructure and land development for sustainable productivity.

(c) Improvement of productive efficiency of the livestock sector in a sustainable manner.

(d) Promotion of fisheries development by ensuring effective utilisation of fisheries resources.

(e) Encouraging private sector participation and farm mechanisation through supply of agricultural equipment, irrigation and agro-processing machinery to improve land productivity and value addition to agricultural produce.

(f) Promotion of competitive, efficient and transparent private sector driven agricultural marketing and input supply system.

(g) Promotion of effective service delivery with emphasis on agricultural research and extension (Mwanawasa, 2006:2).

The government also hopes to create land banks and a Land Development Fund to enable rural-based communities to expand their productive activities. The overall goal in agriculture is to promote a self-sustaining export-led agricultural sector that ensures increased household income and food security. Additionally, there has also been intervention made in poverty reduction through the promotion of commercial agriculture, land and infrastructure development, technological development, and the provision of extension services and targeted support systems for food security. In 2003, a total of K56.9 billion was allocated for poverty reduction programmes of which K46.1 billion, representing 81 per cent of the total allocation, was released. Outgrower schemes received 14.7 per cent while the rest of the programmes were allotted 16.1 per cent. In 2004, a total of K142.3 billion was allocated for poverty reduction programmes. The bulk of the allocation was for the Fertiliser Support Programme, which was 49.2 per cent (Government of the Republic of Zambia, 2004). The following areas also received attention from the government:

(a) Outgrower schemes

The promotion of outgrower schemes was aimed at enabling small-scale farmers to benefit from commercial farmers' expertise in the production and marketing of high value agricultural products. Through the schemes, the Zambian government increased its outreach in delivery of extension services to small-scale farmers.

(b) Irrigation development programme

This programme is aimed at promoting small-scale irrigation schemes, especially for drought prone areas. In 2003, an amount of K6 billion was allocated of which K2 billion was released for the programme. Ten projects were implemented in 2003 under the dam construction/rehabilitation and irrigation development scheme. By the end of 2003, six projects were completed while four were near completion.

(c) Land development programmes

Land development programmes aim at the establishment of new farming blocks at Kalumwange in Kaoma, Nasanga in Serenje and Luena sugar project in Kawambwa. The objective of developing these areas is to increase the land under cultivation in order to expand agricultural production. The areas of concentration in the three farm blocks include land capability, social surveys, crop suitability, lay-out plans, infrastructure development and socio-economic amenities, as well as marketing and agro-processing (Government of the Republic of Zambia, 2004).

(d) Agro research and technological development

In an effort to seek better farming methods and crop varieties, an amount of K500 million was allocated for agricultural research and technological development in 2003 out of which K55 million was released.

(e) Rural Investment Fund (RIF)

The Rural Investment Fund is aimed at supporting community-based development of rural infrastructure. Matching grants were given to farmer groups for the rehabilitation and construction of boreholes, markets, storage sheds, bridges, feeder roads and irrigation facilities.

(f) Agricultural Input Support Programme

The focus of this programme is on supporting vulnerable households through the provision of agricultural inputs. K10 billion was allocated for this purpose in 2003. An additional amount of K21.9 billion was released through a supplementary budget to meet the cost of inputs. A total of 150 farmers benefited, of whom 130 grew rain-fed crops and twenty thousand used wetlands and winter agriculture. A diversified range of agro-inputs were procured and distributed to farmers (Government of the Republic of Zambia, 2004).

(g) Seed multiplication

In order to improve the provision of good seed an amount of K1.06 billion was allocated to the Seed Multiplication Programme, of which K464 million was released. K250 million was disbursed and distributed to eleven districts for the purchase of chemicals and fertiliser, K56 million was used for seed production and the rest of the funds were set aside for final seed inspection, monitoring and sampling of seeds (Government of the Republic of Zambia, 2004). [Note: 1 US $ was equivalent to K4,270 at the time of writing].

(h) Animal draught power

In order to improve labour constraints and guarantee timely tillage operations and increase areas cultivated per household, the Animal Draught Power Programme was launched by the government.

(i) Livestock re-stocking

The objective of livestock re-stocking is to reduce poverty through restoration of breeding stock and increased animal draught power.

(j) Animal Disease Control

Control of livestock diseases aims to preserve the existing population of livestock in the country and in order to have effective livestock-restocking.

(k) Rehabilitation of agricultural training institutions

Money was allocated in 2003 for the rehabilitation of infrastructure at five agricultural training institutions in the country.

(l) Aquaculture and fisheries development

The objective of the programme is to promote food security through protein food for the population (Government of the Republic of Zambia, 2004:21-23).

Tourism

The tourism industry has for years not been effective, primarily because of the government's nonchalant attitude towards the sector and derelict infrastructure in the country. Travelling from the once grandiose airport (which is in need of repair) to the run down hotels and motels, one does not need to be a rocket scientist to figure out why the country has not been able to attract large numbers of tourists despite its huge potential. This is confirmed by the example of the Victoria Falls. For a long time, this wonder of the world was regarded internationally as solely being in Zimbabwe. Many people outside Africa did not know that the Victoria Falls actually had a huge chunk in Zambia and that Dr David Livingstone had 'discovered' the Falls with local tribes from the Zambian side. But these facts could not be sold to the world. Moreover, even if tourists came in droves, there would be few decent accommodation facilities and other services to cater for their needs.

At the height of the Zimbabwean economic boom in the 1980s, the country vigorously marketed the Victoria Falls to the world, and invested heavily in tourism infrastructure in the town of Victoria Falls. It was a common sight those days to see tourists walk or drive from the town of Victoria Falls in Zimbabwe into Livingstone, just to have a glimpse of the waterfalls from the Zambian side and return to Vic Falls for lodging. At the time, Zambia had only one dilapidated hotel, the Mosi-oa-Tunya. Even now, Livingstone has slightly over 1,000 beds as compared to 3,000 beds on the Zimbabwean side of the river Zambezi (The Post, 2006).

For decades, potential revenue was lost in this area. The one-party state was the least interested in bolstering this sector and most of the blame must be put at its doorstep. It is only in the last five years or so that two modern hotels, a couple of lodges and backpackers' hostels have sprung up in Livingstone. However, the breadth and length of the country is still devoid of tourist facilities. For that reason, Zambia is still getting the 'battle-hardened' tourists who unfortunately usually survive on a shoe-string budget. In a nutshell Zambia is still not a tourist friendly destination, mainly because of the lack of infrastructure and high costs emanating from sub-standard services.[2] Indeed, slogans of 'Zambia the real

Africa' will not do if concerted efforts by the Zambia National Tourist Board are not channelled towards raising the quality of infrastructure and services in this area.[3] However, there have been some commendable moves made in tourism infrastructure, such as the rehabilitation of access roads mainly in Mosi-oa-Tunya National Park, Kafue National Park, Lower Zambezi and the South Luangwa National Park. In addition, the Tourism Development Credit Facility (TDCF) established in 2003 was enhanced with 43 small-scale Zambian entrepreneurs benefiting (Government of the Republic of Zambia, 2004). But this is a mere drop in the ocean when compared to other countries in the region or in East Africa.

The national government and local authorities as well as the Tourist Board must mount campaigns to beautify Zambian cities and towns. No tourist will be encouraged by run down facilities. The littering of cities and towns with rubbish must also be punishable by law; for that purpose authorities (especially municipalities) must also make sure that they create structures to collect and destroy refuse. However, when one goes around most towns in the country, there are just no dustbins. Ordinary citizens must also be educated on the need for a clean environment as it seems that consciousness regarding this matter has been eroded over the years and people no longer appreciate beauty or cleanliness. To respond to this need, civic education programmes have to be conducted by both Civil Society Organisations (CSOs) and the government. For instance, whenever one goes to public buildings, one encounters a torn flag or an oxidised sign-post. Surely, does the flag not just require a new cloth and the sign-post new paint? These are simple matters, but in a situation where a thug culture was cultivated by the government (under Frederick Chiluba), perhaps civic education has to start at the top.

Sport and recreation

Zambia does not have modern sports facilities like good stadia for athletics or football. The existing decrepit infrastructure like the Independence Stadium remain a safety hazard – indeed sections of the stadium collapsed in the 1990s, killing scores of football fans. Because of this situation, Zambia has lost out on opportunities to host continental football showpieces like the Africa Cup of Nations[4] and All Africa Games. Lately, President Mwanawasa announced that government would like to develop sport infrastructure in the country so that Zambia benefits from the 2010 World Cup to be staged in South Africa. He also signed an agreement with the Chinese government to build an ultra modern stadium. But the sector still requires a serious revamp.

Sport and recreation are very important for producing a stable nation and healthy individuals, even critically important in regard to children and the youth. At present there are also no public parks one can speak of, where people can go and relax, or where children can play. Now parks have become luxuries for the elite. All the parks that were left by the colonialists have either been turned into grasslands, or 'bought' by some unscrupulous rich individuals building mansions for themselves. Long gone are the days when Zambia used to have public benches where people could just sit and relax in city spaces. Town planning (if it still exists) does not include public squares where all sorts of recreational activities can take place; Zambian cities have ceased to have such spaces. If we have to talk of ponds and waterways, that is another issue altogether. As for public libraries, the situation is also deplorable. Most libraries in Zambia are in a state of disrepair even though there is hunger for information in the country. Once providing a pastime for both young and old people, reading in libraries has altogether become a mission these days. Many libraries have simply been turned into monuments.[5]

Brain drain

Zambia's notoriety as regards the maltreatment and non-appreciation of its professionals and technocrats is a relic of the one-party state that simply does not want to be erased. In such an environment, where most of the political leadership was illiterate, professionals were constantly vilified and hounded by the political establishment; they were viewed as a source of opposition. Infamous pronouncements by political leaders like 'You will die with your degree' or 'Do not bite the hand that feeds you' served to reinforce the notion that intellectuals were a problem for society and not assets. Since the educated were in most cases vocal against the excesses of the single-party rule they were always targeted by the state machinery; such sentiments were meant not only to smother their voices but also to dampen their spirits. Independent thinkers, predominantly from the intellectual class, were anathema to the one-party regime. Because of this negative stance by the ruling party against intellectuals, and the declining standards of living due to worsening economic conditions, many educated Zambians began to leave the country. What was galling to most of them was the fact that they were not remunerated according to their expertise, while uneducated politicians were living very comfortable lives.

In spite of rhetorical statements about 'belt tightening' and 'sacrifice to the nation' from the political establishment, regard to politicians and parasites of the one-party regime always did the opposite and lived extremely lavish lifestyles. In fact it can be argued that this was when the seeds of inequality were sown in post-colonial Zambia. In this environment, even the Zambian masses were not supportive of their intellectuals. The situation became so bizarre that ordinary Zambians would rather respect a drug dealer (because the individual had money and drove a BMW) than a university professor (who in most cases was relegated to walking because he/she could not afford to buy a car from a meagre salary).

When Frederick Chiluba came to power, the culture of undervaluing intellectuals was simply extended and concretised. There was just no respite for intellectuals and professionals in the Third Republic. For example, when medical doctors went on strike to demand better conditions, they were simply fired and even told to go to neighbouring countries if they so wished. Even though Zambia's migration and development situation is more of a structural problem, it should be seen as an attitudinal one as well, whereby successive governments have failed to provide adequate conditions of service to professionals, for unclear reasons. The country's brain drain is acute and deeply rooted, but was accelerated in the last decade by the Structural Adjustment Programme that imposed drastic measures involving civil service retrenchment, voluntary retirements and redundancies. These reforms fostered the departure of qualified professionals from the public to the private sector as well as skills migration across national boundaries (Ammasari, 2005).

The pattern of Zambia's brain drain unfolded in this manner: in the 1980s a large number of teachers left the country to fill the critical skills gaps in the education sector in Botswana. During the same period, the country began to experience the loss of health workers and registered nurses, who started to leave Zambia in significant numbers to countries in the region and abroad. Zambian skills are very much in demand be cause education in the country used to be better than in other countries in the region. The University of Zambia lost 230 professors and lecturers from 1984 to 1994, the majority of whom held doctorates. Also, the School of Law is currently suffering from brain drain as law specialists leave, mostly for Botswana (Ammasari, 2005). A study by the United States Agency for International Development (USAID) in 2003 suggests that out of more than 600 doctors trained after independence only fifty were still in the country. Furthermore, the total number of Zambians residing in wealthy industrialised countries of the Organisation for Economic Co-operation and Development (OECD) is estimated at 34,825. Almost half of these Zambian expatriates are highly skilled as compared, for example, to only 20 per cent among Angolan expatriates. International migration of skilled and highly skilled Zambians increased rapidly during the last ten years. The health sector is the most affected by the brain drain, but institutions of higher education also experienced important skills losses from the beginning of Zambia's economic crisis (Ammasari, 2005).

What is worth mentioning here is that most educated Zambians would have stayed home if there was even some form of appreciation from both the government and the masses of their contribution towards the development of the country. Many want to come back home but are faced with the grim prospect of poor conditions of service. Some have indeed come back home only to join the rank and file of the unemployed. In many instances, the 'returnee' is usually treated with disdain by the 'locals' who feel that he/she does not know what is going on in the country, without appreciating that such an individual has been exposed to different, even sophisticated ways of doing things. The returnee is also confronted with the harsh reality of nepotism: even though one may have outstanding qualifications one needs to have the 'right connections' to get a job. Even in the so called international Non-Governmental Organisations (NGOs), the highly qualified individual will not endear himself or herself to the person who is in charge, usually a semi-literate European who has been given a good package to come and enjoy some sunshine in Zambia while living the life of an expatriate. In many cases, the returnee usually leaves the country after an unsuccessful stint.

The government of Levy Mwanawasa tried to encourage professionalism in the country, but in most instances was non-committal on the question of the brain drain. This problem will continuously hound the country until there are specific policies to stem the tide of emigration on the one hand, and to woo expatriates back home on the other. Zambia lacks a comprehensive and coherent migration policy. This is somewhat surprising given that skills migration and the brain drain are issues that have been on the policy agenda for some time now (Ammasari, 2005). Also, the general attitude of Zambians regarding this matter has to change if indeed they want their intellectuals to come back home.

Therefore, pronouncements in the local press by the Zambian president urging Zambians living abroad to send back home foreign exchange so as to invest in the development of the country can be taken as a good sign. This is the first time a Zambian president has publicly acknowledged the importance of the diaspora in the reconstruction of the Zambian economy. It is hoped that this gesture will not remain rhetoric, but end in the promulgation of a forward-looking policy that will tap into the expertise as well as the finances of Zambians working abroad. Other countries have greatly benefited from their citizens who are working overseas, once local conditions were made favourable for their participation. For instance, the present increased growth in the Indian economy can mostly be ascribed to the technical know-how and financial injections into the country from Indians abroad. In Ghana, contributions from citizens overseas account for the fourth largest source of foreign currency after cocoa, gold and tourism. Their contribution to the national treasury annually is said to be US$ 2 billion, a figure that is only destined to grow in the coming years (Times of Zambia, 2006).

For this to happen in Zambia there has to be a reciprocal relationship between those that remain in the country and the government as well as citizens who emigrate. Ill-treatment of people who left the country for better opportunities should not be encouraged. It is therefore gratifying to hear that the Organisation of Zambians Abroad (OZA) has indicated that it will inject K330 billion into the economy.[6] Whether this will transpire remains to be seen, but the proposal is also a positive indication that Zambians living abroad are awakening to the critical role that they could play in reconstructing their country.

Zambia in Southern Africa

Zambia is located in Southern Africa and is virtually defined by its cultural and geopolitical ties to countries in this part of Africa. To be precise, it is more south-central, geographically, than purely a Southern African country. Thus, it does have certain parts in Central Africa and also Southern Africa.

Cultural affiliation

Most countries sharing a border with Zambia have a close affiliation with communities in the country. In the Eastern Province, the Cewas' and Tumbukas' kin reside in Malawi. The Nsenga of the same province also have kindred in Mozambique, together with the Chikunda of Luangwa. In Luapula, the Lunda have relatives across the border in the DRC, as well as the Bemba of the Northern Province. The Namwanga of the same province also have family ties with Tanzanians across the border. In the North-Western Province, the Chokwe, Lunda, Luvale and Mbundu, all have attachments to Angola through closely related tribes. The Gwembe Tonga of the Southern Province also have ties with tribes in Zimbabwe.

In the Western Province, the Subia have relatives in Botswana and Namibia, while the Kwa-Mashi and Mbunda are closely linked to tribes in Angola. From this general picture, it can be seen that culturally, Zambia is strongly linked to most countries in Southern Africa. Furthermore, the Lozi of Western Province also have linguistic patterns similar to the Sotho and Tswana languages spoken in Botswana, Lesotho and South Africa, while the Ngoni have a similar language to the Zulu and Ndebele, of South Africa and Zimbabwe respectively. Therefore, Zambia's links to parts of Southern Africa is not just political or on paper, but is a truly lived experience spanning hundreds of years.

Geo-political ties

Zambia can be credited for helping to create significant regional organs that played vital roles in the political development of Southern Africa. To begin with, the Frontline States group, set up at the instigation of Zambia and Tanzania, was crucial in providing a platform for charting the course of the liberation struggle of Southern Africa. The late president of Tanzania, Julius Nyerere, and Zambia's president Kenneth Kaunda were the main actors in this body that mobilised resources and provided logistical support to various liberation groups in the region. Created in 1975, the Frontline States group later incorporated Botswana under its late president Sir Seretse Khama into its fold, and with the independence of both Angola and Mozambique the organ co-opted both those countries. Zambia was also a trend-setter in this area when it advocated the Frontline States' reconfiguration into a regional body aimed at harnessing and enhancing the socio-economic potential of the region for the betterment of its people. To this end the Southern African Development Co-ordinating Conference (SADCC) was created in Lusaka in 1980.

One may argue that without Zambia, most, if not all of the Southern African countries fighting for freedom and the overthrow of colonial and white settler rule would not have attained their independence when they did. For many, independence would have been delayed for decades if Zambia had not taken up the responsibility of hosting all the liberation movements in the region that were fighting colonial rule. This may seem exaggerated, but only one who experienced the situation and lived in the context and age can appreciate the magnitude of Zambia's sacrifice in aiding all the liberation movements of Southern Africa. In a world where most of the Western powers were supporting the colonialists, many liberation movements turned to the Eastern bloc for military assistance. Owing to the Cold War, the West had proxy states in Africa that were not willing to help in the decolonisation of Africa. With the threat of isolation from the West looming, Zambia nevertheless went ahead to support all the liberation movements in the region. There were times when there could be two or more organisations from one colony that were ideologically opposed to each other, but Zambia supported them all the same. Zambia's umbilical code to Southern Africa was clearly discernable during the decolonisation process, when it did not abandon any of the political movements that were opposed to colonial rule, even though some countries were not willing or reluctant to help them at all. However, this stance came at a heavy price.

The Southern African liberation struggle

Huge sacrifices were made by Zambians in facilitating the emancipation of Angola, Mozambique, Namibia, South Africa and Zimbabwe from colonial and white minority rule. In many respects, this stance contributed significantly to Zambia's current deplorable economic standing. This issue is not treated seriously by commentators when Zambia's current dim economic fortunes are taken into account. In truth support for the liberation of these countries was a very expensive undertaking on the part of Zambia, but this sacrifice is not given the acknowledgement that it deserves, or when it is mentioned it is put squarely on the shoulders of one man, Kenneth Kaunda, without looking at the broader picture. In fact, it was the ordinary Zambians who sacrificed for the freedom of their brothers and sisters in Southern Africa, and not the president alone. It was the common people: the poor, the marginalised and the rural dwellers living along the border areas close to settler-ruled colonies that died during the military raids of the Portuguese, Rhodesian and South African armed forces. Nevertheless, a good number of Zambians feel betrayed by people they so graciously looked after in the way they reciprocated after they gained their independence. Support for the liberation struggle impoverished the country in many ways and therefore Zambia's poverty should not be erroneously treated as an original condition.

Supporting the liberation movements added to the economic difficulties that made the Zambian government borrow heavily and incur debts from international financial lenders. The human and humanitarian costs were immense, with repeated raids from Rhodesian, Portuguese and South African forces resulting in countless deaths. In the process, infrastructure critical to the country's economy was also destroyed. From 1965 until 1989, villages and people suspected of aiding freedom fighters were attacked and landmines were also planted by the forces of the white minority regimes, resulting in the maiming and deaths of many Zambians. From 1964 to 1990 there were approximately 100,000 war-related deaths in Zambia. The wars in Southern Africa also displaced many people in the region who found refuge in Zambia. From the 1960s up to the late 1980s, refugees streamed into Zambia. By the mid-1980s there were an estimated 300,000 refugees in the country. Zambia lived up to its obligation to support these refugees, both morally and materially, by diverting scarce resources to ensure their protection (Action for Southern Africa, 2005). Zambia's position against colonialism and apartheid is thought to have cost over US$ 19 billion. Without these extra costs the advances made in human development after independence would have been sustained much longer. In addition, Zambia not only borrowed heavily to meet its economic and defence needs (incurring further debt), but it also had to spend heavily so as to carry out extensive repairs to infrastructure damaged in the raids (Action for Southern Africa, 2005).[7]

Kenneth Kaunda, the president, took it upon himself to champion this crusade without consulting Zambians over this issue most of the time. Some critics have pointed out that he never cared for the local people, but for foreigners because he was himself a 'foreigner'.[8] Some Zambians wonder why their country's wealth is always developing other countries or people and not its citizens. As was shown in the previous chapter, Zambia's wealth literally built the Zimbabwean industrial base and then later on, the country's resources were channelled into looking after foreigners as well as propping up liberation struggles in Southern Africa, at the expense of the nation's development.[9]

Zambia's support for the freedom struggle of Southern Africa can be categorised as moral, political, material and financial. Zambia used many platforms and networks for that cause, such as the Frontline States, the Southern African Development Co-ordinating Conference (SADCC), the Organisation of African Unity (OAU), the Commonwealth, the Group of 77 and the United Nations. The costs borne by Zambia were both immediate and long-term. They included death and injury; economic costs; humanitarian costs because of displacement and refugees; military and defence costs; political costs; debt, and debt conditionality impact; and lost opportunities (Banda, 2000).

Zambia incurred high costs in trade, economic action and de-linkage. Billions of dollars were lost as Zambia's economy tried to deal with both sanctions and basic needs. Infrastructure had to be built to deal with transport and energy requirements. The balance of payments was also affected (Banda, 2000). There were social costs as well. Many of the freedom fighters had consorted with Zambian women and a good number of these relationships had resulted in children. Unfortunately these children grew up fatherless as one of their parents was in effect a sojourner. However, it must be pointed out that social policy perspectives have become more regionalised in the last five years. There have been concerted efforts from regional governments to harmonise specific countries' social policies into a regional policy. Such initiatives are welcome as the economic factor was the main issue in regional integration initiatives of the Southern African Development Community (SADC) in past decades.

Social policy and human development in the region

Zambia is a member of the Southern Africa Development Community (SADC) comprising also Angola, Botswana, the DRC, Lesotho, Madagascar, Malawi, Mauritius, Mozambique, Namibia, Seychelles, South Africa, Swaziland, Tanzania and Zimbabwe. The SADC has an organ of ministers charged, among other things, with harmonising social development amongst member states. Although it is relatively new and still grappling with the question of a regional social policy, some strides have been made in order to arrive at a clear understanding around this matter. It was in this spirit that several ministers met in Johannesburg on 23-24 November 2006 to discuss the issue of developing a regional social policy, in the context of the African Union's NEPAD. Forerunner gatherings had tackled various regional social policy concerns in the following manner:

1. The Ministers' meetings of 1999 and 2000 discussed the implementation of the outcomes of the World Summit for Social Development. A SADC Statement of Intent on Copenhagen+5 emanated from this undertaking. Furthermore, the programme on social development from this symposium culminated in the Millennium Development Goals.

2. The SADC Regional Indicative Strategic Development Plan (RISDP) was launched in 2004 and covered social and human development as one of the core areas of co-operation. In the same year, in preparation for the Ten Year Review of the Implementation of the Copenhagen Commitments, the ministers responsible

for social development committed to an ongoing co-ordinated approach to tackling and promoting social development through continental dialogues focused on integrated poverty eradication strategies, social integration and full employment.

3. The ministerial meeting, hosted by South Africa in partnership with UNESCO, in 2004 recommended to the Integrated Committee of Ministers to approve the establishment of a forum for SADC Ministers responsible for Social Development in line with the amended SADC Treaty Article 12 (paragraph 2.1) (Department of Social Development, 2006:1-2).

One of the key resolutions emanating from the ministers' deliberations was that a regional social policy should be based on an understanding that economic and social development cannot be divorced from each other, and that both are critical for comprehensive and sustainable development (Department of Social Development, 2006). The meeting also confirmed the need for a regional social policy that could enable the SADC region to deal with the various social development challenges. The ministers also resolved to mainstream social development and the social policy dimensions of the NEPAD into the SADC regional action plans, and promote this process to colleagues in other regions (Department of Social Development, 2006). This standpoint also links up with social policy education and training in the region as well.

As regards teaching of and training in social policy by universities in the region, much needs to be done in order to have a harmonious outlook in this area. In South Africa, this sphere is still fairly insulated and does not reflect regional and continental issues pertaining to social policy and human development. This situation may still be attributed to apartheid which in effect closed the country from outside influences and in particular from countries north of the Limpopo River. At an academic symposium in Harare in 1998 that brought together scholars from Botswana, South Africa, Tanzania, Uganda, Zambia and Zimbabwe, this issue was put under the spotlight. What emerged from the discussions was that there was indeed a need for synergies in social policy training in the regions of Eastern and Southern Africa if the perennial problems of poverty and social exclusion were to be dealt with. The academics observed that social policy was well placed to tackle the social ills of the regions as it could also give regional governments a rational and scientific route to remove bottlenecks, for example in areas like health, education, social security and employment. The symposium observed that protocols aiming for a common approach in social policy could also help to avoid duplication and dissonance in East and Southern Africa, leading to the empowerment of citizens. Thus social policy could become a vital tool for both East and Southern African politicians and policy-makers to realise social development in the two regions.

At the Harare symposium one delegate clearly pointed out that the role of social policy in the sub-region, as in other developing countries, is fraught with the usual dilemmas of keeping abreast of new knowledge and skills in social delivery, in addition to basic ideological concerns of societal reform versus individual adjustment. He argued that, in order to allow for a co-ordinated approach to social policy formulation and implementation in Southern Africa, governments and civil society should be innovative and creative and use non-traditional patterns of service delivery, while there was also a need for re-examination of the basic philosophy, goals and values of Southern African social policies (Tembo, 1998). Furthermore, Tembo (1998) notes that countries needed to find answers to questions such as: when should social policy adopt developmental, preventative or remedial approaches as it endeavours to meet the needs of the people?

Conclusion

LDCs are significantly exposed to the vagaries of external forces which in turn define, *inter alia*, the promulgation of social policies and the meeting of human needs in such countries. It was this chapter's intention to show how, in such settings, social policy and human development acquire unique characteristics. Using Zambia as a backdrop, the chapter looked at the various exogenous and endogenous forces that ultimately impacted on the wellbeing or contributed towards the ill-fare of Zambians. The next chapter closely examines Zambia's human development imperatives.

Notes

[1] As regards corruption, the then president of Transparency International Zambia (TIZ), the late Professor Alfred Chanda, had this to say: 'This position of Zambia poses a challenge to all concerned citizens that corruption is a major problem that poses a huge risk to the

development of the country. We all need to take proactive responsibility in the fight against corruption and much more needs to be achieved, if we are to translate political will by government into sustainable and tangible achievements.'

2 These sentiments and experiences are based on the author's travels in Southern Africa and other parts of the world.

3 Even the song used to advertise Zambia's tourism potential on television is not palatable to the ears. Honestly, could not those charged with this responsibility just have hired professionals, or better still have conducted a national contest where everybody voted for the best song? The problem with Zambia is that the merit system is so denuded that things are just imposed on people, even if they are below standard. It is the same with the national football team. Instead of engaging the nation in choosing a name for the country's football team the name *Chipolopolo*, a mouthful, was thrust onto Zambians, in all respects.

4 Zambia was fined and barred from participating in the Africa Cup of Nations finals in the 1990s when it failed to meet the required infrastructural standards after bidding to host the continental event. There were no stadia that the country could use and one wonders why the government of the day had embarked upon this foolhardy quest in the first place. Such policy mishaps in the sports arena were also evident in the one-party state when then president, Kenneth Kaunda, ordered that one of the important stadia in the country, The Dag Hammarskjöld Stadium (named after the United Nations Secretary General who died in a plane crash at Ndola, Zambia in 1961, whilst on a peace mission to the Congo), should be razed to the ground in preparation for the erection of a new and better stadium on the same site. After the stadium was demolished nothing was done; to date, the area is just a grass field. That is how simplistic national development issues were in the one-party state.

5 The Chairperson of the Zambian Library Association pointed out in the local press that libraries in Zambia are in a deplorable state. He said the situation was worse in public libraries as there was inadequate funding to libraries and that the materials stocked in libraries were outdated.

6 The local currency had taken a heavy blow after the elections, when it had performed well for most of 2006 as it had reached at least the

K3,000 to 1 US$ mark. However, after much fluctuation, at the time of writing, it had risen to 1 US $=K4,270.

7   Gabriel C. Banda undertook a detailed study 'Zambia Against Apartheid: A Case on Apartheid Caused Debt', documenting Southern Africa's liberation struggles and how these impacted on Zambia.

8   Despite having parents who originated from Malawi, Kaunda was born in Zambia, in the Northern Province town of Chinsali. This issue was contentious for a long time in Zambia as many people felt that they were not supposed to have suffered the one-party state's excesses that were in fact perpetrated by a 'foreigner'. In 1996, a constitutional amendment clause was instituted by President Chiluba barring all people of foreign origin from contesting the presidency. Some commentators assert that this measure was solely directed at Kaunda who had made a strong political comeback and was about to challenge the incumbent at the polls.

9   It always baffles the mind that citizens of countries in the region that continuously harp on Zambia's supposed backwardness benefited morally, financially and otherwise from the country's pure generosity. Furthermore, Zambians lost out on many economic opportunities due to this moral stance. Some Zambians wonder why their hospitality has been rewarded for ill-treatment. For many Zambians, it is not a question of 'pay-back' but an issue of brotherly and sisterly love. They also observe that Zambians are rarely illegal immigrants in these countries, but only go there for business or are professionals propping up their economies.

Chapter 5

ZAMBIA'S HUMAN DEVELOPMENT IMPERATIVES

Introduction

This chapter casts light on Zambia's human development imperatives and attempts to cluster them into the following thematic areas: social services, rural development, civil liberties and equal opportunities, and populations at risk. The assumption is that once these areas are fully functional and sustained over a considerable period of time, Zambia will then experience a social atmosphere that is devoid of stress and deprivation. These thematic areas are further categorised as sub-themes in the following manner:

1. *Social Services*: including education, housing, health, water and sanitation.
2. *Rural Development*: focusing on raising the living conditions of rural dwellers.
3. *Civil liberties and equal opportunities*: relating to human rights, social and economic justice (socio-economic opportunities), and gender parity.
4. *Vulnerabilities and populations at risk*: encompassing people with disabilities, the aged, children (orphans and /or street children) and the youth.

Zambia is currently in the lowest category of human development as defined by the United Nations Development Programme (UNDP). Adverse human welfare indices such as reduced access to a nutritionally adequate food basket, to name just one, are not encouraging. What is even more disconcerting is that poverty and its severity have been fast worsening as the majority of Zambians continue to subsist on the equivalent of less than US$1 a day (Government of the Republic of Zambia, 2006). Social strife remains a central feature in the lives of many Zambian citizens, owing to lack of socio-economic opportunities. For instance, access to social services (which were a universal right in the 1960s and 1970s) is increasingly becoming extremely difficult for many poor Zambians.

Social Services

Social services are instrumental in shaping a country's human development path in the way that they help to harness and ultimately contribute towards the sustenance of people's livelihoods. They help in the reduction of life threatening aspects like diseases and enable people to participate in other productive activities. Social policy and social services intersect at the core of human development, hinging on the raising of people's capabilities. This section begins to examine in detail various subcategories of social services in Zambia that are critical to the country's human development.

Education

At independence, education standards were appalling in Zambia and the country only had about a hundred university graduates. Very few of these had received their education by virtue of official British foresight; most had attracted the support of private charities or private scholarships, or had attended the universities of other developing countries, themselves newly independent, like India (Chan, 1985). This situation is attributable to British colonial policy which had sought to colonise Africa in such a way that while, on the west coast, educational provision for the indigenous population extended as far as university education, in East Africa and Northern Rhodesia, the emphasis was on primary education, as this would help the white employers of the eastern countries, but anything higher was deemed superfluous, if not dangerous (Chan, 1985). After independence, as explained in Chapter 2, the first African government expanded the educational sector in profound ways. By 1966, the University of Zambia was already complete and ready to welcome its first students. Schools, at both primary and secondary levels, were erected all over Zambia, extending to the remotest parts of the country. Colleges were also built and emphasis was placed on the construction of technical, teachers' and nurses' colleges around the country.

For this study, education is regarded as one of UNIP's and Kenneth Kaunda's successful projects, especially in the two decades after independence. Social policy's efficacy in the First and Second Republics was best exemplified by the highly successful education sector. Indeed, one social project that will endear Zambians to Kenneth Kaunda and UNIP is the way education was prioritised after independence. For instance, Kaunda took advantage of the good relations he had with the Eastern bloc by signing various bilateral agreements on education. A good number of these spilled over into the Third Republic, whose education record was dismal. These agreements, mostly in the science and technical fields, enabled Zambians to study at universities in China, Bulgaria, Czechoslovakia, Cuba, the German Democratic Republic (GDR), North Korea, the Soviet Union, Romania, Yugoslavia, etc. Scores of agricultural specialists, doctors, engineers, and other professionals were being churned out of foreign universities and coming back home to participate in the development of the country. The University of Zambia and various colleges were also producing various graduates for the country's industries. It seemed like nothing could go wrong. Indeed, this was Zambia's golden age as the economy was also on the upswing. During this period, many citizens would beat their chests and declare loudly how proud they were to be Zambians.

The only limitation to Zambia's educational expansion was the fact that it could not be sustained over time. For example, institutions of higher learning were not self-sustaining and were solely dependent on government subsidies to operate as well as offer high quality education. Therefore, it was not accidental that when the economy faltered and began to tumble the education sector followed suit. From primary all the way to university level, the education sector felt the reverberations of the economic collapse. There were also no mechanisms created to make sure that the gains made in education could benefit future generations. For instance, all the students who were educated on government bursaries did not pay back these loans. Today, the higher education sector is experiencing difficulties and is unable to educate the mainly poor students who are on government bursaries owing to lack of funds. The Bursaries Committee, falling under the Ministry of Science, Technology and Vocational Training, has records on who was on a government bursary or scholarship from 1964. In fact there were few students that were self-sponsored in Zambia; even students from affluent families were on a government bursary (there was a shift in policy from free and universal education to bursaries at tertiary level as the economy declined). It is proposed here that government needs to be proactive in this regard and begin to trace all the students who were on this scheme who never paid back their loans to the state; in fact very few have done so, and there was no system to ensure repayment; and while students signed bonds to work for the government for a number of years after graduation, many in fact began joining the increasing army of the unemployed.

The one-party state in its benevolence forgot to plan for the future, thus the current funding crisis in higher education. Now the government could create a kind of Solidarity Fund where all those who were educated by the government can begin to voluntarily pay back funds to the state, and this money could then be used to bolster the sector, while efforts are made to recover money owed by graduates – though repayment should merely be a civic responsibility on the part of the graduates. Even foreigners residing in the country benefited from free and universal education from primary school to university; but unfortunately there is nothing that can be done about this, unless some of these individuals pay money into the Solidarity Fund for moral reasons, which is most unlikely.

After 1991, the Zambian government attempted to restructure the education sector through various measures such as decentralising administration and encouraging participation of communities and the private sector in the provision of education services. In addition, rural and urban schools as well as tertiary institutions were rehabilitated (Government of the Republic of Zambia, 1994). However, the performance of the sector was hampered by low morale among the teachers due to unfavourable conditions of service, which led to continued migration of teachers to neighbouring countries. There were cost recovery and cost sharing schemes established in all learning institutions, encompassing user charges levied by Parents Teachers Associations, boarding fees at secondary level and student loans at university. Primary school enrolment continued to increase in the same period, in spite of government not building new structures. It rose from 1,452,264 in 1989 to 1,574,129 in 1992 (Government of the Republic of Zambia, 1994). The Transitional National Development Plan (2002) reported that enrolment had increased from 2 per cent in 1990 to 24 per cent in the year 2000. But in 1998 only 8.4 per cent of children going into Grade 1 could access Early Childhood Care, Education, and Development (ECCED) services. Rural areas had received little attention, with only 2.7 per cent of children having ECCED experience, compared with 23.6 per cent in urban areas.

Despite this gloomy picture, there are glimmers of hope. The government's ongoing Education Sector Public Expenditure Review programme seems to be bearing fruit. It is the first of a series of programmes intended to assist the government to consider issues of intra-sectoral allocations and the share of the budget that would need to be allocated to the sector. According to a World Bank Report of 2006 entitled Zambia

Education Sector Public Expenditure Review, the country has recorded rapid progress towards achieving universal primary education before the target date of 2015 set by the United Nations. The report also shows that enrolment in basic education has grown rapidly in recent years, almost reaching universal benchmarks; 96 per cent of Zambian children were enrolled, and for those aged between nine to twelve years, it was almost universal (Zambia Daily Mail, 2006). The completion rate for Grade 7 increased from 64 per cent in 2001 to 72 per cent in 2004.

However, the learning achievement at the basic school level has remained low. Several hurdles are also identified in the report, such as too few trained teachers and instruction materials, less government spending on the sector (only 3.2 per cent of the GDP), a high pupil-teacher ratio of 56:1 in public schools, double-shifting of teachers and short pupil instruction hours in Grades 1 to 4, and lack of housing for teachers, especially in the rural areas (Zambia Daily Mail, 2006). Higher education has also its own set of challenges; the institutions are in arrears to various creditors and are behind in financial reporting and audit requirements set by law (even though the government provides grants to two of the country's public universities), there are imbalances between academic and non-academic staff and within academic disciplines, and the labour market experience of graduates is generally unfavourable (Zambia Daily Mail, 2006). Nevertheless, strides were made in the setting up of an open university in 2002. The Zambia Open University is an appropriate gap-filler and outlet for many citizens unable to undertake full-time studies for a number of reasons. The offering of long distance education in the country is indeed a laudable initiative which must be consolidated and expanded.

The education sector has also attracted significant support from Co-operating Partners through the sector-wide approach, benefiting in particular basic education at district levels. Major programmes implemented in the sector were the expansion of infrastructure, curriculum development, provision of education materials, provision of bursaries to vulnerable children and orphans, equity and gender, and HIV/AIDS related interventions. These initiatives led to improvements in terms of access to education at all levels. For example, there was a positive result in terms of basic enrolment, 75.5 per cent for girls and 77.2 per cent for boys. In 2003, completion rates increased to 66.7 per cent for girls and 80.3 per cent for boys, from 63 per cent and 77 per cent respectively in 2002 (Government of the Republic of Zambia, 2004:5). Education is an important pillar of human development and therefore needs to be harnessed, by government and organs of civil society, through various targeted interventions if the sector is to enjoy the prestige it once commanded in the 'glory' days.

The government made an important decision in 2002 to remove user fees in primary schools throughout the country. Many people, parents, educationists and development advocates, hailed the move as a step in the right direction. Even though education was made free from Grades 1 to 7, many children drop out of school because they cannot afford to buy requirements such as books. The situation is even worse in rural areas where schools are very few. According to a Jesuit Centre for Theological Reflection (JCTR) report, although the abolition of school fees increased the net attendance rate at primary levels from 71 per cent in 2000 to 85 per cent in 2004, approximately 15 per cent of Zambian children, almost 300,000 girls and boys between the ages of seven and thirteen are simply out of the educational system, missing training in the basic literacy, numeracy and reasoning that are essential for their own and the nation's full human development (The Post, 2006).

However, the government has pledged to pay particular attention to the provision of quality education in the next five years by addressing the shortage of teachers through the recruitment of 8,000 at the end of 2006 and 6,500 in 2007, as well as an additional 5,000 in 2008. These measures will lead to the elimination of double shifts and improvement of teacher-pupil ratios at basic and high school levels. The government also envisages that quality education will be addressed through the revision of the existing teacher training curriculum and through increased procurement and equitable distribution of learning materials (Mwanawasa, 2006).

Housing

There is a critical shortage of housing in Zambia and little has been done in this sector since independence. This problem has been further compounded by the high rural-urban migration after 1964. Most of the residential areas such as the suburbs and the older townships were left by the colonial government, while new housing schemes were also constructed in the First and Second Republics. Shelter is an important basic need and when people are without this necessity, they are impeded from functioning properly in society. The housing problem is a relic of the colonial era and can be attributed to the non-committal attitude of the colonial authorities to building houses for Africans. The African in towns in those days was referred to as a temporal sojourner as his home was deemed to be in the village where he would return. Therefore, makeshift structures were erected for Africans by the colonial authorities. After independence, there was a huge influx of people from the hinterland to the cities, which ultimately resulted in the mushrooming of squatter settlements in all urban centres. The UNIP government promoted home-ownership, on the assumption that long-term solutions to the need for shelter were dependent on resources available both to the nation and to individuals within the context of self-reliance (National Housing Authority cited in Siamwiza et al., 1993). In spite of support for private ownership, however, the housing sector did not perform satisfactorily two decades after independence. Targets were not met in terms of units constructed and the change from 'tied' housing to owner-occupied accommodation. The provision of housing remains fragmented, discontinuous, and, at times, contradictory. Several administrative divisions of the government are responsible for housing, together with the National Housing Authority established by an Act of Parliament to promote home ownership through the provision of affordable shelter and the provision of technical assistance to local authorities (Government of the Republic of Zambia, in Siamwiza et al., 1993).

The rise in the urban population since independence, partly due to the rural-urban migration and also to the natural population increase in the country, has led to the burgeoning of squatter settlements. This situation has meant that urban housing development as well as town planning is haphazard and remains inconsistent, owing to the sprouting of many of these habitats in undesignated zones. Meanwhile, the illegal allocation of plots by some local authority officials has for decades only exacerbated this chaotic situation. As they are unregulated, these settlements also face water supply and sanitation challenges. Many remain health risks and prone to annual outbreaks of cholera due to unsanitary conditions. Certain steps which were taken in the Kaunda era, continued in the Third Republic to improve these areas. The squatter upgrading programme is one initiative that was spearheaded by the government with the help of the donor community. Efforts were made to construct better roads and flush toilets, sink boreholes and install piped water, and connect households to electricity in these settlements. There was also the Site-and-Service Scheme initiative that involved the allocation of plots of land and loans by the government to Zambians from the low-income brackets, so that they could build their own houses. The loans were mainly in the form of building materials such as bricks, sand and cement. Local authorities were also supposed to facilitate the setting-up of vital infrastructure such as roads, electricity and piped water in various towns and cities.

Most housing was provided by the government, parastatal organisations and local authorities. Those who were not accommodated by their employers could claim a housing allowance, whereby they could then rent accommodation privately. This arrangement was drastically changed in the Third Republic. During Frederick Chiluba's rule, all houses were sold to 'sitting tenants' under the Presidential Housing Initiative (PHI) scheme. This meant that most public servants and workers in parastatals bought these houses at concessionary rates. The government of the day argued that this was one way it was filling the housing gap. However, this process was fraught with irregularities and was seen by many Zambians as a political ploy to buy Chiluba political time. It was neither sustainable nor practicable, because when the existing housing stock was depleted there were no houses to meet new demands.

Until 1996, the country had no housing policy that could guide the sector. The National Housing Policy was adopted in the same year with the overall aim of providing adequate and affordable housing to all income groups in the country. However, this policy has not been fully implemented because of the absence of an implementation plan. Therefore, it is not surprising that housing still remains inadequate in the country. For instance, in 1991, the total national housing stock was estimated at 1,501,898 dwelling units; this increased to 2,311,988 in 2001; 80 per cent of the houses are informal and poorly serviced or not serviced at all. The main problem in the housing sector is lack of adequate finance. Prior to 1996, investment in housing was less than 3 per cent of GDP (Government of the Republic of Zambia, 2006). Today, the government has recognised the need to expand and enhance this critical area and envisages that it will strive to create a conducive, private sector environment, to allow for the construction of decent houses for Zambians. For public service workers, there is already in place a comprehensive housing loan scheme.

The government introduced the national housing bonds programme which is aimed at raising affordable long-term finance from the capital market rather than from government resources. It has also proposed the preparation of integrated development plans in order to guide construction in the country's towns and cities. In addition, the programme to upgrade urban settlements will continue, as well as the development of a peri-urban strategy to upgrade squatter settlements in a systematic rather than random manner (Mwanawasa, 2006).

Health

The health sector has suffered many years of neglect and decay after initial successes in the 1960s and late 1970s. Because of outright disregard by the UNIP government during its last years in power, the health sector almost completely collapsed. There was a critical shortage of essential medicines and equipment in most hospitals and clinics around the country, while the number of doctors and nurses was not enough to meet the needs of a growing population. After 1991, the government endeavoured to restructure the health system through the reconstruction of dilapidated physical infrastructure, increasing the supply of drugs and reorganising the health sector's management boards and decentralising the functions to the district level. Cost recovery schemes or user fees were introduced to supplement government resources and the private sector was encouraged to play a role in this area. Also, medical fees in the form of private insurance, user charges and community-based insurance schemes for rural areas were introduced (Government of the Republic of Zambia, 1994). The human resources situation continued to deteriorate in the same period, owing to unfavourable working conditions. For instance, 35 doctors resigned from government in 1993, with the majority migrating to neighbouring countries where conditions of service were more favourable (Government of the Republic of Zambia, 1994).

Owing to the various problems faced by the health sector, the trend these days is for politicians and the wealthy to seek medical attention in either European or South African hospitals. Even the former president Frederick Chiluba was attended by South African doctors after suffering a heart condition, having done little to stem the decay in the health sector and pay health professionals competitive salaries while he was president of Zambia. Chiluba was airlifted to South Africa at the expense of the same taxpayers who suffered under the former president's economic austerity measures as well as his plunder of national assets. However, certain quarters (including the first president, Kenneth Kaunda) also criticised president Mwanawasa when he was rushed to a London hospital in 2005 after suffering a mild stroke for medical treatment, saying he should have gone to the University Teaching Hospital (UTH) in Lusaka; Kaunda said he used to have his medical reviews at the UTH when he was president, though he forgot to mention that the rot in the health sector had set in when he was president.

One disease that increases Zambia's mortality rates is malaria, which also incapacitates Zambians and lowers their productivity in contributing to the national economy. It is the country's leading cause of death, even though it is both preventable and curable. There are about three million cases of malaria reported on an annual basis in Zambia. According to the National Malaria Control Centre, estimates are that malaria was responsible for nearly 4.3 million clinical cases and an estimated 50,000 deaths per year in Zambia (The Post, 2006). The Zambian government has sought to respond by initiatives such as the Indoor Residual House Spraying (IRHS) campaign, flagged by the government through the Ministry of Health, and efforts are made to entrench an integrated approach to the prevention of malaria. Also, there is 'child health week' from 4 to 8 December each year, when children are immunised, de-wormed, given vitamin supplements, and more importantly, screened for malaria. Treatment is undertaken for those who are sick, and mosquito nets for malaria prevention are dispensed. In addition, the days from 17 to 23 November have been declared SADC Malaria Week, marked by Zambia with other member states. Belinda Gates (the wife of the Microsoft billionaire Bill Gates) has visited Zambia to add impetus to the anti-malaria campaign by donating mosquito nets to Zambians, among other things, especially in the rural areas.

IRHS uses Dichloro-Diphenyl-Trichloroethane (DDT), even though DDT has serious ramifications for the environment. The Minister of Health, in a public statement to the nation, argued DDT's case in this way: 'DDT has been associated with a lot of concern especially on its impact on human health and the environment. The Ministry of Health has taken these concerns seriously and measures have been put in place to ensure that DDT does not leak into the environment and is used judiciously.' These assertions did not convince many people given the fact that DDT has been banned in many parts of the world and only dumped in LDCs.

Despite a poor performance in the past, the government has also made significant strides in the fight against HIV/AIDS. In 2006, about 70,000 HIV patients had their lives saved with free Antiretroviral Therapy (ART) services. The number of centres providing ART services increased from two in 2003 to over 85 throughout the country. The Home Based Care (HBC) approach was also scaled up to all the 72 districts in the country. The government also envisages the strengthening of Prevention-of-Mother-to-Child-Transmission (PMTCT) activities through integration with reproductive and child services as well as routine testing in antenatal clinics. Further, it envisages the development and implementation of HIV/AIDS workplace policies at the district and provincial level. But there have still been problems over budgetary allocations towards the dispensing of coartem and Anti-retroviral Drugs (ARVs) (The Post, 2006).

Major interventions in this arena have also included HIV/AIDS prevention campaigns, Voluntary Counselling and Testing (VCT), Prevention-of-Mother-to-Child Transmission (PMCT), Anti-Retroviral Therapy (ART), home-based care, care for Orphans and Vulnerable Children (OVCs) and work place programmes. Most of these initiatives were implemented using a multi-sectoral approach. As a result of the continuous efforts, HIV/AIDS prevalence rates fell from 20 per cent in 2001 to 16 per cent in 2003. There is evidence that young people have started delaying sexual activity; at least the age for starting it rose for males, from 16 years in 1998 to 17 in 2003, while it still remained stagnant for females at 17 years. Condom use increased among males from 28 per cent in 1998 to 43 per cent in 2003, and from 24 per cent to 34 per cent among females (Government of the Republic of Zambia, 2004:5). In regard to other diseases, Zambia was declared a polio-free state in 2005 and immunisation coverage for one-year olds improved from 75 per cent in 2003 to 82 per cent in 2005.

Mental health

Mental health deserves some attention in this section as it is mostly overlooked when Zambia's human development trends are duly examined. Mental health services date back to the colonial era when they were introduced in 1962. By 1978 (in line with a World Health Assembly resolution of the previous year) the Ministry of Health established a multi-sectoral National Mental Health Co-ordinating Group, which outlined priorities for mental health services in Zambia. Mental health services in Zambia are mainly hospital based (Directorate of Public Health and Research, 2002:8). Mental health is perceived as the ability to cope with demands of living in Zambia. It also pertains to sound or stable minds which mean that the individual is seen as living in harmony with his or her surroundings, and doing things that society expects from its general membership. Mental illness, on the other hand is when an individual is seen as a danger to self and society in such a way that he/she disturbs the peace of the family and community (Directorate of Public Health and Research, 2002).

It has been established that there are certain approved ways of life among the people of Zambia that contribute towards positive mental wellbeing, for example, initiation ceremonies that equip young people with knowledge and skills in order to cope with the challenges of adulthood. However, the aged are quite vulnerable to mental health problems. It is encouraging to note that even if they have mental illness or dementia, they are usually accepted in the community. The family takes on most of the social burden of looking after their aged as this is regarded as a noble act and a responsibility of every sibling or member of the family (Directorate of Public Health and Research, 2002:8).

Depression or anxiety can have significant negative effects on people's mental health. Zambians, owing to the bad economic situation that has existed in the country for decades, have had to endure all forms of humiliation and incapacity due to lack of income. For lack of financial resources, people live sub-standard lifestyles. In some situations, such as loss of employment (through retrenchments, etc.), many Zambians' living conditions were drastically changed for the worse, almost overnight. An example was the liquidation of Zambia Airways, the monopoly air carrier, in the Chiluba era. Pilots, flight engineers, air hostesses and stewards, and other employees of the airline woke up one morning to a rude shock: they had lost their jobs. These individuals were not only jobless, but had few outlets for their skills and experience, except for a few who were fortunate to get jobs outside the country. It was said that many died from depression; some resorted to heavy drinking in order to numb their depression. People's mental health is severely compromised under such stressful and trying conditions.

Water and sanitation

Access to clean running water is still a major challenge to many Zambian communities, several decades after independence. This situation is even more acute in the rural areas which have remained almost in the same state as in the colonial days. Despite early successes in the 1960s and 1970s, development in this area stalled and access to water, even in the urban areas, became erratic. Water and sanitation still remain critically below par in the country. For instance, public toilets are virtually non-existent in many parts of the country and where these facilities are available they are in a deplorable and unhygienic state. It always seems as if this issue is treated as an afterthought whenever public spaces are created such as bars, restaurants, bus stops, airports, schools, train stations etc. Surprisingly, this is not only a Zambian problem but is quite manifest all over Africa. This nonchalant approach to public sanitation cannot continue as it has done all these years; it affects personal hygiene and cleanliness. Public campaigns need to be mounted by government and civil society in schools, family settings, and traditional leadership structures, so that hygiene and cleanliness are maintained in the country. This issue also calls for self-discipline. It is unacceptable that water and sanitation become donor-driven initiatives. Some of these anomalies simply rest on certain officials' incompetence. For example, it is simply ludicrous that in a town such as Kafue, where there is a huge river merely a stone's throw away, people experience an erratic supply of water. Honestly, how can this be?

The primary legislation prescribing the development and management of water resources in Zambia is the Water Act, Cap 198, originally enacted in 1948. Other related statutes are the Environmental Protection and Pollution Control Act, Cap 204, which is primarily concerned with control of water pollution, and the Zambezi River Authority Act (1996) (Government of the Republic of Zambia, 2003). With respect to water supply and sanitation, the Water Supply and Sanitation Act, No. 27 of 1997 anchors the sector's legal framework. According to the Act local authorities, under the Ministry of Local Government and Housing (MLGH), acting by themselves or through commercial utilities or the private sector, are responsible for the provision of water and sanitation services to all areas in the jurisdiction of local authority (Government of the Republic of Zambia, 2003). But legislation alone, whether outdated or not, will not solve the problems of critical water shortages in Zambia. There is need for planning and judicious formulation and implementation of policies that deal innovatively with the problems of clean water provision.

The problem lies in the failure to construct water infrastructure, through digging of new boreholes, erection of water tanks, piping of water, etc. The same infrastructure that catered to a population of about 3.5 million in 1964 is now supposed to supply water to a population of about 11 million. Most of the water infrastructure is obsolete. There has not been any major overhaul of the water works systems in years, so that supply in most towns has been extremely unreliable, with disruption taking place after certain hours. Although Zambia is endowed with numerous natural water systems that would be a source of envy to her neighbours south of the Zambezi, access to clean water remains a distant prospect in the country. Things of this nature should surely not even be debated in this day and age. If the Romans were already using flush toilets, and tapping water via sophisticated systems of distribution, honestly is there even a need to flounder over this issue?

Rural development

Despite increased rural-urban migration flows[1] before and after independence, Zambia has continued to remain extremely rural, with most of its population still located in this sector. The most urbanised provinces in Zambia are the Copperbelt and Lusaka. The rural areas were and still remain highly impoverished with virtually no existing social services in certain parts. Most rural people earn a living as subsistence farmers or simply live a simple type of existence. Many remain marginalised; for example, in 2000 more than 40 per cent of rural youths were classified as excluded from the world of information and unable to assimilate strategies to move themselves out of poverty (United Nations Development Programme, 2003). Poverty is simply more widespread in rural settings than in urban areas. For instance, after 2000, the total percentage contribution by province show that the population in rural areas accounted for 72 per cent of the overall poverty. There are also other challenges that erode the capacities of rural people; regarding rural and micro financing, for example, there has been a gap in the provision of financial services in these areas, following the collapse of most of the subsidised and public funded rural financial institutions in the mid-1990s.

This problem has been further aggravated by the closure of many bank branches in peri-urban and rural areas, due to stagnation in the rural economy and poor infrastructure. The lack of financial services in the rural areas has remained one of the constraints to rural development (Government of the Republic of Zambia, 2004:43). The pervasive rural-urban divide that motivated interventionist policies in the 1970s still looms large. Investment policies and practices have favoured urban areas, with most rural facilities having deteriorated beyond repair. The quality of socio-economic infrastructure in rural Zambia is not conducive for human development and the fall in the livelihood security in rural areas is attributed to this. The rapid rise in urbanisation is also ascribed to this rural-urban divide (United Nations Development Programme, 2003).

Zambia's first government was really concerned with the state of the rural areas at independence. In spite of being confronted with a host of development challenges, the government of the day sought ways and means to raise the quality of life of rural people. This vision was crystallised into policy when the First National Development Plan (FNDP) was finally put into operation in 1966. The precursors of the FNDP, the Emergency Development Plan (EDP) and the Transitional Development Plan (TDP) just after independence, served as initial pivots for policy formulation and implementation and laid the foundation for future policy interventions in Zambia. The FNDP had eight objectives relating to development. Out of the eight, two objectives, numbers one and five, directly addressed the situation of rural areas – to diversify the economy so that the copper industry was not the only main employer in the economy, so that a greater proportion of domestic demand satisfied local production from a large industrial base; and to minimise the inherited economic imbalance between the urban and rural sectors, with a view to raising the capacity of the latter for transforming resources into social and economic growth (Government of the Republic of Zambia, 1966).

One of the major objectives of all the development plans in the First and Second Republics was to reduce the urban-rural disparities in regard to quality of life. The major strategy for doing this, since independence, has been to improve social services through increased public investment, and to increase employment opportunities by encouraging agricultural production and locating industrial projects in the rural areas (Ndulo, 1985). The intentions towards rural development were usually noble but the realities of lack of funds and the necessary expertise to execute such projects bogged down their implementation. In most cases, implementation was also hampered by lack of political will. This problem has haunted Zambia since the colonial period and continues unabated to this day. The magnitude of socio-economic development envisaged by the government was also bedevilled by high expectations following independence among the rural population, who felt that they were entitled to the promised 'fruits of independence' and an immediate change in their socio-economic situation. Thus, the priority given to rural development by the new government was also a political necessity (Chikulo, 1985). Before proceeding further, an elucidation of rural development is required.

What is rural development?

The idea of rural development has undergone profound transformation in the past decades. It evolved from signifying just modernisation and capitalisation of the countryside in the 1960s to a more balanced approach nowadays, in which it is seen as a multi-sector strategy for simultaneously addressing questions of economic growth, poverty alleviation and livelihood support (Hall and Midgley, 2004). What is commonly referred to as 'rural development' should be defined less in terms of certain 'inputs' (interventions) or 'outputs' (results), as it so often is defined in current exercises of planning and evaluation, than as a particular arena of interaction or struggle. It is a struggle, first of all, between rural producers on the one hand and representatives of government or parastatal agencies on the other (Crehan and von Oppen, 1994). After the consequences of structural adjustment and the rise of the Washington Consensus on Agriculture (WCA) in the 1980s and 1990s, a new paradigm for rural development (which stressed a flexible, broad-based approach) came to the fore. From a social policy perspective, the new approach is epitomised in the adoption of the Sustainable Livelihoods Framework (SLF) as a comprehensive, analytical device that prioritises the interests of those rural groups traditionally neglected by mainstream modernisation policies (Hall and Midgley, 2004).

Which way forward?

The present government seems quite serious about rural development and it is only hoped that this position will be emboldened via clear policies and adequate resources. President Mwanawasa was quoted in the local press as wanting to take development to the vulnerable people in the rural areas that gave him a massive vote in the last presidential and parliamentary elections: 'Every time I go around the country, I see a lot of poverty and despair on the faces of the people despite the economy recording growth in the last five years' (Zambia Daily Mail, 2006). Meanwhile, the government envisages that it will consolidate the gains it has made in agriculture by expanding interventions in marketing, extension services, animal disease control and livestock development, and attend to infrastructure, especially feeder roads and irrigation facilities, so as to increase productivity. The agricultural strategy in this area will involve the development of markets, provision of infrastructure, and agricultural and financial services. In this regard small-scale farmers will continue receiving support under the fertiliser support programme. For instance, in the 2006/7 season, beneficiary farmers were only required to contribute 40 per cent of the cost of inputs while the government covered the remaining 60 per cent (Mwanawasa, 2006).

There have been some encouraging signs in this area which need bolstering and sustaining. For example, community-based infrastructure has improved through the Rural Investment Fund (RIF), and there has been increased stakeholder participation through institutionalised consultative bodies such as the District Agricultural Committees (DACs) and the Agricultural Consultative Forum (ACF) (United Nations Development Programme, 2003). There is also a rural allowance given to professionals working in these parts, such as doctors; something that has never happened since independence though it had been proposed before by various progressive actors. The government also hopes to enable the private sector to undertake detailed mineral exploration work and the setting up of more mines in the rural areas, which might create employment and turn some rural areas into urban communities with modern social and economic facilities. The rural electrification programme has been implemented by the government and has paid dividends. In 2006 alone, 43 projects drawn from across the country were implemented at a cost of K48 billion (Mwanawasa, 2006). It is argued in this text that rural development is intertwined with the wider agendas of civil liberties and equal opportunities; realisation of the latter is a critical factor in the implementation of rural development strategies.

Civil liberties and equal opportunities

Human rights

Concerns relating to human rights became global after the Second World War when the United Nations Organisation (UNO) endorsed the Universal Declaration of Human Rights of 10 December 1948. This was the first time in human history that countries consciously sought to at least begin to enforce such rights, following the Second World War when Nazi Germany, Fascist Italy and Japan had been responsible for gross human rights violations (Noyoo, 2004).

In Zambia, the Human Rights Commission acts as a watchdog seeing that people's rights are not trampled over. Despite its existence, there are numerous human rights violations in the country. They include violence against children, child abuse, gender-based violence and police brutality. Lately, the police had to be called to order when certain officers were involved in gunning down citizens in unexplained circumstances. The Human Rights Commission condemned such acts by the law enforcement officers. Political intimidation during elections from different parties also constitutes a violation of rights. This area still needs more intervention from both state and non-state actors.

Social and economic justice

Apart from the above, social and economic inequities are promoted in several sectors of the society when citizens are denied their basic needs through exclusionary mechanisms. For instance, in the area of labour, Zambians have been denied social and economic justice by unscrupulous foreign investors, who pay workers slave wages and subject them to inhuman conditions of work. For example, there is the phenomenon of casualisation of labour. Even the Zambian government has taken note of this with grave concern. The Minister of Labour was quoted as saying that most investors were deliberately flouting labour laws to disadvantage Zambians. He noted that the 'mushrooming' of short-term contracts, inadequate in terms of social security coverage and rights of employees to a safe and healthy working environment, have contributed to high turnover of employees continuously seeking 'greener pastures', which perpetuates casualisation (The Post, 2006). The gravity of this situation was discerned in 2005 when fifty workers were blown to pieces in a foreign-owned dynamite factory. It was discovered upon inquiry that many of the workers were locked up by the employers and treated inhumanely. They were also not entitled to protective clothing, and safety standards were brazenly disregarded by the employers. This is what is meant by denying people's social and economic justice, and more important, their basic human rights.

One social injustice on an economic level is income inequality. Zambia is a highly unequal society with the richest 10 per cent of the population, having 41 per cent of national income (United Nations Development Programme, in Gaynor, 2005). Social injustices that have economic connotations lie in poor people's inability to access both educational and health services. Social injustices are also exacerbated by unequal allocations of resources in these areas (Gyanor, 2005).

Gender parity

Gender parity refers to relations between women and other groups in society firmly based on equality, reciprocity, mutual respect, equity and dignity. Gender equality also rests on an understanding that women should not be barred from participating fully in the social, economic and political domains of their society. This outlook then extends to the girl-child who needs to be accorded an equal status with male children in Zambia. A child's gender should not be an impediment to the attainment of livelihood. Gender parity is closely linked to human development in that oppressive conditions affecting women should not be treated in isolation, but must be seen in the broader context of national development. Gender oppression ultimately retards a country's progress and hinders families, groups, and communities from functioning optimally in society.

Zambia is signatory to various international protocols on gender development, especially of the United Nations, but usually falls short on the implementation side. The government acknowledges that gender issues are a critical component of Zambia's overall development as the Transitional National Development Plan of 2002 rightly admits:

> Gender plays a significant role in the socio-economic development and planning for development of any particular nation. Economic development and gender are interrelated through the contributions of both men and women. Gender plays a very important role in developing a sustainable strategy for economic development, employment creation and poverty reduction (Government of the Republic of Zambia, 2002:199).

Earlier, the government promulgated the National Gender Policy in 2000. In the introductory part of the policy, it conceded that there had not been an explicit gender policy since Zambia's independence in 1964. However, the document highlights efforts made to increase the role of women in socio-economic development in the Fourth National Development Plan of 1989-93, which included a chapter on women (Government of the Republic of Zambia, 2000). This policy also recognises that gender is a cross-cutting issue and that there is need to mainstream gender in government programmes. The following critical areas are addressed in the policy:

(a) the power relations between women and men in the domestic, community, and public domains which are impediments to the advancement of women;

(b) the feminisation of poverty as reflected in women's limited access to and control over productive resources, social services, remunerative employment opportunities and minimal participation in political and managerial decision-making processes;

(c) cultural and traditional practices that systematically subject females to male subordination;

(d) limited access by women and girls to and use of basic health services, inadequate reproductive health facilities, maternal and child health care;

(e) lack of access by women and girls to adequate food, safe water and sanitation;

(f) lack of access by women to credit, improved technology, and land and extension services which constrain agricultural productivity;

(g) disparities in access to and limited opportunities for education, science and technology, skills development and training;

(h) lack of appreciation by society that there is structural linkage between gender and the environment;

(i) the dichotomy between domestic and industrial energy requirements, which has left issues of domestic energy requirements largely in the hands of women;

(j) statutory and customary laws and practices which hamper women's and men's full participation in national development; and

(k) prevalence of gender violence (Government of the Republic of Zambia, 2000:2-3).

The government also formulated a Strategic Plan of Action for the National Gender Policy (2004-2008) containing policy measures and interventions, activities, expected results and actors for specific sectors to facilitate the effective implementation of the gender policy through comprehensive gender planning/programming, advocacy, monitoring and evaluation (Government of the Republic of Zambia, 2002). On paper, Zambia's gender policy is quite impressive indeed, but there remains a huge chasm between what is purported in the policy and what is actually happening in society. If we take the last part of (b) and closely examine (k), above, for consideration, it is apparent that women in Zambia still face major hurdles in being elevated to political and managerial decision-making processes and are subjected to arbitrary gender-based violence. Despite having eminent women who are leaders in various fields, Zambia has failed to meet the SADC target of 30 per cent of female appointees in decision-making positions. For example, since independence, Zambia has never had a female Vice-President and has only managed to have a woman as first Deputy Speaker of the National Assembly. Despite this, the Zambian government has been following a focused appointment policy that has resulted in an increase in percentages of women in decision-making positions from 10 per cent in 1997 to 18 per cent by June 2004 (Government of the Republic of Zambia, 2004).

Women have always contributed positively to the development of the country. For instance, they have significantly played a role in agricultural production. In the 1992/93 season they provided about 50 to 80 per cent of labour in the production of food and cash crops. The majority of women are in the category of small-scale farmers identified with production (Government of the Republic of Zambia, 1993). In 2006 the Zambian government created the position of minister of Gender in Development, but it was widely condemned by gender activists and certain quarters of civil society as simply 'opportunistic', etc.; they suggested this would undermine their cause and deflect interventions away from gender, and said the best option was actually the mainstreaming of gender perspectives into line government ministries. The government argued otherwise and observed that the Gender Ministry was going to be in the forefront of conceptualising and advocating for gender programmes in all government ministries. It still remains to be seen whether the new portfolio will be a toothless organ or a viable one.

Vulnerabilities and populations at risk

People with disabilities

According to the Zambia Persons with Disabilities Act Number 33 of 1996, disability is defined as any restriction resulting from an impairment or inability to perform any activity in the manner or within the range considered normal for a human being. It is generally accepted that disability is both a cause and a consequence of poverty. The Disability Act also ushered in the Zambia Agency for Persons with Disabilities (ZAPD) (Government of the Republic of Zambia, 2006). The mandate of the ZAPD revolves around the following activities:

(a) to plan, promote and administer services for all categories of Agency persons with disabilities;

(b) to keep statistical records relating to incidences and causes of disabilities, which may be used for the planning, promotion, administration and evaluation of services for persons with disabilities;

(c) to keep a register of persons with disabilities;

(d) to provide rehabilitation, training, and welfare services to persons with disabilities;

(e) to promote research into general rehabilitation programmes for persons with disabilities;

(f) to promote public awareness relating to the prevention of disabilities and the care of persons with disabilities;

(g) to co-operate with ministries and other organisations in the provision of preventive, educational, training, employment and rehabilitation and other welfare services for persons with disabilities;

(h) to co-ordinate rehabilitation and welfare services provided to persons with disabilities by ministries, and voluntary associations;

(i) to monitor and supervise the provision of services to persons with disabilities;

(j) to promote, directly and indirectly, the development of human resources in the prevention of disabilities and in the provision of rehabilitation, education, training and the general welfare of persons with disabilities;

(k) to advise the Minister on matters relating to social and economic development and the general wellbeing of persons with disabilities; and

(l) to do all such things as are incidental to or conducive to the attainment of the functions of the Agency (Government of the Republic of Zambia, 1996:5-6).

There are several social barriers that people with disabilities face in Zambia in achieving their potential. They include cultural taboos, myths, traditions, societal discrimination and biases (*Times of Zambia*, 2006), and also lack of income brought on by unemployment, lack of skills, and minimal or no economic opportunities that are available for them. The question of skills is directly related to the ability or inability of people with disabilities to access education services. For example, despite the country instituting a free education policy, indications are that it seems to have favoured able-bodied children. The education of people with disabilities in Zambia has been undermined by inadequacies ranging from inaccessible buildings to lack of learning materials and specialised teachers to handle different kinds of disability; there are also too few colleges to train specialised teachers for the disabled in Zambia, so that numbers of disabled children getting enrolled in school are low (*Times of Zambia*, 2006).

In a recent study focusing on the living conditions of people with activity limitations, by the Zambia Federation of the Disabled (ZAFOD), it was discovered that more than 23 per cent of children with disabilities of five years old and above have no chance to attend school (*Times of Zambia*, 2006). In addition, households with disabled members who are also suffering from the harsh economic situation Zambia is currently experiencing are facing huge barriers in accessing education. Unfortunately, negative stimuli from society have also been translated into a phenomenon referred to as 'self discriminating tendencies' by families looking after children with disabilities, who feel that educating them will expose them to ridicule (*Times of Zambia*, 2006).

The visually impaired

There are approximately 100,000 blind people in Zambia, according to the 2000 Census of Population and Housing Report. The majority of these people are not in formal or informal employment and are living in abject poverty. A good number of the blind are children, 10 per cent of whom attend some type of formal or informal education (Zambia Daily Mail, 2006).

The aged

Government policy on the situation of the aged in Zambia centres on promoting the role of the family in the care of its older members and the protection of their rights. Programmes created for the protection of older people also take into account the country's social, economic, cultural and historical factors. To this end, the government has been reviewing its national population policy to incorporate issues of ageing. The social welfare policy also envisages a refocus in approach so as to spell out the special needs of older persons. The country is also implementing safety-nets to address the basic needs of vulnerable aged persons. In spite of these initiatives, older persons in Zambia experience huge challenges ranging from lack of income, neglect and sickness to abuse. Older people in

Zambia are also exposed to high levels of stress due to a number of factors. For instance, Zambia's sharp economic decline has seriously eroded the country's traditional support system for the elderly (Muzyamba, 2002).

The changing cultural values, amplified by the negative effects of globalisation, are also undermining traditional values of respect and support for the aged. As a consequence, some of the aged are left to fend for themselves, in both urban and rural areas. The HIV/AIDS pandemic has again impacted negatively on support for the elderly. The high death rate among the productive age group of 15-49 years has resulted in old people, particularly elderly women, being heads of households and carers. In addition, they have taken up responsibilities for the upkeep of orphans. The effects of this development on the aged and the orphans are far-reaching (Muzyamba, 2002). The aged continue to remain at risk in Zambia and the model of the traditional family is not so feasible nowadays, especially when these new factors are duly considered. The government has to come up with creative strategies of protecting this age group, for example, a pension system. Furthermore, homes for the aged should not be regarded as an anathema to the Zambian way of life, because society is dynamic and constantly changing; family patterns also change as society evolves.

The youth

The youth are a critical component of Zambia's human development and need to be nurtured as well as harnessed because they are an important generation that will lead the country into the future. In many countries, this category of people is usually in the majority. In Zambia, the young constitute 68 per cent of the population. Globally, 1.5 billion people are between the ages of 12 and 24 with 1.3 billion of them living in developing countries (World Bank, 2007). A youth in Zambia is defined as a male or female person aged between 15 and 25 years of age. This definition is a radical departure from the previous one that was adopted by the UNIP government; a youth in those days was any person between the ages of 15 and 35. Such a conception had negative consequences as regards the mindsets of certain Zambians who chose to remain dependent on societal systems with the view that they were still youths, even though they were not really so.

It is crucial that institutional mechanisms and policies are tilted in the favour of youth development if this population group is to be allowed to flourish. At present, a significant number of the group are school dropouts at the levels of Grades 7, 9 and 12 (and, to a certain extent, college level) (Department of Youth Development, 1994). In Zambia, youth development (as a comprehensive process through which the youth will grow up to full adulthood in consonance with contemporary social, economic and political ideals and aspirations of the nation) has been hampered by a number of problems (Department of Youth Development, 1994); critical among them are:

(a) The youth lack guidance necessary for their lives especially given their tender age.

(b) Owing to lack of proper guidance and counselling, some of the youth are engaged in drug abuse, alcohol, crime, prostitution and teenage pregnancies.

(c) In most cases, the youth indulge in these illegal practices because of lack of recreational facilities and the disintegration of the family as a nucleus of socio-economic development.

(d) Most of the youth lack life skills; training and experience to enable them obtain formal employment and/or finance to engage in self-employment activities.

(e) It is felt that the youth have been socially, economically, and even politically alienated from national development (Department of Youth Development, 1994:3).

In addition, the current educational system does not guarantee this group's continued education as its provision at every stage gets significantly narrower, which means 'kicking out' armies of school-leavers who cannot get school places (Department of Youth Development, 1994). The following building-blocks have therefore been put forward as essential for global youth development, which Zambia can also link to local initiatives:

1. *Opportunities* - Broaden the opportunities for developing human capital by expanding access to and improving the quality of education and health services; and by giving young people a voice to

articulate the kind of assistance they want and a chance to participate in delivering it.

2. *Capabilities* - Develop young people's capabilities to choose well among these opportunities by recognising them as decision-making agents and by helping ensure that their decisions are well informed, adequately resourced, and judicious.

3. *Second chances* - Provide an effective system of second chances through targeted programmes that give young people the hope and the incentive to catch up from bad luck or bad choices (World Bank, 2007:2).

For young people to succeed in today's competitive global economy they must be equipped with advanced skills beyond literacy; to stay healthy, they must confront new disease burdens, such as sexually transmitted diseases and obesity. Having survived the scourges of childhood, young people confront health threats at a very vulnerable time, initiating sexual activity and entering the age of identity-seeking and risk-taking. In 2005, more than half of the estimated five million people who contracted HIV worldwide were young people between 15 and 24, the majority being young women and girls (World Bank, 2007).

The youth question in Zambia is further complicated by the phenomenon of streetism. Most street children in the country graduate into youths bereft of social skills and the critical forms of socialisation that shape young people into adulthood. Not only are they vulnerable, they are extremely 'untamed' and lacking in values of dignity, respect for elders and authority, love and civility – all alien concepts to them. This army of street youths is what Zambians will have to depend on to carry the legacy of the country into the future. This situation is actually frightening if it is seriously considered. The street youths are a diverse group, but they have in common the problems they face which include negative perception by the public, health problems, deviance and psychopathological symptoms (Mufune, 2000).

There have been various government attempts to address problems of the youth since independence, ranging from sending young people to rural reconstruction centres or agricultural rural resettlement schemes to national youth or military service[2] (especially for secondary school leavers). All these initiatives failed to deal with the negative forces impacting on the youth. One of the key failings at the time was that the youth question was not treated holistically, but in a segmented way. Furthermore, there was no clear youth policy to guide programmes from the government and the civil society sector aimed at offsetting young people's undesirable living circumstances. To this end, the National Youth Policy (that was launched in 1994) attempts to deal with some of these challenges faced by the youth through the promotion of their welfare and safeguarding their rights to better existence and self-development as well as meeting their needs in accordance with international requirements. It aims to highlight youth problems and design programmes or projects with a view to improving the quality of their lives in line with national development aspirations, and to create the much-needed environment that is conducive to youth development, socially, culturally, spiritually, politically, economically, as well as to other areas of human development (Department of Youth Development, 1994).

While outlying the government's five-year vision, in October 2006, President Levy Mwanawasa committed his administration to an emphasis on skills training and youth empowerment. In the same vein the government also began to revise the national youth policy and also established the Youth Employment Fund that is now fully operational as a permanent feature in youth development in Zambia. An amount of 40 billion kwacha has been set aside for this endeavour. The government has also secured about 500 hectares in various parts of the country for resettlement of former street kids who have graduated from the Zambia National Service (ZNS) training camps. Land was secured on the Copperbelt and in the North Western, Eastern, Central and Southern provinces. The Ministry of Youth, Sport and Child Development was also going to provide the youth with the necessary requisites to develop the allocated pieces of land. Retirees and other vulnerable people would also be earmarked for this venture as well (Zambia Daily Mail, 2006).

It must be pointed out that many initiatives targeting the youth, or street youths in particular, are still not holistic and tend to focus on one dimension. In most cases there is an over-emphasis on skills training or the economic factor as opposed to life skills, or other psycho-social aspects. Most of these young people are psychologically damaged because of their precarious lifestyles on the streets and hazardous conditions that they were exposed to. The situation of Zambian youths in general and street youths in particular requires a multi-sectored and integrated approach (Mufune, 2000). Thus, the revision of the country's youth policy by the Ministry of Sport, Youth and Child Development is an encouraging undertaking. It aims not only at making the policy relevant, but also at bringing it in line with new global and national trends. Furthermore, the policy change is driven by the need to attain the Millennium Development Goals and is also based on the principles of equity, participation, human rights, partnership and networking (Mwanawasa, 2006).

Children

The majority of children in LDCs are vulnerable and remain at risk. A number of children in Zambia fall under the categories of either orphans[3] or street children. Many are exposed to various shocks, for instance hunger. The levels of child malnutrition in Zambia were showing steady improvements throughout the 1990s, but since 1999 there has been quite a significant deterioration, from 25 per cent being underweight to 31 per cent in 2002. The levels of malnutrition vary significantly across Zambia. However, it appears that those deemed better off (i.e. in more urbanised areas) showed a greater degree of child malnutrition. The levels of stunting in Zambia are some of the highest in Africa – 51.9 per cent of children less than five years of age (United Nations Children's Fund, 2004). Children continue to face life-threatening situations with negative impact on their wellbeing. For instance, recent media reports referred to a 100 per cent increase in violence against children in the country (The Post, 2006). Lately, child defilement is also proving to be a serious problem. According to the Young Women's Christian Association (YWCA) 85 per cent of cases of defilement reported in the country resulted in HIV/AIDS. The Executive Director of the YWCA reported that the organisation had received cases of defilement on a weekly basis and that the victims were getting younger. In 2006, the organisation had recorded 32 cases of defilement in the country, indicating that these were on the increase in Zambia. However, she also attributed the rise in reported cases of defilement to the sensitisation of communities, by both the government and Civil Society Organisations, whereby people were becoming aware that defilement 'was a crime and that things should not just be settled out of court' (The Post, 2006).

Because of these problems the country's Parliament approved the Children's Rights Bill in 2005. The government also went on to revise the National Child Policy so as to provide adequate protection and development for Zambian children. It has put in place stiff penalties to deter the abuse of children either sexually or through violence. The sentence for child defilement has been increased to 15 years' imprisonment, while for child battery it is between five and ten years.

Zambia ratified in 1976 the International Labour Organisation (ILO) Convention 138 on the Minimum Age, the United Nations Convention of the Rights of the Child in 1991, and ILO Convention 182 on the Worst Forms of Child Labour in 2001. Zambian laws pertinent to child labour are somewhat inconsistent and no comprehensive child labour laws exist. The Zambian Constitution (1991) addresses the protection of young persons from exploitation and forced labour and defines a young person as anyone under the age of 15. However, the Employment Young Persons and Children Act (1993) defines a child as anyone under the age of 14 years, and establishes 14 as the minimum age. Numerous laws make mention of children's rights, and several, including the Labour and Industrial Relations Act and Employment Act, also focus on working children. However, children engaged in subsistence agriculture, domestic service or the informal sector, are not covered by law (Bureau of International Labour Affairs, 2004).

The problem of street children is not a new phenomenon but what has changed in the last ten years is its acuteness. This issue has actually existed since the mid-1980s (see Tucon and Lungwangwa, 1992), although at the time, the situation was not so stark as many were absorbed into petty trading, car-minding and other survival-types of jobs. The majority were children 'on' the streets rather than 'of' the streets. They would come and work or beg on the streets during the day and return to their respective homes in the evening. Thus, the problem was fairly invisible and did not cause much public concern. The issue would have been nipped in the bud had the government been more astute in handling this matter. However, owing to the UNIP government's attitude of denial as well as sticking to clichés of the role of the extended family, the problem spiralled out of control. The rise of the HIV/AIDS pandemic was to amplify this problem tenfold and it still continues to grow at an alarming rate. The rise of child-headed households and orphans has only aggravated the phenomenon of children living on the streets. Many commentators ranging from NGOs to international organisations such as UNICEF have put forward proposals to cope with this problem. Nonetheless, a well-funded, holistic and multi-sectoral strategy, primarily co-ordinated by the Zambian government in concert with other partners, needs to be quickly put in place. Efforts in this arena have been inchoate and fragmented for decades and now these initiatives have to be streamlined in order to have ample impact.

Some media reports have referred to the fact that at present, there is no specific legislation that deals with the welfare of street children in the country as this is still regarded as a new phenomenon (even though it has been in existence since the 1980s). The government (in collaboration with NGOs and development partners) is said to have been working towards strategies that would see fewer children on the street, although the problem may not be completely eradicated (Zambia Daily Mail, 2006). In 2004 an Inter-Ministerial Committee of Ministers comprising Youth, Sport and Child Development, Defence, Finance and National Planning, Community Development and Social Services, and Science, Technology and Vocational Training was established to spearhead the Zambia Youth Empowerment Programme. The Committee of Ministers was supported by a body of experts who developed a concept paper, outlining the implementation framework of the programme. The overall aim of the programme was to empower vulnerable children and out of school youths aged between 15 and 25 through the provision of life skills. Consultative meetings were held with stakeholders to examine the Zambia National Service Act in order to determine the possibility of using ZNS infrastructure and equipment for skills training to non-military people. In September 2005 a Statutory Instrument was issued by the Ministry of Defence allowing the Ministry of Youth, Sport and Child Development to use ZNS infrastructure for the purpose of training young and vulnerable Zambians (Zambia Daily Mail, 2006).

It is suggested in the present work that there is a need for stronger child protective laws, as well as other measures governing the plight of children in Zambia. Statutory work must be enhanced and co-ordinated throughout the nine provinces of Zambia. This work at present has serious gaping holes that need to be plugged. For instance, the establishment of orphanages remains a contentious issue between government and civil society. The issue should not be much of a problem if it is backed up by contemporary, relevant and child-friendly policies and legislation. Clear set guidelines and norms and standards for their establishment must be arrived at by the Ministry of Community Development and Social Services. This Ministry should also increase the numbers as well as capacities of officers so that they conduct effective inspections of such facilities in order to enforce norms and standards amenable to the care and protection of children.[4]

Despite prevailing problems in regard to children's livelihood, there are also some heartening accounts. According to the United Nations MDG Annual Report (2003) Infant Mortality Rates (IMRs) in Zambia, though still high, decreased between 1992 and 2002. In 1992, the IMR stood at 107 deaths per 1,000 live births, but it dropped to 95 deaths per 1,000 in 2002. This was attributed to improved childhood immunisation rates and provision of micronutrients such as Vitamin A, and early medical attention (IRIN, 2004).

Conclusion

The above-mentioned spheres are taken as imperatives of human development in Zambia, and progress in these areas remains critical to the country's ultimate wellbeing. When these sectors are not functioning properly, then human development will be impeded, while the opposite would mean that it is indeed taking root in Zambia. All vulnerable populations find it difficult to meet their basic needs and continue to suffer in many ways. Such challenges are also contributing to the erosion of human development in the country. The question has proved quite elusive to Zambia's policy-makers as they have failed to come up with innovative strategies to address this problem. In concluding the chapter, it must be reiterated that the eradication of vulnerabilities is cardinal to the realisation of human development in Zambia. Social policy can play a leading role in creating conditions that enable vulnerable populations such as children, the youth, women, senior citizens and rural dwellers to move out of difficult circumstances, by providing them with viable alternatives so as to improve upon and sustain their livelihoods. The next chapter pays close attention to the process of monitoring and evaluation in the context of human development.

Notes

[1] Rapid and large scale urbanisation has been taking place in Zambia since independence, in most cases, to the detriment of rural development. For example, the proportion of the population that lived in urban areas almost doubled during the 1965-80 period from 23 per cent to 43 per cent. The annual rate of increase for the urban population averaged 6.6 per cent during this period (Siamwiza et al., 1993).

[2] The national youth service question needs to be revisited and be informed by better strategies. There are various models from other countries that can be explored by government. Different categories of youth have to be designated for various national service activities. For example, university graduates should also be earmarked for national service as well. This would help them have a practical

orientation and be able to engage in some productive activity, while they are waiting to be employed. Ghana and South Africa have a national service that is targeting university graduates. There are some lessons that can be learnt from these countries. The notion of graduates having an elitist mentality, whereby they think that the nation owes them something because that they have attained intellectual competencies, can be addressed through the national service scheme. A sense of responsibility and patriotism on the part of graduates can be fostered via a national service programme. Programmes for former street children and street youths have to be conceptualised in a way that enables such individuals to be re-educated, conscientised and instilled with discipline, responsibility and self-reliance. These young people have no sense of tradition, decorum and etiquette as they grew up on the streets with no concept of respect for authority or culture. So interventions should not only be at the skills level but should go beyond this.

The education system that was inherited from the colonialists was tilted in the direction of 'white collar jobs'. This legacy has to be erased so that students are radically oriented in a curriculum that fosters self-reliance, innovation and creativity. In the same vein, the country's economy must also be patterned in such a way that it is able to create spaces for these individuals when they fall out of the education system at different levels. For instance, the industrial base must be expanded so that it is able to incorporate individuals who have had some training in vocational trades but did not make it to universities, such as artisans, welders, joiners, plumbers, carpenters, etc. However, if there is no industrial expansion in the country, it will be difficult to incorporate out-of-school youths (possessing some skills) into productive activities. Concomitantly, the agricultural base needs to be expanded to also absorb youths who have been exposed to agricultural subjects at school.

3   Orphans from all causes can be described as follows:

(i) single orphan — a child who has lost one parent;

(ii) double orphan — a child who lost both parents;

(iii) maternal orphan — a child whose mother has died (includes double orphans);

(iv) paternal orphans — a child whose father has died (includes double orphans) (UNICEF, 2006:4)

[4] At the time of writing, the Minister of Community Development and Social Services had expressed sentiments on national television relating to the sudden increase in the number of orphanages in the country. Obviously her concerns were not misplaced, but there was no feasible alternative that was offered. Yes, orphanages that are abusing children have to be closed down, but we cannot beguile the nation that orphanages should be an option of last resort. There are simply no families or communities that can take on this societal burden any more. As things stand, most families and communities have almost reached breaking-point. They have been heavily encumbered by the bad economic situation that does not seem to be easing at all. The country cannot afford to over-glorify the extended family, which is almost becoming extinct. This type of rhetoric only scored points in the 1960s and 1970s. The reality is that Zambian society has dramatically changed with the extended family also being stretched beyond capacity by various socio-economic forces, for instance, the AIDS pandemic. Institutionalisation (though not so desirable) is the only option available to normalise the present deplorable situation of Zambian orphans.

The state should invest heavily in this sector if the country is to avert a national catastrophe. The problem of children in Zambia must not be treated lightly or laced with political rhetoric. This issue concerns all Zambians. Thus, the government through the Ministry of Community Development and Social Services should come up with workable solutions to stem the tide of this social crisis.

Chapter 6

MONITORING AND EVALUATION: OUTCOMES, IMPACTS AND POLICY ANALYSIS FOR HUMAN DEVELOPMENT

Introduction

The discussions in this chapter focus on the mechanism of Monitoring and Evaluation (M&E) as it relates to human development in Zambia. The chapter argues that the country could reap huge dividends from human development endeavours if various government and civil society interventions are constantly monitored and evaluated. In order for organisations to rectify, modify and improve upon strategies aimed at accelerating human development in the country, M&E should play a pivotal role in their programmes and projects. When new circumstances or challenges emerge, while implementing, for example, certain programmes aimed at raising the living standards of Zambians, M&E could be used as a back-up tool so as to provide alternatives or solutions to unworkable policy options. This chapter also focuses on public policy formulation and implementation as these processes are also directly linked to M&E.

Data on human development have long been treated as a poor cousin to those of economic performance. While considerable effort has gone into the collection, compilation, and standardisation of economic statistics, data on human development have received scant attention. This trend appears to represent a paradox as human development is universally regarded as the ultimate objective of economic development. This situation can be explained in part by the, often unstated, assumption that the process of economic growth is synonymous with the improvement of social welfare (Ghai and Westendoff, 1993). This discussion argues that interventions that try to engender human development in Zambia can only be effective if there are means of measuring inputs as well as outputs stemming from previous investments. Furthermore, easy ways of ascertaining and then quantifying human progress (or retardation) are needed to guide policy formulation and implementation in Zambia. This goal can only be attained if governmental or non-governmental interventions, through projects and programmes, are monitored and then evaluated. Monitoring and evaluation is crucial to human development because the effect of an intervention may be subjected to different interpretations due to incomplete information, inherent conceptual obstacles in correctly assessing the impact, and normative considerations grounded in belief or ideology that colour conclusions (United Nations, 2001). In effect, monitoring and evaluation can also be an invaluable tool for public policy formulation.

The concept of Monitoring and Evaluation (M&E)

In order to clearly define M&E, it is fitting to firstly separate the two concepts of monitoring and evaluation into two components.

Monitoring defined

Monitoring is a continual, methodical process of data collection and information gathering throughout the life of a project. The information collected can be used for regular evaluation of progress, so that adjustments can be made while the work is continuing. Monitoring is also used to mean the systematic 'tracking' of a particular condition or set of conditions, for example political events, environmental change, the situation of women and so forth, in order to identify trends (Rubin, 1995). During monitoring, information for 'tracking' progress against previously agreed plans and 'milestones' is routinely gathered. The changes, relating to both the effects and impacts, that are emerging from project activities can be identified. If there are discrepancies between the actual and planned progress, corrective action can be taken. This process may include changing the overall purpose and plan of the activity. Monitoring can also mean keeping a check on the use of resources. Questions for latter evaluation can be identified during monitoring (Rubin, 1995:16).

Evaluation conceptualised

Mwansa et al. (1990:166) point out that there are several definitions of evaluation, depending on the intellectual background of the person defining the concept. The manner in which the term is defined determines or conditions how evaluation is conducted and influences its possible utilisation. They argue that three types of definitions of the term can be distinguished:

> There are various definitions whose major concern is with outcomes. The focus here is with output related to the achievement of the programme's goals. This exercise is usually referred to as outcome evaluation. Some definitions have a broader view of evaluation that include outcomes

(impacts) as well as analysis of effort (programme input). However, such definitions exclude considerations of programme activities (i.e. process evaluation). The third definition is much broader and is conceptualised as a comprehensive evaluation of the whole system in that it combines the effort, the outcome, the process, and all related issues.

The third definition focuses on the degree to which a project/programme is meeting its associated goals and any unanticipated effects created. Actually this view is a systems approach to evaluation. The third definition has better application in a country like Zambia that is dealing with a host of developmental challenges. Also, this type of evaluation is appropriate to the country because of its holistic nature as it originates from a systems appraisal of issues. Taken further, evaluation means to 'assess the value or worth of' something. Also, it means to understand the value of something in order to do things better in the future (Rubin, 1995). Evaluation uses information gathered during regular monitoring, but may need other information as well. It often uses 'baseline information', which is information collected at the very beginning of a project, against which progress can be measured. Evaluation happens at set times in the life of a project. In addition, evaluation looks at the relevance, effectiveness, and impact of a project, with the aim of improving it or influencing future policies, programmes and projects (Rubin, 1995:16).

Furthermore, evaluation is a learning and management tool in that an assessment can be undertaken of what has taken place in order to improve work. Measuring, analysing and interpreting change helps people to determine how far objectives have been achieved and whether the initial assumptions about what would happen were right; and to make judgments about the effectiveness, efficiency, impact, and sustainability of work (Rubin, 1995:15).

After defining monitoring and evaluation separately, one important question concerns the relationship between the two. Although it is customary to refer to them together (as in the term 'M/E'), many aid agencies and project-implementing entities treat them as distinct activities conducted by separate organisations and having separate objectives (Valadez and Bamberger, 1994). However, monitoring and evaluation should be considered complementary parts of an integrated system. Evaluation is concerned as much with the lessons of project implementation as with the degree to which intended impacts have been achieved (Valadez and Bamberger, 1994). Consequently, evaluation should take place either continually or periodically from the time the project is formulated right through implementation and the operational phase.

The World Bank (2004) presents an elaborative though not exhaustive list of several data collection methods, analytical frameworks and types of evaluation and review. They cover (a) performance indicators; (b) the logical framework approach; (c) theory-based evaluation; (d) formal surveys; (e) rapid appraisal methods; (f) participatory methods; (g) public expenditure tracking survey; (h) cost-benefit and cost-effective analysis; and (i) impact evaluation. These tools and approaches are complementary while some are alternatives. Some have broad applicability and some are quite narrow in their uses. The choice of which is appropriate for any given context will depend on a range of considerations, including the uses for which they are intended, the main stakeholders who have an interest in their findings, the speed with which the information is needed and the cost (World Bank, 2004). For instance, *performance indicators* measure inputs, processes, outputs, outcomes and impacts for development projects, programmes, or strategies, while the *logical framework* helps to clarify objectives of any project, programme, or policy by aiding in the identification of the expected causal links (World Bank, 2004). *Theory-based evaluation* has similarities to the logical framework, but allows a much more in-depth understanding of the workings of a programme or activity. On the one hand, *formal surveys* can be used to collect standardised information from carefully selected samples of people or households, while on the other, *rapid appraisal methods* are quick, low-cost ways of gathering the views and feedback of beneficiaries and other stakeholders, in order to respond to decision-makers' needs for information (World Bank, 2004).

Valadez and Bamberger (1994) further observe that at the national level, information should be fed into the national monitoring and evaluation system to build up a national data bank that can be used to improve the selection and improvement of future projects. The central monitoring and evaluation requirement is therefore to track systematically the key variables and processes over time and space, and see how they change as a result of strategy activities (Spellerberg cited in Organisation for Economic Co-operation and Development, 2002). The execution of this activity requires measuring and analysing sustainability; monitoring implementation of the strategy; evaluating the results of the strategy; and reporting and dissemination of the findings (Organisation for Economic Co-operation and Development, 2002).

Measuring and analysing sustainability are necessary to determine the state of the society, the economy and the environment, the main strengths and weaknesses and the issues for the strategy to address underlying factors. The most productive way to approach this exercise is to undertake an indicator-based sustainability assessment, supplemented by spatial analysis and possibly other contributing measurements and analyses. The indicators chosen for the assessment need to be monitored on a continual basis to identify trends, detect (and, if possible, anticipate), change and track progress. Monitoring implementation of the strategy is necessary to ensure standard management oversight and accountability (Organisation for Economic Co-operation and Development, 2002). The following also need monitoring:

(i) inputs in terms of financial, physical and human resources applied to the strategy and its related activities;

(ii) process quality in terms of how strategy principles are satisfied (e.g. people-centred, participation, integration, and commitment generation);

(iii) outcomes in terms of access to, use of, and satisfaction with strategy products (which are not necessarily under the control of agencies involved in the strategy); and,

(iv) the performance of individual actors in implementing the strategy, in terms of the effectiveness and efficiency of their service provision and management (Organisation for Economic Co-operation and Development, 2002).

Evaluating the results of the strategy is necessary to correlate actions with specific changes in human and environmental conditions, test the strategic hypotheses (choice of priority issues, analysis of underlying factors, prescriptions of action), assure accountability, capture lessons, and develop capacity through learning. Furthermore, reporting and dissemination of the findings are necessary to feed back critical messages to key stakeholder groups, and thus enable them to continually improve their behaviour, the strategy itself, and its component activities (Organisation for Economic Co-operation and Development, 2002:309-10). Both monitoring and evaluation require skills in implementation management (Bowden, 1988). In terms of human development, there are several levels at which monitoring and evaluation activities could be undertaken – the macro, institutional, strategy and micro or local levels. Again, as with any social issue, monitoring and evaluation of a particular development intervention cannot be isolated from the wider political, institutional, and cultural context (Oakley et al., 1998:29). Monitoring and evaluation should not be seen as 'ends' but as means to better understand present and future quality, effectiveness, and impact. To be confident of the future direction of human development initiatives, it is necessary to understand fully what has happened in the past (Oakley et al., 1998). Furthermore, monitoring and evaluation activities should not be treated in isolation, but linked to the overall policy formulation and implementation processes in a country. They must also be guided by a theoretical perspective.

Oakley and associates (1998) point out that the lack of an overall framework can be and often is the major obstacle for initiating monitoring and evaluation. This framework should have several main components: structure, methods, indicators, data storage, retrieval and analysis, and interpretation. The following broad principles should at least underpin systems that monitor both social and human development:

(a) The system should be minimum but cost-effective, it should be intelligible to both staff and project partners at all levels and should not require onerous and unnecessary reporting.

(b) The system should be designed in such a way that it is able to develop the reflective and analytical capacities of those involved and not merely result in the mechanical undertaking of pre-programmed activities.

(c) The system should be able to feed consistent, quality information on output, outcome and impact into the (annual) project cycle – for both accountability and learning purposes – leading to the ongoing adaptation of plans and objectives.

(d) The system should emphasise decision-making and analysis, and not merely be geared to the collection of information and data.

(e) The system should be based on the assumption that change as a result of social development may be unpredictable and that its evaluation, therefore, cannot always be based on predetermined expectations of likely outcomes.

(f) The system should also be based upon as wide an involvement as is realistically possible and necessary, valuing the contributions of various stakeholder groups; it should recognise gender diversity and should seek to ensure that both women and men are able to contribute.

(g) The system should recognise that the most crucial aspect of the monitoring and evaluation of social development is monitoring, and should emphasise this function as opposed to the ex-post evaluation approach.

(h) Finally, the system should acknowledge the value of alternative sources of information, both oral and visual, and of the perceptions of local people who have been directly involved in the project (Oakley, *et al.*, 1998:49-50).

Countries use monitoring and evaluation to establish the performance of operational projects and programmes, but the United States and some European countries have been applying monitoring and evaluation in policy analysis and strategic planning for a while (Valadez and Bamberger, 1994). Bowden (1988:2) identifies five components, which are essential to the effective operation of national monitoring and evaluation. These are:

> An administrative unit to monitor and evaluate developmental projects and programmes. It will ideally be located in a central agency of the government. The administrative unit necessary to carry out this work needs not to be large. Often numbering half a dozen or fewer persons, the unit should be located in an influential agency of the central government. An information system for monitoring a number of key progress indicators on selected projects in the country. The system includes a reporting of the major difficulties that the projects are facing. Methods by which the unit would identify problems, which had a high impact on development achievements, together with procedures for joint resolution by concerned agencies. The creation of the political and administrative support necessary for analysing the issues that arise, and for implementing responses. The inclusion of an evaluation capability in the system, able to answer questions on the impact, or long-term achievements, of the projects.

Monitoring and evaluation ensures that projects or programmes spearheaded by organisations function towards the meeting of their goals and objectives, and that there is optimum utilisation of available resources. Indeed, in a context of constant flux like Zambia, there is no guarantee that programmes and projects will work as planned. The cardinal point to note is that M&E allows some room for clear parameters to be established so that a needs assessment can be executed. This means that the needs and the perceptions of the consumers will be incorporated into the implementation of the project or programme (Noyoo and Mamphiswana, 2003). This understanding again brings into focus the importance of consulting relevant stakeholders in the intended change process, which ultimately calls for full participation of the intended recipients of the service. In the past, M&E was mostly top-down with technocrats 'knowing what was best' for the people. Clearly, such a stand had to be questioned, especially when the projects or programmes were not working. The rise of participatory methods can partially be explained from this premise.

Participatory Monitoring and Evaluation (PM&E)

Participatory Monitoring and Evaluation (PM&E) is not a new concept and has been utilised by different professionals for almost four decades. It is increasingly being used for different purposes and varying sectors. PM&E thinking and practices are widespread and diverse (Noyoo, 2005). PM&E draws from various participatory traditions, including Participatory Action Research (PAR); participatory learning and action, encompassing Rapid Rural Appraisal (RRA) and later Participatory Rural Appraisal (PRA); and Farming Systems Research (FSR) or Farming Participatory Research (FPR) (Estrella and Gaventa, 1997). Ultimately, monitoring and evaluation should solidify policy analysis stratagems that should then inform the policy implementation process.

The domain of public policy

A sojourn into the field of policy analysis would first require a re-examination of the terrain of public policy-making. The idea of public policy presupposes that there is a sphere or domain of life that is not private or purely individual, but shared by the broader community. The public comprises that dimension of human activity which is regarded as requiring governmental or social regulation or intervention, or at least common action (Parsons, 1995). Anderson (1997) observes that public policy may also be viewed as whatever governments choose 'to do or not to do'. The special characteristics of public policies stem from their being formulated by authorities in a political system. Furthermore, it should also be noted that all public policy formulation unavoidably reflects normative positions (Nussbaum, 2000). In this sense, public policy formulation is not a value-free activity. Bekker (1999) underscores this point and puts across the three dimensions of public policy formulation. First, it communicates what a government values; secondly, it provides direction to those who make and take decisions in government; thirdly, it is a measure against which a government may be held accountable and be evaluated, particularly if it is subject to regular democratic elections.

Usually, public policies follow a sequential pattern: identification of goals, selection of a procedure and policy consequences. In identifying policy goals, a problem is brought forward for public consideration. The second activity involves placing the issue on the political agenda. In order to receive public attention, the problem must be invested with 'publicness' – for example, unemployment. The third issue in the identification phase will be related to the publication of the problem (Heffernan, 1979). In the stage of selecting a procedure there is application, where expert analysis takes place and costs and benefits are derived, and the negotiating of a plan unfolds, so that tradeoffs and compromises are brought to the fore. Finally, policy consequences will speak to the administration of the plan. In this regard, the choice of administration must be in line with the diverse supporters of the policy innovation (Heffernan, 1979). There are various models of policy analysis that could be used by policy-makers in order to make informed choices, for instance, the *Elitist Model* whereby public policies evolve according to the perceived self-interests of those at the top; or the *Pluralist Model*, where groups advocate alternative desirable ends; or the *Neo-Elitist Model* that focuses not on the politically active, but on the politically quiescent (Heffernan, 1979).

The need for policy analysis

As a policy-maker, one cannot deal with policies or even intelligently apply them without a clear, systematic understanding of what they are and how they operate. Part of the competence of a professional is systematic knowledge of one's roles and the reasons for one's work (Ginsberg, 1994). The term policy analysis takes on many characteristics and different authors have provided different interpretations over time. It is prudent, therefore, to pinpoint certain competences that may go hand-in-hand with the policy analysis exercise before arriving at a definition.

Whilst looking at social policies, Gill (1994:69-70) identified three objectives that could ideally lead to the systematic analysis of existing or proposed policies and for the development of alternative interventions:

> The first objective is to gain understanding of the issues that constitute the focus of a specific policy, which is being analysed or developed. This step involves exploration of the nature, scope, and distribution of these issues, and of causal theories concerning underlying dynamics. A second objective is to discern the chain of substantive effects resulting, or expected to result, from the implementation of a given policy, including intended, unintended and short, and long-range effects. This process involves, among other things, the explication of policy objectives with respect to the focal issues, of value premises underlying these objectives and hypotheses guiding the strategies, and provisions of a policy. A third objective of policy analysis is to suggest alternative policies aimed at the same or different objectives concerning the focal issues.

There are different perspectives to policy analysis. Weiner and Vining (1992:4) provide a schema of different perspectives to policy analysis (see Table 4).

Popple and Leighninger (1998:44-52) have identified several approaches to policy analysis.

Descriptive analysis

This type of policy analysis can be further subdivided into four types. These are content (which should not be confused with the research methodology of content analysis, in which qualitative data, such as words or themes in a text, are subject to quantitative analysis), choice, comparative, and historical analyses.

(a) Content Analysis

This type of policy analysis is the most straightforward. It is simply an empirical description of an existing policy in terms of its intentions, problem definition, goals, and means employed for achieving the goals. This analysis is mostly employed by the agencies charged with administering a policy.

Table 4: Approaches to policy analysis, adapted from Weiner and Vining (1992:4)

Policy Analysis Approach	Purpose	Consumer	Method
Academic Social Science Research.	Constructing theories for understanding society.	Academic community.	Rigorous empirical methodology, often quantitative.
Applied Policy Research	Predicting or evaluating impacts of changes in variables that can be altered by public and/or private programmes.	Decision makers in the policy area.	Formal research methodology applied to policy-relevant questions.
Social Planning	Defining and specifying ways to ameliorate social problems and achieve a desirable future state.	The 'public interest' as professionally defined.	Survey research, public fora, and expert and/or citizen panels.
Agency Planing/ Policy Management	Defining and clarifying agency goals; explicating alternatives for achieving those goals; evaluating outcomes of attempts to achieve those goals.	Boards of directors, funding agencies, interested citizens.	Data bases, management techniques (PERT, flow charting, decision analysis), survey research, public fora, expert and/or citizen panels.
Journalistic Analysis	Focusing public attention on social welfare problems.	General public.	Existing documents, expert sources (professionals, scholars, people affected by the problem).
Practitioner Policy Analysis	Understanding the policy context within which an individual social worker functions.	The social worker doing the analysis.	Existing literature, government, and other documents available in microform and documents division of large libraries, expert sources.
Citizen Policy Analysis		The citizen involved in the analysis of elected officials that the citizen wishes to influence.	Existing literature, elected and appointed officials.

(b) Choice Analysis

Choice analysis is a systematic process of looking at the options available to planners for dealing with a social welfare problem. The analytic focus of such studies is upon issues of choice: what is the form and substance of the choices that compose the policy design? What options did these choices foreclose? What values, theories, and assumptions support alternatives? There are four primary dimensions of choice: bases of allocation, types of benefits, delivery structures, and financing benefits (Popple and Leighninger, 1998:44).

(c) Comparative Analysis

This type of policy analysis involves systematically comparing policies across two or more settings. The most common form is cross-national analysis: the policy in one nation (for instance Zambia) is compared with the policies of other nations regarding the same problem. More limited comparisons, between states/ provinces, communities or between public and private service provision for example, are possible and useful. This approach is a very rich one because it provides policy analysts with 'natural experiments' of alternative approaches.

(d) Historical Analysis

It is difficult, if not impossible, to analyse any current policy without at least a brief review of preceding events. Historical analysis, as a policy analysis type, goes well beyond this stage and is based on the assumptions that current policies can be fully understood only if we have a thorough understanding of their evolution. If a policy is the continuation of a long trend, historical analysis seeks to explicate that trend and to understand why it has continued (Popple and Leighninger, 1998:44).

Process Analysis

This analysis is less concerned with policy content than with how a policy comes into being. The focus of this analytic approach is on the interactions of the many political actors, which include public officials, bureaucrats, media, professional associations and special interest groups representing those likely to be affected either positively or negatively by a policy (Popple and Leighninger, 1998).

Stages in the policy analysis cycle

Various authors have suggested different analytical frameworks for specific situations. Emphases differ from model to model. Parsons (1995) asserts that despite a growing unease with the dominant framework of policy analysis, (rational decision-making), the policy cycle or stagist approach continues to be the basis for both the analysis of the policy process and of analysis in/and for the policy process. This approach incorporates the following stages:

(i) problem definition;

(ii) identifying alternative responses/solutions;

(iii) evaluation of options;

(iv) selection of policy options;

(v) implementation;

(vi) evaluation.

Analysing policies presupposes a variety of kinds of knowledge. One cannot analyse a policy by simply understanding and applying a policy analysis framework. Instead, the person must have some knowledge of the public policy-making process, politics, public opinion, public finance, the structure and function of many facets of the public sphere such as the social welfare system, and economics (Ginsberg, 1994). Furthermore, frameworks must enable an analyst to have a critical lens to discern and comprehend social reality so as to provide workable solutions to prevailing societal problems.

Implementing policy

The implementation of any extensive public policy usually requires a programme and collective action of many people. Not all of these will favour the goals of the policy, and the self-interest of some may call for a return to the previous policy or at least an extensive modification (Quade, 1982). Policy implementation is no mere afterthought to policy-making; rather, implementation determines whether enacted policies are actualised. Critically, effective implementation of the activities of government requires the formulation of a myriad of policies that deal with all aspects of the way the state operates. Perhaps of greatest interest are policies that shape the way the state seeks to discharge its obligations to maintain law and order, ensure national defence, engage in international relations, promote economic development, and ensure the wellbeing of the population (Midgley, 2000). The implementation phase is generally a time of filling in the details through regulations, personnel procedures, programme guidelines, and other specifications, all of which further shape the policy. This administrative process is often referred to as 'secondary legislation' (Popple and Leighninger, 1998).

Jansson (1994:378) refers to the implementing stage in this way:

> During this phase of the policy cycle, people want to know whether leaders charged with implementing a policy invest energy and political resources in doing so. It is also necessary to know whether they believe the policy is important and whether it furthers their values, prestige, resources, or power. In addition, it needs to be ascertained if specific leaders fear negative consequences, such as reprimands or loss of funding, if they do not vigorously implement a policy. In the case of multi-faceted policies, it is necessary to determine which facets they support or oppose. Finally, it also needs to be established how decision makers and implementers interpret specific policies in the light of the vagueness of many written policies.

Smith (1973:202-205) also highlights four areas that are crucial to policy implementation:

1. The idealised policy, that is, the idealised patterns of interaction that those who have defined the policy are attempting to induce;

2. The target group, defined as those who are required to adopt new patterns of interaction by the policy. They are the people most directly affected by the policy and who must change to meet its demands;

3. The implementation organisation, usually a unit of the government bureaucracy responsible for implementation of the policy; and

4. Environmental factors, those elements in the environment that influence or are influenced by the policy implementation.

The implementation of policies is also about changing systems or attempting to provide impetus for that change. It is a complex undertaking and may be obstructed or facilitated by various factors, for example, political interference or lack of skills. Implementation is concerned with the design and management of systems to achieve the optimum integration of people, structure, processes, and resources essential to achieving the agency's purpose (Kabat, 1983). There are different methods involved in the analysis of the implementation phase. For purposes of this discussion the focus will be on what is termed as delivery analysis.

Delivery analysis

This activity refers to the analysis of the following processes: implementation, evaluation, change, and impact. The framework of public policy is consequently being shaped by continuing and increasingly common concerns about cost-effectiveness, delivery of policies and services, improving human resource management, and better monitoring and evaluation (Organisation for Economic Co-operation and Development in Parsons, 1995). Modes of delivery or 'systems' of policy delivery have become a central concern of analysis in the public sector. The focus on the increasingly diverse intergovernmental and inter-organisational network of delivering public goods and services (Parsons, 1995) is crucial to an informed understanding of specific ways of making the policy processes for example, in Zambia, propel a country's human wellbeing, specifically in the area of poverty reduction. In explicating this phenomenon, this discussion heavily borrows from Parsons' (1995:492-523) discussion, which looks at mixes of delivery, and which are explored hereafter.

Four 'mixes' are looked at, bearing in mind that Zambia's choice of policy mix is not static and may change with novel circumstances and operational parameters. These are: *governmental mix, sectoral mix, enforcement mix,* and *value mix.*

1. The governmental mix

In the first instance, the territorial dimension needs to be taken into consideration. What part or level of government is responsible for the delivery of a programme? How is responsibility shared in terms of administrative and financial arrangements? The mix of levels will, of course, vary from policy arena to policy arena. The mix will also be determined by the political and constitutional traditions, and arrangements between centralised unitary states and decentralised systems (Parsons, 1995:492). Although political systems may share policy goals, the level of government which is deemed responsible for actually providing a service varies widely between national, regional/state, local and neighbourhood levels.

Since 1964, successive Zambian governments have only paid lip-service to the devolution of power from the centre. Localised decision-making is still yet to be attained in the country. So the central government promulgates all public policies as well as setting the norms and standards for government interventions. There have been no moves towards regional or state governance in Zambia since independence. Indeed, power has remained concentrated at the centre, with vast powers still vested in the president. In the one-party state, things were worse off; people's participation in the governing of their country being a mere side-show. This was also the case with local government (notwithstanding various window dressing overtures by different governments). Hence service delivery has been hampered by ineffectual systems or inexistent institutions at the centre, coupled with lack of trained personnel. At the local level, many functionaries are oblivious to their operational mandates and how they are supposed to discharge their responsibilities. It is hoped that the ongoing decentralisation programme will begin to reduce some of these problems at the local level. For instance, its focus on fiscal decentralisation aimed at empowering Zambia's 72 local authorities so that they improve programme implementation and service delivery is one way of ensuring that decentralisation is realised.

2. The sectoral mix

The mix of levels (or spheres) of government must also be considered alongside the sector which is involved in the delivery of public goods and services. Here again, the pattern is complex. The relationship between the public, private, and voluntary sectors, for example, is one that has undergone considerable change since Zambia gained independence. In the colonial setting the public, private and voluntary sectors were tilted towards the needs of Europeans and not Africans. However, with the reconfiguration of political institutions in the 1960s and 1970s, services took on a national character with regard to raising people's livelihoods. Services may comprise a mix of public and private responsibility, as well as a mix of the voluntary sector and community agencies. Under this configuration flow the public-private mix partnerships (Parsons, 1995:497). The setting up of partnerships between the public and private sectors, better known as Public-Private Partnerships (PPPs), has not gained considerable ground in Zambia, although the opening of political spaces after 1991 led to their emergence. Examples of PPPs can be in the areas of social welfare and housing. They are also found in infrastructure development, urban renewal, regional development, training and education, and the environment.

3. The enforcement mix

Policy is all very well, but without an enforcement or compliance capability, the delivery of public policy is unlikely and uncertain. The mix of enforcement methods may range from brute force and 'fixed bayonets' to information broadcasts which seek to change behaviour. Markets, bureaucracy and communities, for example, may be viewed in terms of different ways of enforcing policy. The market achieves this goal through supply and demand prices, and the interaction of buyers and sellers; bureaucracy relies on rules, whilst community enforcement relies on such modes as shared values, reciprocity, trust and gossip (Parsons, 1995).

4. The value mix

Under this mix the following is considered: what is the distribution of values, which frame and inform the delivery mix of a given policy or programme? The governmental, sectoral and enforcement mixes are ultimately manifestation of values or the 'assumptive world'. The value mix involves choices and priorities regarding the allocation of resources between policy and problem areas as well as between different programmes directed at common problems and policies (Parsons, 1995). The present approach to policy formulation and implementation in Zambia is more transparent and participatory than it was in the Second and Third Republics.

Zambia's public policy arena

The domain of public policy formulation and implementation primarily rests with the government of Zambia. Currently, government policy formulation is overseen by the Policy and Central Administration sector, which comprises institutions and organs in the Public Service dealing with overall public policy formulation, co-ordination, monitoring and evaluation, national planning, financial and statistical services, regulation and legislation, general administration, human resources management and development, and general services (Government of the Republic of Zambia, 2002:189). However, this trend has taken on new nuances in the current political dispensation. One cardinal shift in public policy-making has been the willingness on the part of the government to bring a cross-section of the Zambian society onto the policy formulation platform. This did not happen before. In the past, when the one-party state was in existence, policy formulation and planning were the sole preserve of the government and the participation of civil society was rarely elicited or even encouraged. In most instances planning was top-down, and consultation with stakeholders relevant to the policy process was again an aberration in a single-party setting. In most instances, key policy decisions originated from one person, the president. At the time, Kenneth Kaunda would make far-reaching policy pronouncements at public rallies. Citizens would be bewildered after such an occasion as the country would be in a state of uncertainty, or the country's future would be sealed, without their input; this usually happened through the country following a certain detrimental development path.[1] In most cases, policy decisions were never mulled over, were emotional or not rationally thought out.[2] Of course, the president and his coterie saw fit to make crucial policy decisions without consulting Zambia's cardinal stakeholders, its citizens. On another level, policy-makers and planners also did not engage with the Zambian populace.

Planning in Zambia was linked to policy-making in the 1960s, 70s and 80s. The justification for planning in the Zambian situation, as elsewhere (in those times), was that the direction and allocation of resources would be unacceptable without intervention from the state, through the planning process. The plan therefore set out to establish a co-ordinated set of investment decisions to achieve specified objectives so as to contribute towards the improvement of the country's standard of living (Ndulo, 1985). At independence the responsibility for planning was concentrated in a Central Planning Office, which was initially a government department. Afterwards, it was elevated to a ministry in the 1970s, and later on moved to the Office of the President, as the National Commission for Development Planning (NCDP). The NCDP became the main actor in the planning process and prepared Zambia's development plans and oversaw their implementation (Ndulo, 1985). The NCDP ultimately faced obstacles due to the way government was structured and became overshadowed by the Ministry of Finance. After the return to plural politics, public policy formulation and implementation in Zambia became a shoddy affair, to say the least.

During Frederick Chiluba's reign, everything seemed to operate on an *ad hoc* basis. Even the top-down policy formulation and implementation that had taken place in the single-party[3] system was denuded during the ten-year period of Frederick Chiluba, as the Transitional National Development Plan (2002:189) admits:

In the last ten years, public policy management and government were weak due to limited numbers of adequately qualified personnel, inadequate mechanisms for public debate and insufficient information dissemination of the policy process itself. This resulted in unco-ordinated policy formulation and implementation, unsystematic budgetary management leading to wastage of scarce resources and loss of public confidence in the Public Service. In financial management, several factors compromised accountability and transparency in the management of public finances, contributing to large budget deficits on a more continuous basis. It was characterised by wastefulness and imbalanced expenditure patterns caused mainly by weak internal control systems and incompatible regulatory frameworks.

The link between public policy formulation and implementation, on the one hand, and the redressing of socio-economic deficiencies, on the other, has not been well defined by different Zambian governments. The policy arena is limited and has not been expanded extensively in order to provide alternative models with varying solutions. For a long time, this area has remained bereft of rigour and innovation. It is therefore not surprising that Zambia has faced many development hurdles over the years. Policy-making is an extremely important area of national development that requires not only expertise but also dedication from those that discharge this responsibility. Policy-making is not for all and sundry, but must be an area that is set aside for those with the right competences. When a nation allows some of its mediocre citizens to take charge of all of its policy-making activities, it is most unlikely to succeed in maintaining the smooth functioning of its social units and facilitating systematic development, nor can it really promote and preserve human dignity. Those who aspire to leading positions should have had attained a high degree of intellectual adroitness and thereafter have been properly assessed as to their suitability for the positions. In short, the aspiring candidates should meet two basic requirements: (a) familiarity with the traditional policy-making procedures and (b) acquisition of a high degree of intellectual sophistication (Mwaipaya, 1980).

Surprisingly, despite the importance that should be attached to policy-making as well as the identification of captains of this arena, Zambians still seem to prefer people of low calibre at the helm. In 2005, during the Constitutional Review Commission's sittings, certain quarters expressed the sentiment that future Zambian presidents should at least have a basic university degree as a prerequisite. Astonishingly, there was quite a furore from certain segments of the Zambian populace that felt this requirement was not necessary as, so the argument went, 'education is not important'. Now, one wonders why even people looking for so-called simple jobs like cleaning, gardening or child-minding, are required to have a Curriculum Vitae (CV) or resumé and reference letters from previous employers. Such individuals are expected to possess certain qualifications and experience fitting the position applied for. Every Zambian who applies for a particular vacancy is required to furnish his/her Curriculum Vitae at the job interview, together with original copies of academic certificates (apart from those who are appointed by friends or relatives). Why then should the highest position in the land not be subjected to heavy scrutiny and rigour? Just because somebody is able to be a rabble-rouser or has an ability to manipulate, and hijack people's emotions, should he or she be made president? No! This is simply not right. Zambia has got so many intellectually capable men and women who can lead the country; some of them are leaders in well-renowned institutions abroad, but were never given the opportunity to excel in their own country. Zambia can ill afford shoddy work in the highest policy-making office in the land, the presidency, after more than four decades of independence. Past mistakes by presidents who did not possess the *tools of critical analysis* should be warning enough. No wonder the country is inundated with people who only possess primary or secondary school levels of education in the political realm.

This attitude to educated people must be weeded out of the Zambian public space. Without a doubt, the public sector is still in need of intellectuals, but such persons have not been vigorously recruited by the government. The recent assertions by the Secretary to the Cabinet, supposedly bemoaning the low numbers of professionals in the public service, just do not hold water. There are many Zambians with the right qualifications who are roaming the streets looking for jobs, while the public service chooses to ignore them. With regard to public positions, this chapter reiterates earlier calls from progressive Zambians that the president should have a university degree, while Members of Parliament and councillors should possess at least a certificate or diploma after twelve years of both primary and secondary education. This is the only safeguard to guarantee the proper promulgation of public policies as well as their interpretation and implementation. If graduates have been turned into market traders for lack of employment opportunities, then why should their representatives not have any education at all? Institutional mechanisms have to be put in place so that Zambia has the right people in policy-making positions.

Curiously, the shielding of uneducated leaders from public scrutiny is sometimes supported by public institutions such as the broadcasting service. For example, after 2000 the Zambian National Television decided to broadcast live coverage of the country's Members of Parliament's debates to the nation. For the first time in Zambia's post-colonial history, the nation was treated to visual impressions of their leaders as they articulated themselves in Parliament. Even the uneducated were glued to television sets as they watched parliamentary deliberations. However, what became apparent from the live broadcasts were the deplorable and appalling standards that were exhibited by many leaders. The majority were simply an embarrassment not only to themselves and their constituencies, but to the whole nation. Even though there were a few shining examples, the rest of these sessions were not inspiring at all. Many Zambians were beginning to be awakened to the reality that their leaders were simply doing nothing in Parliament. Just when citizens were catching on, the programme was suddenly discontinued. To date, there have been no explanations to the nation as to why televised parliamentary sessions were discontinued.

It is encouraging that the Fifth National Development Plan was published in 2006 by the government. This could be a vital signal that Zambia has reached another learning curve as regards policy-making and planning. Additionally, such initiatives as the Sector-Wide approaches used in development interventions in various areas like education, health and transport are also important indicators pointing to seriousness in public policy initiatives as well. Also, the *Zambian Human Development Reports* (ZHDR) produced by the United Nations Development Programme Resident Office in collaboration with the Zambian government and a cross-section of professionals are crucial in shaping public policy discourse in the country. These reports, which have been produced in Zambia since 1997, have also helped in influencing government policy towards recognising the centrality of human beings in development initiatives. Further, the global *Human Development Reports* have also contributed to the conceptualisation of development pursuits in Zambia and have allowed for a greater appreciation of the multi-dimensional nature of human deprivation, a greater focus on the people in national priority setting, and a greater acceptance of the need for broad-based participation (United Nations Development Programme, 2003).

According to the United Nations Development Programme (2003), policy formulation in Zambia is now much more human-centred. Human-centred policy-making approaches are valuable in as much as they allow the maximum participation of all relevant stakeholders in the policy-making cycle.

However, policy formulation in Zambia is still vested in the hands of the president, and then Parliament. Presidential pronouncements at public rallies are still taken as official policy. Once this occurs, government officials in a certain ministry responsible for the specific issue concerned will be compelled to arrive at a working policy and thereafter present it to Parliament so that it is backed up by legislation. In cases where the president has not made any pronouncements relating to policy, government ministries will research an area of concern that may be lacking or requires certain changes, and then present proposals to Parliament. Also, a Member of Parliament can pass a private motion on an area that needs serious attention. Parliamentary Committees are also important in informing policy processes in the country as citizens are given opportunities to participate in policy-making by engaging with such bodies.

Profile of monitoring and evaluation in Zambia

The need for monitoring and evaluation is on the increase in Zambia. It can be argued that the bulk of M&E activities result from the donor or non-governmental-led initiatives. Donor-driven demands for delivered targets (either to keep track of disbursed monies for projects or to ascertain the viability of specific programmes) seem to be the main rationale for the exercise in Zambia. However, the thrust for monitoring and evaluation is also gaining ground in government agencies as well as Civil Society Organisations (CSOs), owing to a number of development initiatives in the country that require M&E expertise in both sectors, for instance the Poverty Reduction Strategy Papers (PRSP).[4]

With regard to the PRSP, the Zambian government assigned a significant role to civil society in its formulation. The avowed intentions and expectations are that in order to sustain the participatory nature of the PRSP process that began with its formulation, civil society will continue to be an integral part of the government's monitoring and evaluation process as well (Seshamani, 2003). In the past, National Development Plans, Surveys and Censuses, Social and Economic Reports of the Ministry of Finance and the Annual Reports of various government ministries were in a way used as tools to monitor and evaluate government performance. These instruments were helpful in providing base-line information for government planning. It is safe to say that the need for planning at independence in 1964 also necessitated the quest for M&E, albeit the culture had not been as elaborate as in the present times.

However, between 1991 and 2001, again it seems that all care was thrown to the wind as planning, through the Development Plans was abandoned for 'crisis management' in the name of 'adjustment' and 'stabilisation'. The government in its Fifth National Development Plan of 2006 seems to echo these sentiments:

> The re-emergence of planning following nearly two decades of the preoccupation with stabilisation and adjustment signals the realisation of several realities that the government shares with like-minded bilateral and multilateral bodies as well as civil society. Principal among these is the recognition that in spite of reasonable growth during the years of structural reforms, poverty still remains pervasive (Government of Republic of Zambia, 2006:18).

For the present government, instruments like the PRSP, the Transitional National Development Plan (TNDP) and the Fifth National Development Plan (FNDP) all help to serve as frameworks to monitor and evaluate progress in the various sectors of the country. However, the government through the Cabinet Office and the Public Service Management Division also attempts to strengthen policy formulation, implementation, monitoring and evaluation procedures (Government of the Republic of Zambia, 2002). Consultation with stakeholders in the policy development process is slowly gaining ground in Zambia, after fifteen years of political pluralism. Also, civil society's efforts that were blunted during the one-party state have also found expression in the present era.

Conclusion

Both the government and organs of civil society need the mechanism of monitoring and evaluation to help them gauge or measure the impact of their programmatic interventions on the recipients' livelihoods as well as the outcomes of such initiatives. In concluding this chapter, it is reaffirmed here that monitoring and evaluation development activities provide government officials, development managers and civil society with better means for learning from past experience, improving service delivery, planning and allocating resources, and demonstrating results as part of accountability to key stakeholders. Within the development community, there is a strong focus on results. This helps to explain the growing interest in M&E (World Bank, 2004). Furthermore, M&E is strongly linked to policy development which is also tied to human development. This chapter examined the process of monitoring and evaluation, and how it plays a critical role in aiding human development efforts in Zambia. It also looked at the related activities of policy formulation and implementation, and analysis.

Notes

1. For example, the Mulungushi Reforms that led to the nationalisation of Zambia's industries were announced at the Mulungushi Rock of Authority in Kabwe, at one of the various UNIP General Councils.

2. Kenneth Kaunda was a very emotional president and had a quick temper. At press conferences, he would immediately tell journalists who had asked him tough questions to 'shut up' and 'sit down'. One classic case involved a journalist from a Western news agency who provoked this paraphrased remark from him: 'Young lady, you are very beautiful but have no brains, sit down!' Kaunda would also publicly refer to rational thinkers or anyone that dared challenge him as 'stupid idiots'. He was also known to openly weep in public, especially when speaking on the liberation of Southern Africa.

3. During this era there was a strong emphasis on social and economic planning via the various development plans. The Emergency Development Plan (EDP) was launched in 1964 by the government, and a year later, the Transitional Development Plan (TDP) was finalised. In 1966, the First National Development Plan (FNDP) became operational. The last Development Plan in the single-party period was the Fourth National Development Plan of 1989-93.

4. The Poverty Reduction Strategy Paper (PRSP) approach, initiated by the IMF and the World Bank in 1999, results in a comprehensive country-based strategy for poverty reduction. It aims to provide the crucial link between national public actions, donor support, and the development outcomes needed to meet the United Nations' Millennium Development Goals (MDGs) centred on halving poverty by 2015. The government of Zambia approved the country's PRSP in 2002. Five core principles underlie the PRSP approach. It must be:

    1. *Country-driven,* promoting national ownership of strategies through broad-based participation of civil society;
    2. *Result-oriented* and focused on outcomes that will benefit the poor;

3. *Comprehensive* in recognising the multidimensional nature of poverty;
4. *Partnership-oriented*, involving co-ordinated participation of development partners (government, domestic stakeholders, and external donors); and
5. Based on *a long-term perspective* for poverty reduction (IMF, 2005).

Chapter 7

THE SOCIAL WORK PROFESSION AND HUMAN DEVELOPMENT IN ZAMBIA

Introduction

This chapter discusses the profession of social work as it relates to human development and also pays attention to another allied discipline, community work. It then shows how social work helps to foster human development; by the way social work practice elevates human wellbeing in society, and argues that social work, among other professions, is pivotal to the reduction of life threatening conditions in Zambia and is a *sine qua non* for the country's overall development process.

The helping professions

Helping professions are primarily tilted towards the enhancement of human functioning and progress in society. Their raison d'être is human wellbeing and in this case social work, community work or social development are best suited to offer solutions to various social problems affecting individuals, families, groups and communities in Zambia. Falling in the orbit of helping professions, there are also a number of disciplines whose work dovetails with social work's scope of intervention – social welfare, youth work, child work and mental health. From praxis to intervention, these helping professions can be looked upon as playing important roles in creating necessary conditions for people to be helped or to help themselves in order to attain better and well-functioning lifestyles. These professions can all be said to operate under the ambit of social welfare; in most cases, it is the social welfare system that sets the norms and standards for them. It sanctions the work of helping professions via government legislation. In the same vein, social policy provides the overarching agenda for those professions as they seek after the improvement of human conditions.

Social work is a normative profession, perhaps the most normative of the helping professions. In contrast to professions such as psychiatry, psychology and counselling, social work's historical roots are firmly grounded in concepts such as justice and fairness. Throughout its history, social work's mission has been anchored primarily, although not exclusively, in conceptions of what is just and unjust and in a collective belief about what individuals in society have a right to and owe to one another (Reamer, 1999). The evolution of social work over the last two centuries involved the formulation of distinct methods of social work intervention. These methods are all based on the use of personal skills and the application of scientific knowledge by trained professionals who work directly with clients (Midgley, 1996).

Social work has the essential attributes that make it a profession, such as a high degree of generalised and systematic knowledge, primary orientation to community interests rather that self-interest, a high degree of self-control of behaviour through codes of ethics – internalised in the process of work socialisation and through voluntary associations organised, and operated by the work specialists themselves – and systems of rewards (monetary and honorary) that are primarily a set of symbols of work achievements and thus ends in themselves (Greenwood, 1957). Any dynamic profession will develop and change according to the context it has to operate within. These changes might affect the status of the profession at any given time, but need never lead to any doubt as to the professional status of social work.

Social work's rationale

The status of social work as a helping profession is directly linked to its origins. Indeed, social work originates from humanitarian and democratic ideals. Social work practice has since the beginning been focused on meeting human needs and on developing human potential as well as resources. Therefore, social workers find themselves preoccupied with planning, estimating, applying, evaluating and modifying preventative social policies and services to individuals, groups, and communities. They intervene in numerous functional sectors, using various methodological approaches, working within a broad organisational framework and providing social services to various sectors of the population at micro, mezzo and macro levels (United Nations, 1994). These different methodological approaches or theories available for use have been developed in different situations for application in a variety of circumstances.

It is important to understand that social work steps into the breach when individuals, families, groups or communities fail to deal with stressful situations. People have different coping mechanisms and thresholds in withstanding difficulties. Modern society has its host of social problems or stressful situations which can negatively impact on people's functioning capabilities. Unemployment, illness, bereavement or divorce can all lead to people breaking down socially and psychologically. Once people are unable to deal with these problems, social work interventions can help them with some coping mechanisms.

Social work is different from other helping professions in specific ways, including the overarching mission, the client system, the focus on client-in-situation, the target of practice, and the complex of values, knowledge, and skills that make up the ethical stance of social work practice. Social work intervention, although it may include intrapsychic therapy, goes beyond personal problems of emotional or mental health. Social work's original mission was not personal but social intervention and the reform of poverty and its causes. Although this has changed in many ways, the mission is still social in nature and dealing with elements beyond the individual client (Day, 1997). Social work's efficacy lies in the professional relationship established between the social worker and the client, i.e., the person experiencing the problem:

> This relationship exists for a certain purpose and is linked to the client's needs. The relationship also has duration and is terminated once the intervention's objectives have been met. At times, the objectives may not be realised and the relationship would need to be reviewed or a referral could be made. Unlike clients in other helping professions, the social work client may be an individual, a group, a family, an organisation, neighbourhood group, or a political body. Moreover, the focus of practice is the client-in-situation. The importance of the social environment in the helping process is a stated and formal criterion unique to social work, although other helping professions surely deal with these relationships less formally. Social work considers the complex of systems that affect clients, influence their behaviour, and may create, and maintain their problems (Day, 1997:49).

According to the International Federation of Social Workers (IFSW) (2000), social work focuses on promoting social change, problem-solving in human relationships, and the empowerment and liberation of people to enhance wellbeing. Using theories of human behaviour and social systems, social work intervenes at the points where people interact with their environments. Principles of human rights and social justice are also fundamental to social work. Hepworth *et al.* (2002) delineate core elements that lie at the heart of social work, irrespective of where it is applied. These facets can be subsumed under the following conceptual domains:

1. The purpose and objectives of the profession.
2. Values, ethics, and a philosophy of direct practice.

3. Knowledge base of direct practice.
4. Methods and processes employed.

Purpose and objectives of social work

Regarding the purpose and objectives of the profession, social work practitioners serve clients towards specific objectives, while the means of accomplishing them vary according to the unique circumstances of each problematic situation. The activities of all practitioners share common goals that constitute the purpose and objectives of the profession. These goals unify the profession and assist members in avoiding the development of perspectives limited to particular settings (Hepworth *et al.*, 2002). The Council on Social Work Education (CSWE) (1995), cited in Hepworth *et al.* (2002:5-8), describes social work as having four purposes:

1. The promotion, restoration, maintenance, and enhancement of the social functioning of individuals, families, groups, organisations, and communities by helping them accomplish tasks, prevent and alleviate distress, and use resources. Social workers perform preventative, restorative and remedial functions in pursuit of this purpose. Prevention involves the timely provision of services to vulnerable persons, promoting social functioning before problems develop, and includes programmes and activities such as family planning, etc. Restoration is aimed at assisting clients in the functioning of what has been impaired by physical or mental difficulties. Remediation entails the elimination or amelioration of existing social problems.

2. The planning, formulation and implementation of social policies, services, resources, and programmes needed to meet basic human needs and support the development of human capacities.

3. The pursuit of policies, services, resources, and programmes through organisational or administrative advocacy and social or political action, to empower groups at risk and to promote social and economic justice.

4. The development and testing of professional knowledge and skills related to these purposes.

The appropriate social work model for countries like Zambia should build on the following three core themes: (1) the ecosystem (person-in-situation) perspective; (2) the problem-solving process; and (3) client-and-worker partnership. These themes reflect well-established traditions within social work and provide an integrated framework for practice with diverse populations (Compton *et al.*, 2005). Furthermore, social work in Zambia has historically followed the generalist tradition. All professions, including social work, need generalists and specialists. In social work, a generalist is a social worker whose knowledge and skills encompass a broad spectrum and who assesses problems and their solutions comprehensively (Compton *et al.*, 2005). The Zambian social worker is well placed to deal with a multiplicity of social problems on account of this generalist type of training that also allows for eclectic interventions and use of knowledge. Generalist practice is relevant to the Zambian social setting as it utilises practice processes to organise work with client systems; recognises the potential for change at multiple system levels, within human systems, between systems, and among environmental systems; views human behaviour in the context of the social environment; and integrates direct practice with social policy, and social work research activities (Dubois and Miley, 1999).

Values and ethics of social work

Like any profession, social work is underpinned by a set of values and ethics. The practising social worker is therefore bound by a code of conduct determined by these values and ethics. The purpose and objectives of social work and other professions emanate from their respective value systems. Professional values, however, are not separate from societal values. Rather, professions espouse selected societal values, and society in turn gives sanction to professions through supportive legislation, funding, delegation of responsibility for certain societal functions, and mechanisms for ensuring that those functions are adequately discharged (Hepworth *et al.*, 2002:8).

Social workers' understanding of professional values and ethics has matured considerably over the years. In earlier times, social workers' attention was focused primarily on cultivating a set of values upon which the mission of social work could be based. However, with time, the profession has nurtured and refined a set of values that have given meaning and purpose to generations of social workers' careers. Social work's enduring commitment to vulnerable and oppressed populations, and its simultaneous preoccupation with individual wellbeing and social justice, are rooted in the profession's rich value base (Reamer, 1999). Social workers have always been preoccupied with a core group of central values that served as the profession's ballast, such as the dignity, uniqueness, and worth of the person; self-determination, autonomy, respect, justice, equality, and individuation. In the 1960s (especially in the USA), social workers shifted constructs of social justice, rights and reform. The public and political mood of this turbulent period infused social work training and practice with a prominent set of values focused on social equality, welfare rights, human rights, anti-discrimination, and anti-oppression (Reamer, 1999).

Knowledge base of social work

One of the core elements of social work practice is its undergirding knowledge base. Although much of the profession's knowledge is borrowed from other disciplines in the social and behavioural sciences, it is assembled in unique ways. Moreover, many of the profession's basic concepts are unique to social work (Hepworth et al., 2002; Johnson et al., 1997). Social work's universe of knowledge, which also forms the core curriculum areas of social work education, can be subsumed under the following five categories: (i) Human behaviour and the social environment; (ii) social welfare policy and services; (iii) social work practice methods; (iv) research; and (v) field practicum (Hepworth et al., 2002; Johnson et al., 1997). In response to the mission of the profession, social workers strengthen human functioning and enhance the effectiveness of the structures in society that provide resources and opportunities for citizens. Social workers strive to release human power so that individuals can actualise their potential and contribute to the wellbeing of society. One key framework that is complementary to the knowledge base of social work is the Ecosystem Perspective.

The ecosystem perspective: systems theory

Conceptual frameworks used for social work practice should help the client-and-worker understand a problem within the context of the person-in-situation and contribute to the problem-solving process. The systems theory meets some of these requirements by shifting attention from a linear cause-and-effect relationship to the person-in-situation as an interrelated whole. The person-in-situation is a whole, in which the person and the situation are both cause and effect in a complex set of relationships (Compton, *et al.*, 2005). These dynamic interactions, transactions and organisational patterns are critical to the functioning of both the individual and the situation. Thus, the whole is more than the sum of its parts. In order to come to grips with the presented problem, social workers have to strive to understand the complex interaction between the client and other social systems (Compton *et al.*, 2005).

The methods of social work

There are various methods of social work falling within the realm of what is known as direct practice. These include casework, group work, community work, social work research, social policy and social work administration.

Casework

Casework means intervention with individuals focusing on counselling or work to help people overcome personal, intrapsychic, or systemic problems that prevent people from fulfilling their potential. Mental health and child guidance counselling exemplify this kind of social work (Day, 1999). Clifford (1966) is of the opinion that the practice of social casework in Africa, as indeed anywhere else, is more difficult than it appears to the uninitiated. The mechanics or procedures for social casework are difficult to perform externally and they appear deceptively easy. However, what is quite unique in this situation is that Africa has made rather more use of the group in dealing with the individual and the African social worker often has to execute his/her casework through the family or the 'tribe'. Although the tribal issue has diminished in Zambia since Clifford's study, it is quite true that casework does not follow the same patterns as in the West. Even though social work was imported from Europe, certain trends regarding casework emerged in Africa and Zambia, whereby its services were not fragmented into different specialisations like in the West.

Therefore, social casework in Africa or Zambia means helping people and perhaps their families to achieve a measure of independence and self-reliance in contexts that are becoming increasingly specialised and individualistic (Clifford, 1966). However, it would be a mistake to imagine that the African social worker has an instinctive grasp of the 'tribal' landscape on the continent, as he or she will need to study his/her society. The mere fact that people grow up in a particular society sometimes means that familiarity blinds people to the essential patterns of culture. Thus training for social casework in Africa, no less than the casework itself, has to be adapted to meet the needs of the continent. The courses have to be designed in such a way that they produce a caseworker who is flexible in approach and adapts his/her methods to a variety of different circumstances (Clifford, 1966).

Group work

In looking at social work with groups, it is important to bear in mind that a membership group is any setting to which a person belongs. In a sense, membership in a group is clearly defined, as a person either belongs to it or not. Membership is thus a boundary condition. Some people are marginal members of a group. Full psychological membership in a group occurs only when a person is positively attracted to being a member and is positively accepted as a member (Zastrow, 1992). Further, there is a difference between voluntary and involuntary membership. Voluntary membership occurs when an individual deliberately chooses to belong to a certain group, such as a fraternity or athletic team. In other situations a person may have little or no choice about becoming a group member. Social workers often work with groups whose membership is involuntary, as in prisons, mental hospitals and residential treatment facilities (Zastrow, 1992).

Community work

The first major rationale for community work is to help people take action on specific issues of importance to them. These will almost invariably involve the influence of resources, either held, for example, by local authorities, or to be found within communities themselves. The development of political responsibility is the second function of community work, while the third is communal coherence (Thomas 1984, cited in Smith, 2006). Thomas isolated five strands or approaches in his study of community work in the early 1980s:

> *Community Action* focuses on the organisation of those adversely affected by the decisions, or non-decisions of public and private bodies and by more general structural characteristics of society. The strategy aims to promote collective action to challenge existing socio-political and economic structures and explain the power realities of people's situations

and, through this twin pronged approach, develop both critical perspectives of the status quo and alternative bases of power.

Community Development emphasises self-help, mutual support, the building up of neighbourhood integration, the development of neighbourhood capacities for problem-solving and self-representation, and the promotion of collective action to bring a community's preferences to the attention of political decision-makers.

Social Planning is concerned with the assessment of community needs and problems and the systematic planning of strategies for meeting them. Social planning comprises the analysis of social conditions, social policies and agency services; the setting of goals and priorities; the design of service programmes and the mobilisation of appropriate resources; and the implementation and evaluation of services and programmes.

Community Organisation involves the collaboration of separate community or welfare agencies with or without the additional participation of statutory authorities, in the promotion of joint initiatives.

Service Extension is a strategy which seeks to extend agency operations and services by making them more relevant and accessible. This includes extending services into the community, giving these services and the staff who are responsible for giving them a physical presence in a neighbourhood (Thomas 1984 in Smith, 2006:8-9).

From this summary, community development emerges as the most favoured type of intervention in Africa. Given the history of colonial autocracy and post-colonial dictatorships, it is not surprising that community development was preferred over, for instance, community action, though this assertion is not in any way meant to diminish the importance of community development.

Community development

The key purpose of community development work is to build cohesive, active and sustainable communities based on social justice and mutual respect. It aims to re-establish the community as the location of significant human experience and the meeting of human needs, rather than rely on the larger, more inhumane and less accessible structures of among others, the welfare state, the global economy, bureaucracy and professional elites (Ife, 1995). Community development is a process that is important in raising the quality of life of communities, through planned intervention, underpinned skills and knowledge-base that inform the change process. Also:

> Community development can be described as a way of strengthening civil society by prioritising the actions of communities and their perspectives in the development of social, economic and environmental policy and action. It seeks the empowerment of local communities. Community development strengthens the capacity of people as active citizens through their communities, organisations and networks on the one hand, and the capacity of individuals (public, private and NGOs) on the other, to work in dialogue with citizens to shape and determine change in their communities. It plays a crucial role in supporting active democratic life by promoting the autonomous voice of disadvantaged and vulnerable communities. Its core values are concerned with human rights, social inclusion, equality and respect for diversity. It has specific skills and knowledge base (International Association of Community Development, 2005:1).

In Zambia, as in other parts of Africa, community development must also reflect indigenous experience and culture, for example the existence of strong family and community roots. This requires an African/Zambian understanding of the meaning of 'development' at a community level, which recognises and respects basic human rights for all. It also requires appreciation of the fact that rapid urbanisation in Africa has placed great strains on both rural and urban communities and that rural development policies should be strengthened with a view to slowing the rate of movement from the rural to urban areas (International Association of Community Development, 2005). It is imperative that community development workers, trainers and consultants get appropriate support to foster sustainable community development. This should be in the form of:

(i) education and training, including provision of lifelong learning opportunities with appropriate levels of funding and support;

(ii) access to appropriate information technology and learning materials and equipment; and

(iii) access to and knowledge of relevant information and resources to enable continuous learning (International Association of Community Development, 2005).

The historical roots of community development

Community development's origins in Africa and indeed Zambia are traceable to the colonial era when efforts aimed at developing the colonies through projects such as literacy training and nutrition, for example, were mooted. Initially, community development gained ground in West African countries and was referred to as mass education. However, at a major conference of Colonial Welfare Administrators in Cambridge in 1948, the term 'community development' was formally adopted to replace 'mass education'. The conference also formulated a definition of community development which emphasised the importance of self-help and self-determination as its basic theoretical concepts. This definition was widely adopted in the developing countries. Under the guidance of the Colonial Office, community development was extended to other parts of Africa and the British Empire (Midgley, 1995). Already at that time, a number of experiments along these lines had been made by individual district officers and NGOs in various African countries. Governments had already embarked on educational programmes: in Egypt the initiative begun by an NGO was taken over by the new Ministry of Social Affairs in 1941, and made as its starting-point a national programme on rural centres and improvement of societies in 1946. In 1948, the Gold Coast (now Ghana) there were moves towards mass education in the countryside in 1950 (Obbo, 1990:107).

There are two traditions relating to community development's genesis, British and American. In Britain it was taken as a movement designed to promote better living for the whole community with the active participation, and if possible on the initiative, of the community, but, if this initiative was not forthcoming spontaneously, by the use of techniques for arousing and stimulating it in order to secure an active and enthusiastic response (Batten, 1957). In the USA, community development denoted a continuous or intermittent process of social action by which people of a community organised themselves informally or formally for democratic planning and action; defined their common and group 'felt needs' and problems; made group and individual plans to meet their felt needs and solved their problems; executed these plans with maximum reliance upon resources found within the community and supplemented community resources when necessary with services and material assistance from governmental or private agencies, outside the community (Obbo, 1990). From the British definition there was stress on self-help, attention to the people's felt needs and to the social traditions, and other aspects of the community as a whole, while the American definition's focus was on the participation of people, provision of technical and other services in ways which encouraged initiative, self-help and mutual-help.

Many (if not all) Commonwealth African countries adopted the British definition as well as approach to community development (Obbo, 1990).

Social work research

Social work as a helping profession is also predisposed to scientific enquiry as it seeks ways and means of arriving at better and well-informed interventions. Solutions to societies' existing problems cannot be attained if there is no rigorous application of both practitioners' and academics' minds to such anomalies. Therefore, social work's body of knowledge is constantly replenished not only by training and practice, but more importantly by research. Social work research is steeped in the old traditions of social science research that engages in scientific enquiry in order to provide answers about social phenomena (Grinnell, 1993). The scientific method as applied to social work research is sometimes referred to as the positivistic approach or the problem-solving method. The principal alternative to the positivistic approach to social work research is the naturalistic approach (Grinnell, 1993). Naturalistic enquiry studies real-world situations as they unfold naturally and is non-manipulative, unobtrusive, and non-controlling, as well as focusing on openness to whatever emerges. It avoids predetermined constraints on outcomes (Patton, 1990). In social work, the research or structured inquiry is applied to social work problems. Therefore, social work research is a scientific inquiry about a social work problem that provides an answer contributing to an increase in the body of generalised knowledge about social work concerns (Grinnell, 1993). Social work research is goal-orientated in that it seeks solutions to a prevailing societal anomaly:

> The purpose of all social work research is to answer questions or solve problems and each research study is a problem-driven enterprise. The research process is composed of six identifiable and interrelated phases:
>
> 1. Selecting a problem area for investigation.
> 2. Within this problem area, formulating a specific research question and/or hypothesis.
> 3. Choosing an overall research design and sampling plan to guide the collection of data on the research question or hypothesis.
> 4. Selecting one or more particular methods of data collection.
> 5. Collecting and analysing the data.

6. Writing a report of the research findings on the basis of which the research study will be evaluated (Grinnell, 1993:4-5).

Social work research is critical to social policy interventions, especially in its findings, as they eventually inform and fortify social policy's goals. For Zambia, social work research's invaluable contributions are numerous. Some of these could eventually sharpen the focus and rationale of not only social policy, but also of general public policy as well. Indeed, the plethora of social problems facing Zambia, such as unemployment, elder abuse, child abuse and neglect, the plight of pensioners and of street children etc., require solutions that have been ferreted out by social work research among others.

Social policy

Policy implications are evident in professional practice at all system levels. Systematically, decisions are made that affect empowerment in both subsystem structures and suprasystem structures. This reciprocity means that social workers influence welfare policies and, in turn, social policies influence social workers' practice of their profession. Social workers also make policy decisions at the micro level that determine the quality of their interactions with clients (Dubois and Miley, 1999). For example, decisions about which methods and strategies to use with a given client are really policy decisions. Social workers play a vital role in the domain of public policy. For instance, they can and should be committed to promoting citizen entitlements that empower social structures, enhance social functioning, and ensure social justice at the provincial and national levels. Also, direct-service workers are policy-makers. In fact, policy-making is not a casual addendum to direct service. Selecting who receives services and choosing the type and duration of intervention are 'street-level' policy-based choices (Dubois and Miley, 1999).

Social work administration

Social work administration is professional practice to plan programmes, work for legislation, or administer organisations. In this area, social workers direct or become planners in organisations, or they may be legislative advisors or lobbyists (Day, 1999).

Historical development of social work

Social change is one primary force that led to the development of social welfare systems and policies as well as social work practice in industrialised Europe. Social change is not always smooth and is not devoid of casualties, as can be deduced from the debilitating social conditions that followed the Industrial Revolution of 18th and 19th century Europe. The Industrial Revolution, propelled, among other things, by the capitalist mode of production, gave birth to social welfare systems and the profession of social work. The Industrial Revolution was not only related to changes in the economic structure of society, as illustrated by the rise of industrialists and the diminished role of the landed aristocracy, but was also associated with social and political changes. The type of capitalism then could be said to have been 'crude' and was defined at the time by the doctrine of *laissez-faire*, where the market forces were supposed to be self-regulating, without government intervention. Factory owners in this scenario were bent on exploiting the workers who worked and lived in the most appalling conditions.

Social change that gave impetus to the Industrial Revolution also led to population increase. With population rising to unprecedented levels, wealth was created not for the mass of the people but for only the privileged few, while the rest of the populace lived in abject poverty and squalor. The passing of the feudal order to capitalism in Europe saw the emancipation of labour from the landlords. It also meant that people were liberated from rural environments and moved to urban settings. The new urban climate, where there were no guaranteed safety-nets, became a breeding ground for social maladies. The Industrial Revolution was not of great consequence for the form of ownership of the means of production, but was crucial in changing the forms of control over the labour process (the two are not the same). This upheaval created a large population that had nothing to sell but their labour, and received cash wages for work done (Thompson, 1968). The Industrial Revolution imposed a regularity, routine, and monotony which contrasted sharply with the more varied patterns of previous times. The majority of people who had to move to urban areas were not prepared for the massive upheavals that accompanied such moves, or the fundamental changes in their lifestyle. For most working people, the crucial experience of the Industrial Revolution was felt in terms of changes in the nature and intensity of exploitation (Thompson, 1968).

Towards reform and relief

Initially, the church was responsible for looking after the poor in Europe. Thereafter, social welfare was organised by the state. Early social welfare policies in Europe can be traced back to the Elizabethan Poor Laws as was explained in Chapter 1. Day (1997:110) observes that these famous Poor Laws, which were a recodification of earlier laws governing social welfare, legalised and formalised England's responsibility to the poor. She argues that the importance of these laws did not lie in the amount of money spent for the care of the poor, but rather in their defining of social welfare as part of the national labour policy. Social work then emerged after social welfare policies were established by the state. There are two strands of thought that try to explain the beginnings of social welfare and social work. One view is that social welfare policies were designed for circumventing civil disorder and reinforcing work norms. Piven and Cloward (1974) are renowned for articulating this position. They assert that the maintenance of civil order and the enforcement of work were necessary for maintaining stability in the capitalist system. This view argues that the state's purpose was to regulate society. The second strand actually believes in the benevolence of the state in mitigating the plight of the poor. Both views have their merits and demerits, but what is important to note is that there were varying and competing ideas on the part of the state, voluntary associations and the church as to how society could best respond to the negative effects of social change in general, and the Industrial Revolution in particular.

An early British approach to social work is to be found in the Charity Organisation Society (COS), established in 1869 as one answer to the question of how to tackle poverty in the midst of Victorian plenty. This thinking rested on an understanding that charity when given indiscriminately and thoughtlessly demoralised as it encouraged habits of thriftlessness and dependence, which the Society considered the root causes of poverty and pauperism (Woodroofe, 1968). The founders and leaders of the Charity Organisation Society were drawn largely from the middle and upper classes, and the organisation had aristocratic patronage. A large number of the organisation's social workers were well-off, middle class women, who had the opportunity to devote time and resources to charity work (Parry *et al.*, 1979). In these early days, the British government's approach towards poverty was punitive and repressive.

As charity foundations sprung up in Britain, another type of help came through the guilds, which promoted interests like trade, craftsmanship, mercantilism, or simply welfare. Also, wives of factory owners championed other forms of relief work. This gender-biased approach to relief still predominates in present times, as a greater proportion of women than men are still attracted to the profession of social work. Prior to the emergence of the COS, the British government had tried to control poverty, as earlier mentioned, through repressive means, but it later attempted to encourage the church and voluntary organisations to be involved in the amelioration of poverty. Ultimately, the government reluctantly accepted its obligation to help poor people. In the process, the COS was refining its haphazard philanthropic interventions into a more theoretically informed activity that culminated in social work.

The profession of social work came into being initially through the method of casework, which predominated at the time:

> Thus it can be seen that social casework, beginning as a by-product of the work of the Charity Organisation Society, changed quite considerably during the first three decades of its history. By the end of the century, it had broken free from its Lady Bountiful traditions. Originally based on the concept of charity, it had evolved from a set of rules to guide volunteers in their work as friendly visitors of the poor into a philosophy of which embodied many of the principles of modern casework and training from one generation of social workers to another. But in spite of this, social casework was very much the product of nineteenth century individualism (Woodroofe, 1968:54).

The forces of social change definitely created conditions for the emergence of social work in Europe. The situation there in the 19th century is almost similar to the one that unfolded later in Zambia and Southern Africa, although there were unique catalysts for the emergence of social work in the South.

Relevance of social work in Least Developed Countries (LDCs) and Southern Africa

The unique character of Least Developed Countries (LDCs) was explained in earlier chapters. The relevance of social work practice in such environments, regarding its applicability and efficacy, needs to be demonstrated. The beginnings of social work in LDCs, especially Southern African countries, can be seen as an auxiliary of colonialism. The missionary influence in social work's development is also quite pre-eminent in this regard. A cursory appraisal of the emergence of social work in some Southern African countries will bring this fact to the fore. For example, there were no organised services in Namibia until 1951, but owing to the remonstrations by Christian churches in favour of the establishment of social work services, the South West Africa Administration (under South Africa), made moves to create them. It appointed the first social worker in 1953 in Windhoek, the capital city. A home for children in need of care (Children's Home) was later created in 1954 (Grobler, 2007). Later, a separate Department for indigenous Africans was established by the South African regime and referred to as the Department of Bantu Administration and Development. This arrangement formed part of the apartheid regime of South Africa (Grobler, 2007).

In South Africa, the motivation for social work services was racially inclined as well, although there were also various factors that should not be overlooked such as industrialisation. Industrialisation was cardinal in transforming South Africa's social and economic relations, which added impetus to three critical movements. First, a huge influx of foreign, mainly British capital put the mining industry on the world map and spearheaded the highly centralised character of the industry. Secondly, there was a rush of European immigrant labour, which supplied the semi-skilled and skilled labour needed by the mines. Thirdly, there was the dismantling of the African peasantry, which became the chief source of cheap unskilled labour (Marais, 1998). Many Afrikaners (descendants of the Dutch colonisers who first landed on the shores of the Cape of Good Hope in 1652) lost out in the industrialisation of the country. This situation in turn led to what came to be termed as 'the poor white problem'. Also, the economic depression of the late 1920s and early 30s compounded the already difficult living conditions of the Afrikaners.

Initially, responses to Afrikaner poverty came from the voluntary and religious sectors. Religious organisations such as the Dutch Reformed Church or organs of civil society, for example Afrikaner women's groups, were primarily actively involved in the amelioration of the living circumstances of poor white people. The state only became involved in 1910 after the creation of the Union of South Africa. Provisional schemes of relief were used to mitigate the plight of poor whites and concerted efforts got underway to create work opportunities for them. This undertaking was pronounced after the government of General Hertzog came into power in 1924 (McKendrick, 1987:11). Hare and McKendrick (1976:76) summarise South Africa's welfare scene from colonial conquest to industrialisation in the following manner:

> Prior to the 19th Century, there were no organised social welfare services as such. For Blacks, the extended family system provided for the human

needs of all people in accordance with tribal custom. During the first two centuries of colonial rule, White pioneer families also provided for their own needs. In the 19th century the Dutch Reformed Church, to which most Afrikaners belonged, was very active in early efforts to establish a variety of social welfare services, and other religious denominations, Protestants, Catholics, and Jews, followed suit. Gradually, voluntary welfare organisations, some with international affiliations, such as the Red Cross and the Salvation Army, appeared in the Cape Colony.

From the outset, the broader welfare field was defined along racial lines, so that the profession of social work and later on social work education came to be almost the sole preserve of the white population group. Thus in 1928, at the instigation of the Dutch Reformed Church, the Carnegie Corporation of New York was persuaded to fund a new approach to white indigence referred to as 'a scientific investigation into the causes of white poverty, its extent, and the means by which it could be reduced' (McKendrick, 1987:12-13). Thereafter, reasons for establishing social work practice came out of the 'National Conference on the Poor White Problem' which took place at Kimberley in 1934, and resulted in 1937 in the creation of a State Department of Social Welfare, which employed social workers as well as subsidised similar posts in the voluntary sector (Hare and McKendrick, 1976).

Zimbabwe had similar inspirations for introducing a social welfare system and social work services during British colonial rule. During this period, both services represented an almost wholesale transplant of the British experience (Kaseke, 1998). However, in Botswana the racial question was somewhat muted as the British colonialists did not see any economic value in the territory (this was before the discovery of diamonds in later years). The provision of social services under British rule in the Protectorate of Bechuanaland (as it was referred to before independence in 1966) was a response by the colonial power to the emerging social problems associated with the new socio-economic order – the introduction of the market economy, which replaced the subsistence and self-sufficient economy, and the process of urbanisation that resulted in the emergence of towns and the consequent rural-urban drift (Mwansa, 2007). The rural-urban drifters were not guaranteed jobs or accommodation in the towns and this situation created a recipe for social problems such as juvenile delinquency, high unemployment rates, teenage pregnancies, alcoholism and suicide (Hedenquist, 1991 in Mwansa, 2007). It was therefore necessary to introduce social services that would respond to the emerging urban situation. In 1946, a Welfare Unit was created within the

Department of Education that was headed by a Welfare Officer. The fact of employing only one government employee in the Welfare Department reflects the extent of Britain's negligence in developing social services during this period (Mwansa, 2007).

The above description points to the foreign orientation of social welfare services and social work in particular. It also shows that British rule in Southern Africa almost had a uniform approach in regard to the establishment of social welfare and social work, while in South Africa and Namibia there was in addition the racist ideology of apartheid which was more intense than British racism. There were also the Portuguese colonies of Angola and Mozambique that had different sets of institutions. The relevance of social work has constantly been called into question by various African scholars because of this historical fact of its colonial origins. But it is argued in this discussion that social welfare and social work services are critical to the development of LDCs in general and Southern Africa in particular. Indigenisation or locally appropriate practice however requires attention to social work curricula, and more broadly, education. New innovations in social work education that reflect as well as responding to local needs are needed urgently in countries of the South. Tested models and research in areas of human development and social intervention are required so as to proffer local solutions, as opposed to using borrowed and foreign tools, as Nyirenda (1975) rightly asserted. In this way, praxis will be well informed and easily garnered to deal with issues that are prevalent in LDCs such as poverty, social exclusion and gender-based violence.

Social work curricula and education

The word curriculum (a word derived from the Latin *curere*, to run) refers not only to the official list of courses offered by a school, but also to the purposes, content, activities, and organisation of the educational programmes that are actually created in schools by teachers, students, and administrators. Educational curricula should reflect the pulse of a nation, for instance its psyche, culture, traditions, notions, triumphs, aspirations and Indigenous Knowledge Systems. Hence, arguably, the most important influence in social work curriculum planning is going to be the perceptions of the social worker's role in society. In addition, social work curricula should mirror the range of conceptual viewpoints and theoretical perspectives that are germane to the profession; social work's effectiveness depends on the growth of knowledge within the profession and allied disciplines (Nichols-Casebolt *et al.*, 2000).

The domain of social work therefore needs to be delineated in relation to its place in the social structure, its objectives, and the nature of its societal sanction (Osei-Hwedie, 1996). In Zambia the social work curriculum really needs to reflect the changing nature of society and societal problems. This is critical for practitioners as interventions, skills and methods have to evolve continuously and keep abreast with changes in society. It goes without saying that the predominant features shaping the aims of social work education are the purposes of the profession in society, and the roles as well as functions that social workers perform or aspire to perform (McKendrick, 1990). When the changes in the country and the welfare sector are examined, the role of social work educators has to be, among others, that of yeast, to borrow McKendrick's (1990) terminology. They have to give rise to new ideas, critically examine developments and lead practitioner colleagues towards new achievements. Such robust undertakings could essentially lead to new ways of practising the profession, and possibly end up in an Africanised social work practice and professional education that is both constantly touching base with, and questioning, global dimensions.

Africanising social work practice and education

There is an urgent need to deliberately reify the African perspective in regard to social work practice and social work education on the continent. This perspective neatly ties up with the notion of indigenisation of practice. Indigenisation refers to the idea that theories, values and philosophies which underlie practice, must be from local sources to lead development of practices based on the needs and resources of particular people, and their socio-economic and cultural environment. It is conceptualised in terms of appropriateness, which means that social work professional practice must be relevant to the local context (Osei-Hwedie and Rankopo, 2007). Therefore, one of the functions of social work practice and professional education in an African context would be to reconsider the mandate of the profession and then begin to suggest behaviour that directly addresses the conditions of Africa and not that prevailing elsewhere. This intent may be embodied in the conceptualisation of social work's mandate (Ankrah, 1987). Notably, social work needs to actively repudiate as its primary domain of operation the dysfunctioning elements of African populations in this new era. Its mandate should dictate a future and a change orientation, rather than one that constrains it to maintaining systems. Such a mandate, in essence, would reverse a long-standing order priority in social work functioning, from remedial, preventative and developmental functions to development, prevention and remedy, as proposed by the United Nations Conference of Ministers in 1968 (Ankrah, 1987:9-10).

This type of social work will not clash with the quest for an *African Renaissance*, currently being propagated by Africans. Indeed, this brand of social work would reflect initiatives in Africa such as *The New Partnership for Africa's Development* (NEPAD). South Africa's former President Thabo Mbeki has been vociferous on this issue and led delegations from Africa to meet leaders and seek partners in the developed world so as to put NEPAD into motion. Social work in Africa needs to arrive at theories that could help other policy-makers understand the complexities of the African continent as well. For instance, social work's niche, which is the analysis of individuals, families, groups, communities and societies, would be brought to the fore, so as to help policy-makers appreciate the fact that NEPAD cannot succeed on the economic front without due consideration of the social dimensions.

Skill on the part of social workers in comprehending and disseminating social development theories would also add value to the debates as well as offering possible solutions for, among other things, the fight against poverty in Zambia and Africa as a whole. Social development's unique focus on the release of human development potential in order to prevent, eliminate or alleviate social and economic problems and inequalities (Ndonko, 1991) could easily be translated by social workers because of their training. However, such training must again be relevant and be in sync with African ideals, hence the need for informed theories that could enable African social workers to have a broader understanding of African issues. So practice must follow societal knowledge, ideas and resources, and any imported ideas and knowledge must fit the local context. In this way, it translates into practice within a socio-cultural context (Osei-Hwedie, 1993; Midgley, 1983; in Osei-Hwedie and Rankopo, 2007).

The proper basis of social work practice must be knowledge about a society and its needs. This knowledge should form the basis of social theory. At the same time, the issue is not simply to reject wholesale whatever has been learnt elsewhere (Osei-Hwedie, 2002). The people-environment relationship must be defined as a response to a specific psychological, spiritual, economic, social and political context. Increasing social work's effectiveness in Africa means constantly improving professional expertise in relation to local needs, establishing greater legitimacy, and improving social work's contributions to society (Osei-Hwedie, 2002).

Conclusion

To conclude, therefore, it is important to note that adhering to an African form of social work may help to disentangle it from the European value base that was originally woven around the profession. This situation could also allow for a more participatory, emancipatory and context-driven brand of social work to emerge, and push forward human development in Zambia and Southern Africa. The next chapter summarises the discussions of the book.

Chapter 8

CONCLUDING NOTES ON SOCIAL POLICY AND HUMAN DEVELOPMENT IN ZAMBIA

Introduction

This chapter reiterates some points that were raised in earlier discussions relating to Zambia's social policy and human development prospects. Some views that were brought to the fore in preceding chapters are going to be interwoven with final arguments of the book that are presented in this section, in order to chart a way forward in regard to the country's overall development. In undertaking this endeavour, projections will be made and policy alternatives offered regarding human wellbeing in Zambia.

This book has shown that the major obstacle to human development in Zambia is poverty, the main stumbling-block against people's wellbeing in the country. The book's intention was not to collate a litany of failures and ineffectual institutional arrangements in Zambia; it was not a doomsday exercise. However, the sad reality is that there have been few successes to actually report on, and it is hoped that justice has been done to some shining examples of innovations that were directed at removing Zambia from quagmires of hopelessness, despair and dereliction, especially after independence and after Frederick Chiluba was ejected from the political arena. Nevertheless, the main motivation for writing this book was to prick the conscience of Zambia's politicians, policy-makers, academics, civil society actors and the general populace, in order to perhaps spur them into action against the general socio-economic malaise in the country. It is also hoped that Zambians can begin to approach issues related to human development in a more sober and strategic manner, whilst having a high sense of urgency.

The Preamble of this book noted that Zambians have suffered grave indignities due to the persistence, aggravation and the very existence of extreme poverty, mainly characterised by low nutrition rates in the country. However, hunger is but one face of poverty, while discrimination, poor health, vulnerability, insecurity, and a lack of personal and professional development opportunities are all manifestations of the problems faced by Zambians (United Nations, 2006). Do these facts and trends suggest a regression in social justice in the country? The answer to this question, if considered within the framework of the Charter of the United Nations and the Universal Declaration of Human Rights, is unequivocal. Zambians experiencing dire poverty are deprived of a number of fundamental rights invoked in the Charter and enumerated in the Universal Declaration (United Nations, 2006). Furthermore, the notion of human rights, when juxtaposed against human development and poverty, brings forth interesting dynamics. For instance, it can be argued that poverty goes beyond the inability of individuals to meet their basic needs, but is also a silent threat to human security. It also entails a precarious existence subject to hurtful disruptions. Therefore, pervasive poverty in Zambia should also be seen as a threat to security, because it is an element of structural violence that can easily explode into open conflict (Mutesa and Nchito, 2005).

However, the suffering borne by the bulk of Zambians is unnecessary and uncalled for. In many instances, Zambia's poverty trap is self-induced. Zambia is not a poor country when its natural resources profile is laid out. This discussion emphatically states that Zambia should not remain poor and there is no need for this state of affairs to continue. These are not simply outlandish assertions or polemics, but sentiments based on empirical evidence. It is further argued that Zambia should not be typified as a poor country by those who wield political power on the one hand and those who are referred to as 'common people' on the other. Zambians should not continue to cast their country in this mould as it feeds into their psyche and generates a sense of fatalism in the nation. In any event, this characterisation also goes to solidify the notion that Zambians are indeed helpless beings, and yet there are so many natural resources that they can turn into viable economic assets, land being on top of the list.

This text observes that first and foremost, development is an attitudinal issue and is given currency in the way people of a particular country approach it. After travelling the length and breadth of Zambia, as well as residing in certain parts of the country, the author can safely say that there is no province that is poor, when the net wealth of its natural resources is considered. From the sprawling hills and valleys of the Eastern Province, the escarpments and plateaux of Central Zambia, the swamps and rivers of Luapula, the green hills and waterfalls of the Northern Province (which also resembles the terrain around the equator in certain parts, and usually has high rainfall patterns), the forests, rivers and grasslands of the North-Western Province, the waterfalls, rich soils, rivers and lakes of Southern Province, to the forests, sands, rivers and flood-plains of the Western Province, the country is bestowed with the best array of natural resources that nature can offer a people. Literally every province in Zambia has a river system or waterways, fertile soil, grasslands, and forests. The country's agricultural potential is boundless. Some countries have to constantly grapple with nature's negative forces such as desertification, lack of water and infertile soils. This is not the case for Zambia. Granted, there have been droughts here and there, but these have not persisted for decades. Also, Zambia's landmass is huge in comparison to its population density. Indeed, the country's entire population could be relocated into three provinces without even exerting pressure on the natural habitat. So there is no scarcity of land, and the question is not whether it is arable or not as Zambia is blessed with fertile soilsAdditionally, every province in Zambia has mineral potential, ranging from coal, cobalt, copper, diamonds, gold, iron ore, manganese, lead, nickel, silver, zinc to various semi-precious stones such as amethyst, aquamarine, citrine, emeralds, garnets and tourmaline. The country has viable uranium deposits, and now there is talk of oil; the list is endless. In the one-party state era, some areas which were regarded as opposition strongholds such as the Western and North-Western provinces were not considered for development, as a way of punishment. It is no accident that some of the minerals just mentioned have suddenly been 'discovered' in these areas. Therefore, Zambia requires an honest and committed leadership to turn the country's natural potential into a better life for all. The present government is at least trying, but a lot more can be done.

This book declares that Zambians were not ordained to be poor and die from hunger and curable diseases. Zambia should never accept the misplaced 'one dollar a day' description of its people given by the World Bank after it wreaked havoc in the country through earlier short-sighted policies such as the SAP. Zambians should also declare to the world that they want to be free from the misery of poverty. However, the decision to unshackle the country from poverty and misery should begin at the individual level. Without a doubt, the citizenry should take responsibility for its own actions. Individuals have to imbibe the work ethic and help in the building of a better Zambia. It is a fact that very many young and able-bodied persons who are just loafing around in towns are lazy and do not want to live in rural areas where they can till the land and produce food for themselves. Arguably, it is the lack of initiative or laziness on the part of individuals that has led to the abuse of the extended family system. In many instances, the extended family has been a provider for able-bodied people who are just irresponsible. When an individual becomes wealthy in such a system, he or she will be obstructed from progressing to greater heights owing to the continued giving of alms to kin – whereas in a Western individualised type of society, the person might achieve many other things because he or she has the space and latitude to invest energies into productive activities, uninterrupted by constant begging from relatives or so-called friends. The extended family system has been romanticised as well as exploited for so long, and it is high time that it is reconsidered in the light of individual success and national development.

It should not be forgotten that Zambia's poverty trap can only be dismantled by holistic and integrated interventions, with concerted efforts emanating from individuals, families, groups, and communities. It is also important that theoretical and practical dimensions of development and anti-poverty strategies are meshed together so that positive results are achieved in the country. In this regard, it is vital to first identify the point of origin of most of the country's challenges, if solutions are going to be brought to the fore.

The locus of Zambia's socio-economic challenges

The main contention of this book is that Zambia's socio-economic problems emanate primarily from the political realm and if positive change has to transpire in the country, the political establishment must be shaken to its roots and re-awakened to its roles and responsibilities, one of these being to act as the vanguard against indigence. It is this book's central argument that politics play an extremely important and decisive role in creating conditions of wellbeing in a particular country. Therefore, in this concluding chapter it is re-emphasised that Zambia's socio-economic problems, which have persisted for decades, are attributable to the failures or ineptitude of the political establishment.

The political machinery has not been used in such a way that it leads the country towards progress; this is where great efforts have to be made. As pointed out in earlier chapters, politics is vital in charting a country's development path. Those who are charged with the responsibility of managing political institutions also wield considerable power on behalf of the masses. It is these individuals who have to make critical decisions on the management of the country's resources and oversee the smooth running of agriculture, the economy, water and energy, as well as defence and security, among other sectors. Once such people fail in their duties there will be a negative ripple effect on other areas of human endeavour, since public policy and politics remain interwoven. Politics largely mediates the rules and governance structures that enable economic agents to more efficiently, optimally and securely interact to produce the desired effect of economic growth and development (Kalu, 2005).

This point is illustrated by the recent guilty verdict that was passed against the former Zambian president, Frederick Chiluba, in a civil case relating to corruption, brought against him by the Zambian government in the London High Court held in circuit in Zambia. In a damning 220-page judgment, Mr Justice Peter Smith accused the ex-president of 'shamelessly defrauding his people and flaunting his wealth with an expensive wardrobe of stupendous proportions'. The judge singled out as 'the most telling example of corruption' his 'US$ 500,000 purchase of hundreds of suits and monogrammed shirts from an exclusive boutique in Switzerland, as well as seventy-two pairs of hand-made, high heel shoes to extend his 5 feet (1.5 metres) stature. This was at a time when the vast majority of Zambians were struggling to live on 1 US $ a day and many could not afford more than one meal a day' (*The Guardian*, 2007). The Zamnet Communications System (2007) reported the verdict in this manner: 'Zambia's ex-president Frederick Chiluba has been found guilty of stealing US $ 46 million of public money by a United Kingdom court.'

Without sounding dramatic, one has to say that Zambians have only themselves to blame. There were other capable leaders who could have taken up the mantle of leadership after UNIP and Kenneth Kaunda. Rather, Zambians chose to be blinded by narrow parochial lenses of tribalism and parasitism. When delegates were presented with three other possibilities in regard to leadership, at the first convention of the Movement for Multiparty Democracy (MMD), they chose to ignore the voice of reason. These were Zambians with impeccable credentials who were also vying for the leadership of the MMD, together with Chiluba. At this convention, which the author attended as part of the University of Zambia Student Leadership – a section of the mass democratic movement that was slowly gaining ground in the country – it was clear to see that Chiluba was out of his depth. Even his manifesto or presentation did not articulate a vision for a better Zambia, while his colleagues had some 'road map' for prosperity. Intimidation and hooliganism emerged at the convention, mainly perpetrated by delegates from the Copperbelt, where Chiluba was based, and from Luapula and the Northern provinces, where his tribe mainly originates. At the time, he was a labour leader whose headquarters was on the Copperbelt. Chiluba was quite a wily person, having gained experience in underhand politics in the labour movement. Therefore, it is not clear whether it was either by design or otherwise that many voting delegates came from the Copperbelt and allied provinces in terms of ethnic composition and voted overwhelmingly for this individual.

At the same convention, there was a lot of money that changed hands in vote-buying, specifically targeting the block votes. Block votes were mainly from representatives of interest groups such as workers or students. Chiluba was not the best candidate either intellectually or morally. He was also 'tainted' by the UNIP method of co-option. However, he was quick to play the tribal card, that of being affiliated to the Bemba speaking group, which is the largest in numbers and supposedly the most vocal group in Zambia. He would continue using tribalism in the new dispensation of political pluralism, by making key political appointments to this group and speaking in the vernacular at every opportune time, even when addressing the nation or foreign dignitaries.

In Zambia's transition from a one-party state to multi-party politics, the role that the University of Zambia (UNZA) students played is usually treated peripherally by political commentators, and yet they were the main catalysts in the uprising of 1990 that paved a way for the demise of UNIP and Kenneth Kaunda. Even when the famous Garden Hotel Meeting (where incidentally the MMD was born) was convened by Mr Akashambatwa Mbikusita-Lewanika and Mr Derrick Chitala to formally call on all progressive Zambians to defy the one-party state and demand a return to pluralism; the revolutionary fervour and defiance against the UNIP government was already ignited by the students, some of whom were languishing in Kaunda's jails at that point in time. The history of the transition to multi-party politics has been distorted over the years and it is important that a perspective from a former student activist is provided in this book. When the student uprising was unfolding, which led to an open revolt against UNIP in the form of riots all over the country (for almost one week), 32 students were identified as ring-leaders and detained by the Kaunda regime. The insurrection against UNIP has always been ascribed to the increase in the price of the staple food, maize meal. However, the truth is that the students had already been agitating for the re-introduction of multi-party politics in the country prior to this event.

A forerunner and an important trigger to this defiance began with the reported massacre of the University of Lubumbashi students, by the Mobutu dictatorship in the then Zaire (now the DRC). These students had also called for political reform in their country, but, it was widely reported, were brutally suppressed with a good number being bayoneted in the process by Mobutu's security forces. In solidarity, UNZA students marched to the Zairian Embassy to petition the Ambassador, but were snubbed. During the ensuing demonstration aroused by the reports of such a heinous crime against fellow students, the UNIP government did not make any statement condemning the massacre, which further infuriated the UNZA student populace. All these events were happening against a backdrop of fast declining economic conditions, hyperinflation, and wanton misrule by UNIP. In the same period, the UNIP government then made the fatal mistake of increasing the price of maize meal to exorbitant levels. This was the excuse that the students were waiting for and they found a way to demand change of government. The mood at UNZA was that UNIP and Kaunda must go, and it became easy after the price hike to mobilise the masses around one issue: high food prices equals an uncaring government. The rest, as they say, is history.

The point to note is that Kaunda and UNIP had cowed many Zambians into subservience and UNZA inadvertently became an opposition camp. Therefore, the arrest and detention without trial of students (under the infamous Preservation of Public Security Act) opened the floodgates for various forms of opposition. Even a junior army officer announced a 'coup' on the radio in the frenzy. The majority of these young men and women of UNZA were mainly from working class and peasant backgrounds, and had nothing to gain from the one-party's patronage. Although they had benefited from free education, their households and communities were adversely impacted by the worsening economic crisis in the country, which was blamed on UNIP and Kaunda. Furthermore, the students had more to lose in terms of expulsions and being blacklisted by the ruling party in regard to access to life chances, but they threw themselves into the fray of transforming their country.

While the above-mentioned events were unfolding, Chiluba was not even a factor in the political equation. Even those opportunists who emerged to form the first MMD government were not key players in providing impetus for change in Zambia. Many only became visible 'when the dust had settled'. Without the students' involvement in the politics of Zambia, the MMD might have faced an upward battle as Kaunda was very good at the art of divide and rule as well as patronage. It must be stated that even the first MMD rally in Kabwe, which was aimed at introducing the movement to the masses, would have been a flop had students not been invited. Many people were afraid to come to the rally. The author was also present at this rally, where after students chanted anti-UNIP slogans and showed the masses that the 'Hour for Change' was nigh, curious onlookers at safe distances (on top of anthills) began to stream into the ground where the rally was being held. The MMD had to hire six buses to ferry students and especially the ex-detainees (who had nothing to lose by seeing Kaunda and UNIP out of power) to Kabwe for the rally. Arthur Wina, the first Finance Minister of Zambia after the country's independence, was leading the movement at this moment. Indeed, before the opportunists hijacked the revolution, the role of students was appreciated because they were extremely effective in conscientising the masses. As usual, Zambians were sceptical of this new group of people who were challenging the 'old man' and UNIP. Students called for change not to seek personal glory or self-enrichment, but simply because they wanted a better Zambia. So Chiluba is not the 'liberator' as some people wrongly suggested.

Zambians were accomplices to the corruption and plunder of national assets, by the former government of Chiluba, even if they did not actually participate in the actual acts, because they chose to ignore the warnings of some sections of the Zambian populace regarding this individual. When cases of corruption were reported by the then *Weekly Post* (which was the only independent newspaper not controlled by the government at the time), or when other progressive Zambians warned the masses against the excesses of the new MMD government and emerging misrule, many Zambians chose to ignore them. The government of the day simply labelled these progressives as 'malcontents' and so forth. When some politicians of integrity resigned from the MMD (including Mwanawasa) in disgust because of unbridled abuse of power by Chiluba and his sycophants, they were simply vilified by both the government and the masses. The chant then was: 'Give Chiluba and the MMD time'. Even the 1996 general elections, which Chiluba was alleged to have rigged, were arguably free and fair as Zambians went *en masse* to give Chiluba another mandate (to plunder the country), despite increasing hunger, poverty and other ills. So ten years were wasted under Chiluba and Zambians have to look at themselves in the mirror and carry the burden of truth. Those who supped with Chiluba while he pillaged Zambia's wealth are now trying to distance themselves from him. They should also be held accountable.

So it can be seen that Zambia's social problems have arisen from a lack of political will. Political will is a vital essential ingredient in the development enterprise and if it is missing, many of the formulated policies will remain ineffectual as they will not be implemented. Policy implementation ultimately leads to the delivery of services to citizens, who also experience positive spin-offs in the process. When the young

Pan-Africanist Kwame Nkrumah declared to fellow Ghanaians prior to independence, *'Seek ye first the political kingdom and all things shall be added onto you'*, paraphrasing Scripture, he was not just making a rhetorical statement, but was aware of the potency of political power and how it could then be used to redress the colonial legacy of social and economic exclusion, racism, poverty, ignorance and illiteracy. This was before he was exposed to the trappings of power and the way power could be used to retard human progress. The Zambian story fits this scenario. No development initiatives will blossom in a country if the political establishment is inept. Also, no economy will function at all if it is perverted to satisfy the whims of a depraved political regime. But when political power is well harnessed and used to formulate responsive policies, rather than to plunder the country's resources, then the improvement of citizens' lives will become a reality.

Thus it is argued here: *'Get your politics right and everything shall follow'*. However, the opposite has happened in Zambia, even in most of Africa, where the politics have never been right and thus other sectors of the society have also suffered. Zambia almost got it right immediately after independence, but this progress was short-lived. Political will is extremely crucial in defining the development of any country, Zambia included. The *right politics* can only be realised once there is a nucleus of quality leaders who will actually rise to the occasion and lead their people to a better state of existence, by coming up with new ideas, solutions and innovative ways of doing things. This is what the nationalists did when they fought against colonial rule.

It can also be argued that this type of leadership was also exhibited in pre-colonial days. In those times, it was important to have a strong, intelligent and creative king or queen, to rule over large kingdoms in some cases. A king or queen had to prove to his or her people that he or she was wise and could make prudent decisions that would not put the people in harm's way. Those that failed this task were easily deposed. For instance, the Lozi king, Lewanika, was relied upon by his people not only to provide leadership but to chart a progressive course for his kingdom that would benefit all the subjects. His passion was to see his people acquire Western education, and because of this the first school in Barotseland was started by missionaries at his insistence in 1887. However, in all the times that he had faltered, there were rumblings of rebellion (and indeed, he was deposed three times and had to flee into exile before consolidating his kingdom in latter years) (see Mainga, 1973 for details).

So the use of political power for the benefit of ordinary people is not strange or new to Africans or Zambians.

Inevitably, this art of governance was destroyed by colonialists who supplanted the indigenous system by appointing their own 'chiefs', especially in areas which had not had strong political organisation before the advent of colonial rule. Many of these individuals were just rogues, collaborators and so on. They also lacked legitimacy and integrity and usually had voracious appetites for money or material things. Unfortunately, this is the brand of leadership that survived colonialism, and spilled over into the post-colonial state. The post-colonial state has also been dogged by problems of legitimacy which have in turn impeded development pursuits because of its artificiality that can be ascribed to colonialism:

> Arguably, contemporary African states were established by Europeans during colonialism for purposes of expropriation, exploitation and imperial glory. The fragmentation of the continent is a direct result of colonial politics to which Africans were merely pawns in European colonial political chess games. Interestingly, political independence in Africa also came partly as a result of externally-induced European political games of domination and destruction ignited by Adolph Hitler's imperial design. However, Hitler's failed scheme had unintended consequences of Africa's first liberation because most of the old colonialists lost the will and the capacity to hold on to their colonies. Perhaps, part of the unintended consequence of Africa's liberation is at the root of the long-term problem of the unwillingness and/or inability of most African states to institutionalise sustainable processes for solving national and political problems (Kalu, 2005:1).

Chapter 6 mentioned that governance must be underpinned by quality leadership. Mwaipaya's (1980) proposal on this is echoed by the present study. His understanding on this matter fits with this book's arguments that, *inter alia,* regard politics, translated into good governance, as the axis of development and human wellbeing. Whether wrong or right decisions are taken in the political sphere, they will ultimately impact on the rest of the society. Indeed, this issue is taken as a given and not a supposition. Therefore, the translation of political power into a war on poverty, nation-building, or the redistribution of the country's resources, so that each and every person benefits from its wealth, can be important yardsticks for a progressive political leadership. This is synonymous with *visionary leadership* that is characterised by a clean, clear, competent, credible, committed, courageous, and compassionate vision and team spirit (Mbikusita-Lewanika, 2006). Zambia's development cannot be achieved by a leadership that is tolerant of corruption and the corrupt, deficient in intellectual depth, narrow in knowledge, unqualified and inexperienced, populist and demagogic, socially insensitive and unaccommodating, and otherwise, inept and indifferent to national service driven programmes (Mbikusita-Lewanika, 2006).

The above line of thought as regards the leadership criteria for Zambia borrows from Kalu's (2005) analysis on the subject, which expresses the opinion that most of Africa suffers from an absence of *indigenous elites* in the public policy domain. Kalu (2005) argues that it is the lack of productive engagement in the public policy sector by indigenous elites with viable financial, intellectual and patriotic resources that remains an obstacle to the installation and maintenance of institutional structures consistent with modern statehood frameworks. Kalu also distinguishes between *indigenous elites* and *extractive elites*. The former build legacies using ideas and institutions; significant to their roles and functions is the fact that they nurture dreams of current generations and, for the unborn, they leave their marks in sustainable and authentic educational institutions and structures, financial and judicial infrastructural legacies with enforceable norms and stable security. Most important, indigenous elites produce a self-determined citizenry with zeal to serve their country unselfishly. Extractive elites, on the other hand, leave legacies of dug up roads, wasted farmlands, uncompleted projects, corruption, malevolent leadership, false hopes, unfulfilled dreams, institutional decay represented by an externally weak state that is sustained internally by force of arms, while carting away the future of an already alienated, brutalised and emasculated citizenry as personal loot to foreign bank accounts (Kalu, 2005). Zambia and much of Africa have been plagued by extractive elites. Public policy-making is at the disposal of the leadership, and interfaces with a country's institutions, which also require competent decision-makers at their helm.

The policy-institutions nexus

The culture of policy formulation, implementation and analysis has not been embedded in the Zambian public space since independence, and this has resulted in serious social problems in the country. As Chapter 6 highlighted, there has not been robustness in the policy realm, because this area had remained the domain of politicians who in most cases were of humble education but still they continued to be key players, especially during the one-party state. Thus it was always difficult for the government to translate policies into programmatic actions, owing to lack of rigour. Zambia's socio-economic woes can mainly be attributed to both policy and institutional failures. In fact, in certain instances, there were no policies or institutional frameworks to guide development pursuits. The dearth of policies or their non-articulation ultimately led to the public spheres degenerating to such levels that public goods could not be accessed by the citizenry. In this work, effective policies and institutions are taken as vital arteries for delivering wellbeing, in the form of services, to the people. For that reason a closer examination of institutions is required.

Understanding institutions

As part of public policies, social policy should be formulated within a framework that includes economic policy and political regimes. An important determinant of the success of social policies is the recognition of sectoral affinities or synergies between institutions located in different spheres of the political economy. In such situations, the structure and direction of movements in one sector complement those in the other spheres (Mkandawire, 2006). The political-economic system comprises a complex of institutions bearing specific relationships to one another. The constitutional rules are the most fundamental constraints of such a system. Their objective is to be of maximum utility to the rulers by specifying the underlying structure of property rights and control over coercion (North, 1981). They will be developed with the objectives of (i) specifying a pattern of wealth and income distribution; (ii) specifying a system of protection in a universe of competing state; and (iii) laying the framework for a system of operating rules to reduce transaction costs in the economic sector (North, 1981).

Institutions may be defined as the rules, norms and values that shape human behaviour. Sometimes known as the 'rules of the game', they can be both formal (e.g. laws that govern land tenure, market transactions or civil rights) and informal (e.g. social customs and conventions); they may be created (for example as a result of deliberate or policy decisions) or may evolve over time; and they may exist at local, organisational, national and international levels (Department for International Development, 2001). Furthermore, five categories of institutions may be identified:

1. familial - descent or kin-based;
2. communal - grounded in principles of trust and reciprocity;

3. social - norms or codes of conduct derived from societal interests, e.g. definition of gender roles, patron-client relations;
4. collective - common property resource and agricultural marketing institutions;
5. policy/governance - constitutions, legislative, regulatory and administrative norms and procedures, e.g. property rights laws, employment legislation, judicial procedure (Department for International Development, 2001:6).

Institutions provide the framework within which human beings interact. They establish the co-operative and competitive relationships which constitute a society and, more specifically, order. They are a set of rules, compliance procedures, and moral and ethical behavioural norms designed to constrain the behaviour of individuals in the interest of maximising the wealth or utility of principals (North, 1981). It is for this reason that Zambia needs to strengthen existing institutions in order to make them effective. In this sense, effective institutions are those that are incentive-compatible. For instance, institutions with internal enforcement mechanisms are effective because there is a mutually recognised system of rewards and penalties (World Bank, 2002). An important issue in the design of public institutions is ensuring that incentives that are created actually lead to desired behaviour. Therefore, the Zambian government must be preoccupied with institution-building. Focusing on this does not devalue the importance of policy, but good policies alone are not enough.

Springboards for human wellbeing in Zambia

Despite having many socio-economic and political bottlenecks, Zambia also has certain natural endowments that can be exploited to the advantage of its people. Some of these assets were mentioned earlier in this chapter. In spite of this, there are also certain preconditions that need to be met if human wellbeing is to be accelerated in the country. The following proposals are not prescriptive, but are thought of as cardinal launch-pads of human development in Zambia:

The pursuit of a developmental state in Zambia

The first thing that has to be borne in mind is that human development has to be operationalised within a state paradigm. It is proposed in this text that instituting the developmental state is one pragmatic route that the government could take, given the enormity of social problems in Zambia. As regards experiments with neo-liberalism, it is argued in this book that it is not the only route Zambia can follow in its quest to raise the quality of life of its people. The neo-liberal route, for an LDC like Zambia, is not empirically sound or relevant. Furthermore, neo-liberalism clashes with the historical trajectories of Zambia. Neo-liberalism will not liberate the country from its present penury and external dependence on the West, but might even reinforce these unequal relations. This is something that Zambia has flirted with for almost two decades and which currently defines the country's precarious state.

While advocating a developmental state, this work also takes into account that a wholesale transplant of the East Asian experience may not yield fundamental transformations in African terrains. However, it is by no means impossible that a state that is purposefully driven to promote development and utilises the offices of the state in order to facilitate improvement, alongside other actors such as the private sector and civil society, can emerge and prosper in Zambia (Taylor, 2005).

There is also no harm in revisiting some state models that Zambia had tried to put in place after independence. The 'mixed economy' perspective whereby the state is partnered with the private sector can be re-examined and remodelled to suit contemporary times. It is all about innovation and what can work for Zambia, in the fight against poverty that is paramount in this issue.

Debt sustainability

It was mentioned in earlier chapters that Zambia had reached the HIPC completion point. It must clearly be discerned by policy-makers and politicians alike that this is not an end in itself. Many of Zambia's development woes emanate from the debt crisis that affected it for decades. Therefore, it is paramount that careful deliberation and analysis take place at the policy and political levels, so that the country does not fall back into the debt trap. Saasa's (2004:4) warning as regards HIPC needs to be re-sounded:

> The main challenge for HIPCs is that on the one hand, for them to remain within the 150 per cent threshold, they may have to curtail social spending as a consequence of the needed tight fiscal squeeze. On the other hand, if they focus on poverty reduction through less stringent fiscal policy and through foreign borrowing, this could result in increased

external debt stock in a way that could compromise the sustenance of the required HIPC threshold. This dilemma is particularly evident in countries, such as Zambia where enhanced external resource inflows that are required to meet the high levels of poverty, at the casualty level of more than 70 per cent of the population, could easily be curtailed to ensure that the debt sustainability threshold is not breached.

The Zambian government should also sharpen its debt negotiating skills and ensure that new bilateral or multilateral loans or financial agreements that are entered into are henceforth relevant and beneficial to the poorest segments of the country. There is no need to keep on borrowing for the sake of it. The government and the nation must be convinced that there is need to make certain financial arrangements. For instance, the fight against poverty should be at the centre of development co-operation where aid policies revolve around Zambia's determination to reduce poverty and vulnerability with pro-poor growth frameworks, navigating the course in the context of PRSP and MDGs (Saasa, 2007). Past experiences have shown that there has been weak involvement of the government during donors' preparation of the country's support programme. Local ownership of the process is therefore crucial in this regard. However, certain important initiatives that have to be overseen by the government must also take place concomitantly, such as strengthening policy-relevant management information systems in order to secure data integrity in planning, budgeting and financial reporting, and enhancing information and data generation capacity so that accurate, reliable, timely, and user-friendly data are available (Saasa, 2007). The ultimate goal for the country should be its extrication from the debt trap. It will not do any good to revert to unwise borrowing after having undergone severe hardships due to the external debt. In the meantime, Zambia should also arrive at an appropriate forward-looking borrowing strategy that will fulfil its development financing needs in a way that avoids a repetition of the debt from which it is only now emerging (International Monetary Fund, 2003).

Nation-building and a collective national consciousness against all forms of mediocrity

Tribalism, ethnicity, nepotism and all forms of parochial identities are detrimental to Zambia's overall development. Nation-building is important for a multi-ethnic country like Zambia with 72 ethnic groups. At independence, the nation-building project in many instances enfeebled some segments of the Zambian society. Instead of incorporation and careful assimilation, the UNIP government sought to forcefully amalgamate all sectors of the new country into a united nation under the banner of One-Zambia One-Nation. Barotseland is one area that was regarded as intransigent by UNIP and was targeted as an enemy of the new nation. A natural reaction from the people of Barotseland was to oppose the regime or even seek a separate state from Zambia because of either perceived or existing marginalisation after independence. Chapter 2 tried to shed some light on this issue. The nation-building project was flawed from the start as it was imposed on the people by the UNIP government. Even national symbols such as the flag (designed by a British expatriate), the National Anthem (a derivative of South Africa's Nkosi sikeleli iAfrika by Enoch Sontonga, and for decades the ANC anthem) and the currency, the kwacha (also the name of the Malawian currency), are all foreign in orientation and do not bear a Zambian signature. Furthermore, the design of the Coat of Arms (depicting a man in shorts and a woman wearing an apron) is so rudimentary. It is thus fitting that a national debate has to be conducted in order to re-examine these symbols. Everything seems to be so basic in Zambia, and if at the level of national symbols there is nothing inspiring, then how can people be expected to aspire to higher heights? However, that was the case under Kaunda and UNIP, sophistication was unknown to their rule.

Research and Development (R&D)

Research and Development (R&D) is a vital engine for national growth, which must be encouraged at all levels in the country. The myriad ineffectual interventions in the economy, for example in industries and agriculture, can be attributed to lack of rigorous research in Zambia or of appreciation of such research. Even at institutions of higher learning, the culture of research has been seriously denuded. As mentioned earlier, policy analysis is also in short supply in both the public sphere and civil society. There is need for massive investment in this area from both the government and private sector. Research and Development can help Zambia find solutions in many areas through the provision of scientific and technical information services via policy related studies, management studies or efficiency studies, routine quality control and testing, pre-production activities such as demonstration of commercial viability, tooling up and trial production runs, prospecting, exploring or drilling for minerals, petroleum or natural gas, routine computer programming, systems maintenance and software development and application (Statistics New Zealand, 2000). Research and Development can also be regarded as any activity that is characterised by originality. It should have investigation as the primary objective, the outcome of which is the prospect (or expectation) of gaining new knowledge, with or without a specific practical application of new or improved materials, products, devices, processes or services. Basic and applied research as well as experimental development in the natural and applied sciences, and social sciences and humanities will also fall under the umbrella of R&D (Statistics New Zealand, 2000).

There seems to be a direct correlation between the level of development in a country and the value it places on R&D. For instance, the European Union countries seriously consider this issue as intrinsic to their prosperity. In terms of R&D spending, expressed in current euros, the EU rose by an average of 6.4 per cent per year in the five-year period up to 2002, compared with 5.83 per cent in the USA, 6.19 per cent in Japan, and a staggering 18.51 per cent in China (European Commission, 2005). As in past years, the top achievers in R&D intensity were the Nordic countries, headed by Sweden with 4.27 per cent of GDP in 2001, followed by Finland with 3.51 per cent, with over two-thirds of this spending by the business sector. Next in line was Denmark with 2.60 per cent in 2001. Other European countries' GDPs set aside for R&D in the same period were as follows: Germany 2.50 per cent, Belgium 2.33 per cent and France and Austria each 2.19 per cent (European Commission, 2005).

Research and Development can indeed spur human development in Zambia. What needs to be scrutinised for this purpose is the role that intellectuals, scientists and academics as well as all institutions of higher learning can play in this endeavour. What should be their contribution in this whole murky scenario of poverty? Zambia and Africa need thinkers and innovators who can liberate the mass of the people from the bondage of penury. Therefore, liberation theories in the social sciences, humanities and natural sciences are needed. Scientists must innovate and develop new ways of harnessing the country's natural resources. Engineers should be able to design machinery that develops parts for other machines in industry. Zambia should reach a stage where science and technology liberate the country from all forms of backwardness. In the same vein, small-scale development or appropriate technology initiatives should be vigorously pursued.

Education

Zambia's mantra must be education, education and more education. It is important that the nation is educated and enlightened. This is a key that will unlock a lot of the development challenges facing Zambia. It will also mean that there will be a large number of people who will be rational thinkers in the country. Education endeavours should be multifaceted, with formal types of education that go hand-in-hand with adult literacy and other types of education campaigns. The idle youths can also be targeted as well. The path that Zambia took in regard to this matter, after independence, should be pursued vigorously. As shown in Chapter 5, Kenneth Kaunda and UNIP can be credited for having incepted a highly successful project of education, even though it could not be sustained over time. An illiterate and uneducated populace only retards development, and concerted efforts by the government and civil society have to be made in bolstering this sector, through budgetary allocations, clear-sighted policies and voluntarism, whereby Zambian expatriates on holiday from overseas can simply provide their expertise free-of-charge. This point should not be treated lightly and there has to be a policy around the role that Zambian expatriates can play in raising the standards at institutions of higher learning. From the experiences of the author, it has been established that there are many Zambians who are willing to implement such an initiative. However, they get frustrated by unnecessary red tape and a lukewarm approach from such institutions. In certain cases, some functionaries are even hostile towards a Zambian expatriate who wants to volunteer his or her time at these organisations. Indeed, attitudes have to change in this regard.

Political stability, peace and security

Since independence, Zambia has never experienced any civil war or major political upheavals resulting in the displacement of tens of thousands of its citizens. Zambians have never known a life of being political refugees in other countries. The only wars or acts of destabilisation the country experienced were perpetrated by outside forces at the height of liberation struggles of Angola, Mozambique, Namibia, South Africa and Zimbabwe; Zambia had to shelter great numbers of refugees from those wars and from Mozambique's and the DRC's later civil wars. Acts of aggression and sabotage were carried out by Portuguese, Rhodesian and South African forces against the Zambian people, as was explained in Chapter 4. But the only forms of internal conflicts were the Lenshina or

Lumpa Church Sect uprisings just before independence, that were crushed in 1964, and the Mushala Rebellion in the 1970s, which was confined to the North-Western Province of Zambia and which was effectively quelled with the killing of its leader Adamson Mushala by Zambia's security forces in 1982. Political stability, peace and security are important building-blocks of human development in any country and for Zambia, these factors have been in abundance since independence, to a point whereby certain politicians took them for granted. However, ordinary Zambians should be the ones taking credit for the normalcy that has prevailed in the country since independence. Many Zambians do not want unnecessary strife and will do anything to avoid conflict. It is in this environment of peace and security that many development initiatives can be sought after and implemented.

The friendly nature and tolerance of Zambians

Zambians are naturally friendly people and despite experiencing hardships will always find ways to laugh away their sorrows. Many tourists or foreigners have always commented on the fact that Zambians are friendly people. This is a favourable attribute that should not be overlooked in development endeavours. Despite their failings, Zambians have been known to be less offensive towards foreigners. That is why the country was able (and continues) to host so many foreigners and refugees at different periods of time. This quality stems from the African notion of reciprocity and egalitarianism. In the one-party state, it was likened to Humanism, the doctrine of the ruling party. For development, this Zambian quality has to be reaffirmed at a national level so that it can also be linked to tourism as well as Foreign Direct Investment. One thing that the author is sure about is the fact that Zambians are always eager to help. This is a desirable trait that can also be tilted in the direction of socio-economic development.

The resilience of Zambians

The sad reality, as noted in the Preamble, is that many people in Zambia are preoccupied with the satisfaction of physiological needs. Even though the majority of people are poor, somehow life has managed to go on. Children were sent to school by parents who could barely afford to put food on the table. High poverty levels did not translate into, for example, high crime rates. This resilience in meeting adverse human conditions head-on can be turned into strengths which could be used as platforms for sustainable human development. If people can survive and still manage to make a living under the harshest conditions, then they can also play significant roles when they are given incentives to sustain their livelihoods. This is what policy development should aim for.

Lessons from others or 'catch-up' interventions

It is important that politicians, policy-makers and civil society actors take their cue from workable development models in other countries and then adapt them to local circumstances. Zambians must be creative in this regard and learn from other endeavours so as to catch up, after lagging behind in areas of human advancement. For instance, what can be learnt from the experience of Cuba where malaria and illiteracy have virtually been wiped out? Can Zambians begin to think out of the box and implement indigenous, nationally-driven models of development as opposed to parroting the neo-liberal orthodoxy? What lessons can be derived from emerging markets such as Malaysia or Vietnam? Is there anything that can be taken from the models of China, India or even South Africa that can spur development in Zambia?

Thinkers are needed in the country to chart the course of policy alternatives. There is thus a need for 'think tanks' where experts spend time developing and testing alternative models and/or policies in order to embolden various strategies aimed at enhancing human wellbeing. Also, what can the country learn from its past mistakes and triumphs? Is there anything that can be brought back into play? It is therefore pleasing to observe that Levy Mwanawasa's government sought to reconcile with Zambia's past by reactivating development planning and other initiatives from the First and Second Republics which were abandoned by Chiluba's government.

This book argues that Zambian policy-makers, scholars and other professionals have to be daring in their work, instead of, for instance, rehashing the same old theories or ways of doing things. Thus, this text subscribes to the assertions of the late president of Burkina Faso, Thomas Sankara: 'You cannot carry out fundamental change without a certain amount of madness. In this case, it comes from nonconformity, the courage to turn your back on the old formulae, the courage to invent the future. It took madmen of yesterday for us to be able to act with extreme clarity today. I want to be one of those madmen....we must dare to invent the future' (See Thomas Sankara Speaks, 1988). Indeed, Zambians have to dare to invent a future where there will be no hunger, destitution and squalor.

'Smart Partnerships'

'Smart Partnerships', if prudently utilised, could prove vital in the emancipation of Zambia from poverty, as well as Private-Public Initiatives, and should be encouraged by the government. For instance, private companies with a national character that have done well without government support could be earmarked by the state for state investment, for example, buying shares in the companies. In this way, the government could also help in other ways related to capacity-building for such companies. Private firms that are trend-setters could be given tax rebates or other incentives, especially if they are involved in anti-poverty initiatives or social development interventions. Instead of re-inventing the wheel, the government could actually have a stake in already competitive companies and bolster their capacities rather than starting all over by establishing certain industries, etc. The government has to be business-minded and identify performing enterprises for partnerships. Private companies that are offering public goods, for instance, and have proved their worth in terms of high profits could be considered. The relationship must be one of mutual respect. The government should also aim always for minority shares in these businesses and not be tempted to go 'the take-over' route, which had disastrous results earlier.

Regional and continental initiatives

While the foregoing processes are unfolding in Zambia, the country should not be inward looking, but must continue playing decisive roles at both the regional and continental levels, as the country's human development is inextricably bound up with the former. Zambia is in Africa, a continent that is plagued by a plethora of social problems and characterised by despair in every facet of human endeavour. It is this reality which should not escape the minds of Zambians, be they academics, politicians, policy-makers, business people, professionals, farmers or simply ordinary individuals. This realisation will determine the manner in which Zambia forges links with sister countries in the Southern African Development Community (SADC) and the rest of the continent in matters of socio-economic and political development. This is not something straightforward, but is also dependent on many other factors. Some of them are exemplified by the existing neo-colonial relationships of former colonial masters with their past colonies, imperialism, racism, the global oppression of black people and a populace which is defeatist, and at times hates itself. Whether Zambia chooses to follow a Pan-Africanist route as it did after independence, or embarks on a reactionary route, will hinge on the type of leadership it has, and whether such individuals will be adept in reading and interpreting many issues that were addressed in the early parts of this book.

Conclusion

In ending this section and the book, it must be emphasised that not all is gloom and doom in Zambia. There are some encouraging trends in the country which must be given impetus to blossom. For instance, the economy has registered some positive growth. Also, there are some signs of accountability and transparency in the political arena, which is indeed another good occurrence. Furthermore, the first president of Zambia, Kenneth Kaunda, has mellowed into a wonderful great-grandfather whilst championing initiatives against HIV/AIDS, poverty, homelessness, etc. It is just wonderful to see him marching with activists, and standing up for global social justice at various symposia and rallies.

However, the opposite can be said of Robert Mugabe, who simply does not know what it means to retire gracefully. Also, the first court judgment against Frederick Chiluba on corruption has indeed vindicated those sections of Zambia that were never beguiled by this individual. Even if it was a civil case, it actually sends signals to the rest of the country, Africa and the world that Zambia is on a path of moral renewal and will no longer tolerate political thugs who plunder national resources at will. Furthermore, Levy Mwanawasa in all intents and purposes meant well for the country. Despite his shortcomings, which were not many, he managed to steer Zambia towards the road to prosperity. Even if progress is slow, one can actually see development tangibles.

Indeed, Mwanawasa and his government made some key interventions in the economic, political and social arenas (as opposed to the Second and Third Republics) that are already bearing fruit in terms of better standards of living for the people. This positive work must be commended by all right-thinking Zambians. It is worthy of note that most of the votes in the 2006 elections that won Mwanawasa the presidency for a second term were from the rural areas. This is a clear indication of the rural people's appreciation of the progress in their areas. Indeed, a lot of work has been undertaken since 2002, in many parts of the country, some of which had been neglected since independence. Many roads that had been impassable under the past regimes were rehabilitated to normal standards, boosting business through the easy transportation of goods around and outside the country. In the past, Zambia was renowned for potholed roads, but now the road network has been extensively rehabilitated and bridges have been constructed all over the country. This was something that had only happened in the First Republic. There has also been the electrification of certain towns that did not have electricity since independence and had relied on diesel powered generators. Remote districts which had not had television signals (since television transmission started in 1963, just prior to independence) now have this service. The signal network for mobile telephones was also extended to remote parts of the country. Mines that were closed down under the one-party state have been reopened, creating employment and economic prospects. Agriculture is also on the upswing. However, there is no room for complacency. Zambians must remain steadfast in their pursuit of socio-economic prosperity, they should not forget the past, but rather derive valuable lessons from it. Terrible mistakes were made in past eras and these should not be allowed to resurface or continue.

This book has been about social policy and human development in Zambia. While it had concentrated on theoretical issues in disentangling aspects related to poverty and human misery in the country, it also tried to proffer some 'non-academic' avenues for the liberation of the country from indigence. In ending this discussion, it is the firm belief of the author that eventually, everything is going to be well in Zambia; however, in the meantime, there is a lot of work to be done.

EPILOGUE

I congratulate Ndangwa Noyoo for exercising citizen responsibility and applying his scholarship to produce this social science research and analysis. His presentation is made on the premise that Zambia's underdevelopment has evolved from unequal, undermining and exploitative economic relations between Africa and the Western world, and is manifest in the prevalence of extreme poverty, worrisome disease and risk of hunger. He asserts that this arises from 'discrimination, poor health, vulnerability, insecurity and lack of personal and professional development opportunities.' I agree with him that this situation violates human rights and is an affront on human dignity, and is a threat to political and social security. In this book, Noyoo argues that intellectuals and public policy makers can contribute towards an equal, people-friendly and mutually beneficial social order.

In the first Chapter, Noyoo notes that social policy is dynamic and responsive to local and global social, economic and political changes. In relation to this, he acknowledges that social policy has preceded and responded to 'colossal transformations'. According to him, the hallmarks of these transformations are 'the fall of the Soviet Empire' and the political and economic re-configuration of Eastern Europe 'into a democratic sphere', 'the rejection of undemocratic regimes in Africa' and 'the rise of the Right in Western Europe.' He says that this 'new global order' is characterised by the emergence of the United States of America as the sole 'super power'. In this the author falls in line with popular, but questionable, mass media, political and academic discourse. Nevertheless, scholars, political activists and journalists, should applaud Noyoo for opening the challenge for follow-up and deeper and more critical examination of this subject.

This book contributes towards a greater appreciation of social policy, in the broadest sense. It paves the way towards a less Western and Eurocentric focus, and more Afro-centric research into the manifestations of ideas and actions that make up the totality of the 'colossal transformations'. This would discard the popular notions implying that the advance of the African democratic struggle against one party state systems, military regimes and apartheid is founded upon, or inspired by, the intra-European Cold War fought on a world scale. It would show that, as far as the tri-continental of Africa, Asia and South America is concerned, globalisation is an old phenomenon dating back to Christopher Columbus' misled voyage to the Caribbean and Vasco da Gama's trip to India, via the southern tip of Africa, more than 500 years ago.

The required follow-up research, discourse and publication need to expose that the period before the knocking down of the Berlin Wall was an era of power imbalance, but under one overall system. Immanuel Wallerstein revealed that, even during the Cold War, there was actually a one-world capitalist system.[1] It needs to be demonstrated that social policy does not have its origins only in Europe, but existed in pre-colonial Africa, that traditional Africa has much to contribute towards building up the values and contents of even present day and future public policy – while there are democratic shortfalls in the new Eastern Europe and the 'old democracies' of the West, as well as the neo-colonial political economies of current African systems.

This is necessary if firm and decisive steps are to be taken towards the fulfilment of the broad African liberation agenda. For this purpose, it is recommended that scholars, political leaders and mass media practitioners should read and debate this book and resolve to follow through with the issues that it brings forth.

The author traces social policy's historical roots to Europe and North America. He could just as well examine what roots of social policy lie hidden in universal land allocation systems that characterise many African traditional systems. This is because a political system achieves social security if it assures every family and community access to cultivation land, which is the fundamental factor of production in a pre-industrial set-up. This is more effective and more efficient than what is found in Europe and North America, even after the decades and centuries of what the author refers to as Western moves 'toward a comprehensive redress of social maladies in society.'

The tragedies that weigh down on African countries, like Zambia, are due to social policies that have failed to pick up from, and build upon, what is offered by traditional Africa. Instead, they took steps backwards and sought to emulate the piecemeal, gradualist and sectarian approaches of a class-ridden European world. This has undermined social fabrics, as clearly witnessed under the Structural Adjustment Programmes. It has been even more evident with the less than adequate, often quite inappropriate, and belated attention to poverty alleviation, under the dictates of debt relief schemes. Market-based de-institutionalisation approaches to the human development dispensation have further aggravated this situation, which is not always made better by substituting for public institutions, not communities of general citizens, but donor created and sustained organisations led by non-elected, and therefore legally unaccountable, local and foreign elites, presenting themselves as civil society.

The social damage caused by decades of under-spending on and relative inattention to health, education and welfare cannot be fully redressed and improved upon by merely removing school fees and health clinic charges, as has lately been under way. All these are considerations that should be applied to reflecting upon issues in this book, and following through with action for the future.

The follow-up research and policy-making action should visit Noyoo's sketching of the historical background of social policy. This should be with a view to attaining greater accuracy through clearing the blinding smoke and dust arising from political propaganda and popular historical distortions. For example, while noting the racial discrimination and social injustice inherent in the colonisation of Zambia and the demands of some European settlers for the amalgamation of territories on both sides of the Zambezi River, it should be recalled that one important African kingdom on the northern side, Barotseland, had a relatively privileged position under the colonial regime, and that even in the rest of that colonial territory, and in others, British policy sometimes defended Africans against settler pretensions. This trend in British colonial policy, which affected Barotseland and the Northern Rhodesia Protectorate generally, was reaffirmed in the 1920s and 30s. Referring to a memorandum by the Fabian Socialist Sidney Webb (Lord Passfield), Colonial Secretary in the British Labour government of 1929-31, on British 'Native Policy', A.H. Willis notes (1967:259), 'The interests of Africans in the territories concerned, stated the memorandum, must be paramount, and if those interests and the interests of the immigrant peoples should conflict, the former should prevail.'[2]

The historical information in this book, after verification, is a suitable and necessary basis for sound social policy development. The author should be commended for projecting the relevance of social policy beyond classroom audiences to the corridors of political power and unto the national theatre of the general citizenry. He affirms that intellectuals can play a progressive and practical role towards the construction of social policy that solves critical problems such as extreme poverty, threats of hunger and social destitution in general. He notes that the scope of social policy encompasses access to health, education and social welfare as well as broad social security. This includes day-to-day concerns of ordinary people over incomes and wages, pensions and disability assistance, human rights of children, women, and other historically disadvantaged people.

In the era that some have unrealistically declared as being beyond ideology, it is refreshing that the author gives recognition to the value of ideology in social policy. He argues the case for policy to be conceptualised in a clear ideological framework and direction of purpose. In this regard he makes reference to Zambian Humanism. He examines Humanism, and finds it wanting, in terms of depth of content, authenticity of thought and adaptability to broad national consciousness. In this examination, he revisits Timothy Kandeke's writings. This is a helpful start, but there is a need for a more in-depth and more critical review of Kandeke's works – also of the books by Henry Mebeelo.

In terms of political vision, little has been said or done to present a clear and solid national or party ideology. Indeed, Zambian public discourse is distinguished by its lack of ideology content. It cannot be characterised as a contest of ideas based on clear and consistent slates of values and long-term goals. This causes policy carelessness and inconsistencies, some of which the author points out, although not always in proper context. This may not be surprising, but it is a handicap against social policy for long term, wide-spreading, and lasting development. The author correctly states that ideology is a necessary launching pad for human development management. He defines and uses social welfare concepts and the human development approach of the United Nations Development Programme. But, most importantly, he forewarns that successful social policy demands 'not only innovation but a steadfast political will, as well as active support from citizens in general.'

In the second Chapter, Noyoo defines and examines the nature of social change and its impact on the Zambian society, over time, and what social policy has to do with it. He applies theories of Karl Marx and Max Weber, as they depict social differentiations. This is, of course, in terms of social classes, where Marx is concerned; it is in terms of power conflicts, in Weber's perspectives. There are pertinent references to writings by others, such as Montesquieu and Kant. However, the language and some of the historical presentations in the book arise out of propagated perspectives of European colonisers and African post-colonial ruling elites. This does not, in all ways, capture and represent perspectives of African traditional authorities. For example, a more Afro-centric presentation of political changes in Africa would begin with the 1884-85 Berlin Conference and the Scramble for Africa.[3]

That international conference at Berlin, attended by the major European powers but no Africans, addressed and resolved particularly the Congo question and the claim of King Leopold of Belgium over Congo, which became a private territory and business area ruled by Leopold's International Congo Association, and in fact was ruled by Leopold personally, with extreme tyranny over the Africans, for over a quarter of a century. But those Europeans meeting in Berlin also began the slicing and sharing out of African lands, people and governments into shares of monopoly influence, commerce and colonisation, which was completed over the next twenty years.

In this imperialist, racist and exploitation-driven process, Britain claimed right of governance, exploitation and colonisation over African countries, people and governments that included those in territories over which the Zambian Government now claims sovereignty. Britain's European partners in crime approved this essentially anti-African, undemocratic and exploitative venture, which also sought to disarm Africans,[4] to the mutual interest of European governments and economies. The Scramble for Africa was pursued by governments and by European capitalists, such as Cecil John Rhodes, who amassed vast wealth and political dominance in European Southern Africa.[5]

The Euro-centric colonial and neo-colonial legal and constitutional framework for what is now Zambia evolved from Britain's 1889 Order-in-Council which 'empowered the Commissioner and Counsel-General to make what were known as the Queen's regulations for peace, order and good government and for the securing of the observance of any treaty for the time being in force relating to any place to which the said order belongs.' The British South Africa Company (BSAC) accordingly set up administration in territories arbitrarily annexed with or without the Africans' consent – though Barotseland was able to negotiate what were, by colonial standards, fairly good terms. North of the Zambezi the BSAC's territories were at first divided into North-Western Rhodesia and North-Eastern Rhodesia. In 1911 these were amalgamated to constitute the Protectorate of Northern Rhodesia. Barotseland retained its special status after the whole territory came under direct British imperial rule in 1924.

Noyoo mentions the European settlers' agitation for Amalgamation and Dominion Status, despite the British Government's stated policy that 'Native' interests were to be paramount. Throughout the 1930s and 1940s there was ever escalating demands, by European settlers, for the amalgamation between Northern and Southern Rhodesia, with the objective of establishing a European settlers' dominion regime autonomous from the Colonial Office, such as had been arranged for Canada, Australia and White South Africa; the Southern Rhodesia settlers had almost complete self-government already, since 1923. For this purpose, representatives of White workers formed a European settler political party.

There was an African response to this settler campaign. In 1944 the Kitwe African Society, led by Mbikusita Lewanika, issued the Kitwe Resolution. This protested against European settlers' escalating agitation for amalgamation of Northern Rhodesia with Southern Rhodesia, under European settler hegemony. The association also protested against the inappropriate and inadequate representation of African interests in the Legislature. They called for African interests to be represented by Africans elected by Africans, meaning indigenous Africans, but not restricted to those originating within the colonial territory of Northern Rhodesia.

In a parallel move, the Kitwe African Society proposed that the Federation of African Welfare Societies should be transformed into an overtly political organisation. Thus, in 1948, in Lusaka, the Northern Rhodesia African Congress was constituted. Mbikusita Lewanika was its founding President General. The Congress had as its first slogans 'unity in teamwork,' and 'One Man, One Vote'. It represented an escalation in demands for African political rights beyond welfare demands. This marks the earnest beginning of the independence movement. From the start, this struggle was coupled with the fight against plans to impose a European settler dominated Federation between Northern and Southern Rhodesia and Nyasaland. During this same year, the Legislative Council witnessed the introduction of two African members. This Council consisted of the first speaker, nine officials, ten elected members, two nominated unofficial members (European) to represent African interests, all Europeans, and for the first time two African members elected by the African Representative Council. Nelson Nalumango was one of the first two African Members.

At the end of 1951, the Northern Rhodesia African Congress presidency changed hands. This was after Mbikusita Lewanika's second one-year term. This is when Harry Mwaanga Nkumbula became the second President-General. The Congress' name was changed to the Northern Rhodesia African National Congress (ANC) shortly afterwards. It was under this leadership that the African battle against Federation was lost, in 1953. The Federation lasted for ten years, before it was ended in 1963. Despite this setback, the Legislative Council was reformed to consist of eight officials, twelve elected members, two nominated unofficial members to represent African interests and four African members elected by the African Representative Council. Robinson Nabulyato, who had earlier been the first Secretary-General of Congress, was one of the members of the Legislative Council. Then, in 1958, the Congress movement, which had been held together for ten years, split with the formation of the Zambia African National Congress, the forerunner of the United National Independence Party (UNIP). The split was, among other issues, over differences between the militants, who wanted a boycott, and the moderates who accepted to participate in elections based on the less than democratic 1958 Constitution.

In 1959 the Legislative Council consisted of six officials, 22 elected and two nominated unofficial members. Two African members sat on the Executive Council as Ministers (one elected, one nominated) and there were six elected African backbencher members. The ANC had for the first time contested parliamentary elections and managed to have its leader, Harry Nkumbula, enter the Legislative Council as a back-bencher. Of the African members elected, one, Gabriel Musumbulwa, became Minister of African Education, while the other, Mr Mwamba, became Minister of African Agriculture. The next major step in the evolution of African political advancement occurred in 1962. In elections UNIP won 14 seats and the ANC seven seats, and the United Federal Party 16 sixteen seats, after the ANC and the UFP had formed an electoral pact. After much uncertainty and negotiations, the ANC decided to enter into a coalition government with UNIP, as the senior partner. Kenneth Kaunda entered the Legislature and Executive Council, for the first time, as Minister of Local Government. The ANC leader, Harry Mwaanga Nkumbula, returned to the Legislative Council, this time as a member of the Executive and Minister of African Education.

Meanwhile, as this progress was being made, and because of it, the Federation of Rhodesia and Nyasaland was facing mounting opposition from much of organised African opinion. South of the Zambezi River, the opposition to the Federation was conducted under the Southern Rhodesia African National Congress, which evolved through various political formations, including the National Democratic Party and later the Zimbabwe African People's Union, among others. North of the Zambezi Congress first spearheaded opposition, before splitting up, after 1958.

In what is now Malawi, the opposition to the Federation was principally under the leadership of another Congress organisation. This was, in 1958, taken over by Dr Kamuzu Banda, upon his return from his long stay in the USA, Britain and Ghana. With the fire added by the much-acclaimed return of Dr Banda, and after much agitation, the British conceded that Nyasaland had a right to leave the Federation. This removed ground for denying the same rights to Northern Rhodesia, and led to the end of the Federation in December 1963. This further opened the way towards independence for first Nyasaland and then Northern Rhodesia.

Constitutional developments moved fast towards establishing the readiness (in British eyes, at least) of the people of Barotseland and the rest of Northern Rhodesia for independence. This needed to be verified by more democratic elections, which took place on 28 January 1964. UNIP, under the leadership of Kenneth Kaunda, won this last colonial election overwhelmingly in most parts of Northern Rhodesia including Barotseland. The European settler dominated political party, formerly the UFP, and the ANC won some seats also. The results of this election underscored the majority standing of UNIP in Barotseland and the rest of Northern Rhodesia, but also the relevant interests represented by other political parties. Then negotiation towards independence went into the last lap. The British Government indicated that it was not willing to continue to administer Barotseland alone as a Protectorate. Barotse opinion over the way forward was divided. Some demanded total integration of Barotseland with the Zambia to be, others demanded that Barotseland proceed to independence separately. After much agitation and several negotiation sessions, a compromise was reached. On 18 May 1964, the Government of Barotseland and the Northern Rhodesia Government negotiated and concluded the 1964 Barotseland Agreement, with the British Government as a witness. Under this agreement, Barotseland was facilitated to become an integral part of Zambia, with some specified areas of local authority and rights to be consulted, within the Zambia to be.

There was fallout from this in UNIP later. This was manifested at the 1967 Mulungushi Party Conference. At this Conference, elections were conducted on the bases of two competing regionalist groupings. The group consisting of Northern and Southern Province leaders won most seats. Most of the losing leaders came from Barotse Province, North-Western Province and Eastern Province, including the then Vice-President, Rueben Kamanga. Earlier, in 1966 Nalumino Mundia and Mubiana Nalilungwe had been fired, amid allegations of double standard tribal victimisation. In the 1968 elections Mundia, who was in detention, managed to work out an alliance between his United Party and the ANC and to win a seat, while in jail. This alliance managed to win all but two Barotse seats and many of the Southern Province seats. The results of this election indicated that UNIP had lost popularity in Barotseland and that the ANC was far from being a dying party in Southern Province. The status of UNIP as a broad national party and the dream of UNIP establishing a one-party state through the ballot box were dead, at least until different approaches were adopted.

One of the different approaches was the tactic of conducting a national 'referendum to end all referendums'. The UNIP government, in all but the Barotse (or Lozi) parts of Zambia, won the referendum. In an agenda-revealing victory expression, according to Sikota Wina (1985), Kenneth Kaunda:

> Informed the country that several bills were already in preparation, following the referendum victory, for amending the Constitution. Among these was a bill to amend Section 18 in order to give power to Government to acquire property compulsorily subject to payment of compensation. As the delegates cheered the President went on to announce further reforms. Section 99 (3) of the Constitution was to be amended to enable young Zambians who had been in practice for periods of five years to be appointed judges to the High Court. The Legislation would also make provisions for such appointments to take effect before five years were possible. In for repeal came sections 10 and 26 of the Constitution. The former provided for aliens who were Commonwealth citizens to enjoy the same rights as Zambians and the latter which compelled the State to only hold arrested saboteurs for a period of one month was to be repealed in order to allow a detention of twelve months. [6]

Given the blank cheque won in the Referendum, the ruling party leadership had the Constitution amended to delete the limit placed on the number of cabinet ministers. This was followed by constitutional amendments turning Zambia into a one party state, under Act No. 27 of 1973. It was 17 years later, in 1990, that the Constitution was again amended to reintroduce multi-party politics.

European colonialism, even in its protectorate format, meant taking away, or restricting, authentic African governments and people's power. Africans lost power in the areas of self-governance, land and natural resources, as well as economic development. This was in addition to being subjected to unequal trade and other exploitative economic relations and confinement in inappropriate territorial boundaries. Colonial Africa's formal independence, as in Zambia, was not intended to liberate Africans under traditional governments. The end of colonialism has not reinstated native people's power over their own governance, land and natural resources. This is the essence of neo-colonialism. The 1964 Independence Constitution dispensation was a product of a negotiated compromise between contending interest groups represented by the ANC, UNIP, the UFP and Barotseland. In this Zambia-founding constitution, none of these groupings got everything they wanted, or the way they wanted it.

The 1964 Independence Constitution provided for a Referendum Clause, under which no aspect of the Constitution could be amended without at least approval of a majority of eligible (not just registered or voting) voters. This was in order to maintain a balance of the contending interests, and to seek to establish political stability, to promote national harmony and to provide for mutual confidence building between the contending political and social interest groups; its aim was to prevent any sectarian group from abusing or otherwise changing the Constitution without national consensus. However, this protection was uprooted in the 1969 Referendum.

This derogation from democracy and people's rights to be consulted was accomplished in a veiled fashion, billed as a *'Referendum to end all Referendums'*. In practice this meant a blank cheque for the all-powerful Zambian presidency to be able to change the Constitution without necessarily, consulting citizens genuinely through a national referendum. Both the 1969 abrogation of the Barotseland Agreement and the 1972-73 imposition of the one-party state were accomplished by taking personal and partisan advantage of this blank cheque provided by the removal of the Referendum Clause. UNIP was given this blank cheque everywhere, except in Barotseland. There, the Referendum was recognised for what it was and nicknamed *Lifu la Ndambo*, meaning 'the death of the common man'. The repeated doctoring of the Zambian Constitution was due to intentionally inbuilt defects in the Constitution, which begged to be changed fundamentally.

For Zambia's constitutional deformation virus, injected by the UNIP Government, to be completely rectified, there must be a total reversal of all the human rights and freedoms derogations since 1964. Otherwise, the Zambian Constitution can at any time, for almost any personal or sectional purposes, be changed by any dominant grouping in Parliament, as in 1972 and 1996. Many national leaders and political actors in Zambian politics are not concerned about the full extent to which the erosion of democracy since 1964 is due to the constitutional cancer arising out of the removal of the referendum clause of the 1964 Independence Constitution. Indeed, for short-term purposes, even from some of today's self-proclaimed democracy advocates there are loud calls for doing away with the referendum clause. These calls ignore the danger of reverting back to the precedent set by the original removal of this clause.

This reveals that there are still too many among the leaders and would-be leaders of Zambia whose democratic concerns do not go beyond moving particular individuals to or from the state presidency and parliamentary membership, without changing the system. On the other hand, in the guise of championing democracy, rich and influential persons ambitious to acquire political power posts, in both ruling and opposition parties, without any record of fighting for a social cause, in year 2001 claimed that there was no time to embark on a comprehensive and democratic review of the Constitution, ahead of presidential and general elections scheduled for 2001. But, since then, in infantile left-wing fashion, they do even think that any voice other than theirs should be heard over the content and mode of adopting the next Constitution. They are militant for only one way of reforming the Constitution, because they are not the ones who made it to State House, and because they are blinded by self-interested mistrust. Under the circumstances, care needs to be taken before concluding that any one part of the constitutional debate has a monopoly of the spirit of working on behalf of broad national interests.

Noyoo expresses the view that 'Kenneth Kaunda and his colleagues, with all their shortcomings can be said to have had Zambia's best interests at heart.' He couples this with an assessment that in the struggle for the reintroduction of plural and competitive party politics many Zambians were euphoric about the 'change'. He also makes a sweepingly negative portrayal of former President Chiluba's personality and the leadership performance. Facts and justice demand acknowledgment that corruption, with its cancerous nature, and neo-liberal economic policies, with their anti-social impact, had already taken root before the change of administration at the end of 1991. This can be done even while noting how situations may have got worse after 1991. It is necessary that agents of change should be comprehensively factual, fair and balanced in passing judgment upon, and learning from, records of leaders and governments.

The third Chapter depicts how social policy can be developed and applied in social and economic management and political leadership. Noyoo illustrates how some social policies have failed, while others have succeeded, and how even among those that have succeeded, there have been difficulties in sustaining the success. I was particularly happy that he makes reference to my late and much missed comrade, Guy Mhone, with whom I have long shared the view that, in some cases, the failure of social policy in post-colonial Zambia rests on its inability to 'seize upon traditional systems as stepping stones for developing a new support system.' The Chapter charts the evolution of social policy in Zambia, and how it was enhanced after independence, which underscores the importance of political will. In the fourth Chapter, the author begins to dive into the meat of his subject, as he points out the characteristics of social policy and human development in Zambia, as an example of an ex-colonised and least developed country. The context the author takes account of includes the critical and all-influential 'exogenous factors such as the terms of international trade'. The social and economic development challenges that Zambia faces are extensively revealed and reviewed in the Fifth National Development Plan (2006-11) and Vision 2030, which are referred to in the book. I had occasion to make a presentation to the final public consideration of both these documents, before they were launched.[7]

The accumulated impact of past decades of economic regression and social devastation, together with factors of corruption, mediocrity and lack of ideological clarity, make it very difficult to achieve even this minimum vision. But the possibility of achieving the vision is increased by improvements in economic management and performance over the last half-a-decade, of which the author says:

> Consistent economic growth was recorded, averaging 4.9 per cent per annum; macro economic stability strengthened with inflation falling to single digit levels, while budget management also improved. The country also succeeded in obtaining substantial debt relief through the Heavily Indebted Poor Countries (HIPC) mechanism and the multilateral debt relief initiative, relieving it of the previously high debt burden. Lower inflation increased stability in prices of goods and services as well as preventing the erosion of incomes. Fiscal discipline, through reduced government borrowing, now meant that the private sector could borrow more from the banks for further investment (Mwanawasa, 2006).

Noyoo reports this as part of President Levy Mwanawasa's public 'pledge to continue the commitment to constitutionalism, human rights, transparency and accountability' as well as the fight against corruption, giving hope that the vision can be attained, even in the face of exogenous and endogenous forces that make the task very difficult, as indicated in this book.

The fifth Chapter illustrates Zambia's human development status and prospects in the areas of social services, rural development, civil liberties and equal opportunities, and populations at risk. By implication, the prospect of significant improvement in human development depends on sustained economic growth with development that is targeted to have a direct impact on education, housing, health, water and sanitation facilities accessible to an increasing number of citizens, among rural dwellers, women and young persons. The author contends that social policy can play a positive role in ensuring such developmental success.

Then the author focuses on the importance of monitoring and evaluation, in enhancing the chances of social policy success, in terms of an improved human development score. What is emphasised in Chapter 7 is that social policy can achieve very little without being complemented by the work of implementing professionals, such as social workers and ordinary civic-minded community members.

In the last Chapter, Ndangwa Noyoo points to the way forward, having concluded that 'the major obstacle to human development in Zambia is poverty', after noting that 'the sad reality is that there have been few successes to actually report on.' He holds on to the hope that 'justice has been done to some shining examples of innovations that were directed at removing Zambia from the quagmires of hopelessness, despair and dejection, especially after independence and when Frederick Chiluba was ejected from the political arena.' He then confesses that his 'main motivation for writing this book was to prick the conscience of Zambia's politicians, policy-makers, academics, civil society actors and the general populace, in order to perhaps spur them into action against the general social malaise in the country.'

Well, in this regard, Noyoo has demonstrated bravery in putting forward his social concerns, and making them available in book form to all, at home and abroad. If this does not spur people on, it shall not be him to blame. I, therefore, strongly recommend this book to all Africans and all other concerned people, within and outside academia.

Akashambatwa Mbikusita-Lewanika*, BA, MPS, MA, MLS
Lusaka, Zambia, Africa, 15 June 2007

* He is now the Presidential Adviser for Political Affairs; former Commissioner of the Anti-Corruption Commission (ACC); former Chairman, National Economic Advisory Council (NEAC); former Cabinet Minister, Science, Technology and Vocational Training; initiator and Founder National Secretary, Movement for Multi-party Democracy (MMD); former Group Director of Projects, Industrial Development Corporation (INDECO); former General Manager, Zambia Ceramics Limited and Blackhood Hodge Limited; Vice-President, Pan-African Students' Organisation of the Americas and President of African Students' Association of Cornell University. He has been educated in Northern Rhodesia, the United Kingdom, the United States of America and Canada.

Notes

[1] I. Wallerstein, *The Capitalist World System*. Cambridge: Cambridge University Press, 1979.

[2] A.H. Wills, *An Introduction to the History of Central Africa*. London: Oxford University Press, 1967, p. 259.

[3] J. Reader, *Africa: A Biography of the Continent*. Vintage Press: Random House Inc., New York, NY, 1999, pp. 541-3 and 551.

[4] R. Hall, *Zambia*, London: Pall Mall Press, 1965, pp. 71-2.

[5] Ibid. p. 55.

[6] S. Wina, *A Night Without a President*. Lusaka: Kenneth Kaunda Foundation, 1985.

[7] A. Mbikusita-Lewanika, 'A Vision of Zambia' (Submission to the National Stakeholders Meeting on the 5th National Development Plan, 2006-2011 and Vision 2030, Lusaka, July 2006).

BIBLIOGRAPHY

Action for Southern Africa (ACTSA) (2005), 'On the front line: Zambia indebted for her anti-apartheid stance.' www.actsa.org/Debt/zambia frontline.htm, (Retrieved 20/07/2005).

Aina, T.A. (2004), 'Introduction', In T.A. Aina, C.S.L. Chachage and E. Anna-Yao (Eds), *Globalization and Social Policy in Africa*. Dakar: Council for the Development of Social Science Research in Africa (CODESRIA), pp. 1-20.

Amin, S. (1999), 'Economic Globalism and Political Universalism: Conflicting Issues?' (Part 2), *Southern African Political & Economic Monthly*, 12 (7), pp. 31-43.

Ammassari, S. (2005), *Migration and Development: New Strategic Outlooks and Practical Ways Forward. The Case of Angola and Zambia*. Geneva: International Organisation for Migration (IOM).

Anderson, J. (1997), *Public Policy Making, An Introduction* (Third Edition). Boston, MA: Houghton Mifflin Company.

Ankrah, M.E. (1987), 'Radicalising Roles for Africa's Development: Some Evolving Practice Issues', *Journal of Social Development in Africa*, 2 (2), pp. 5-25.

Appadurai, A. (1990), 'Disjuncture and Difference in the Global Cultural Economy', *Theory, Culture, and Society*, 7: pp. 295-310.

Bailey, J. (1975), *Social Theory for Planning*. London: Routledge and Kegan.

Ball, A.R. (1993), *Modern Politics & Government* (Fifth Edition). London: The Macmillan Press.

Banda, G.C. (2000), 'Zambia Against Apartheid: A Case on Apartheid Caused Debt' (Unpublished Report).

Barrientos, A., S. Hickey, N. Simutanyi and D. Wood (2005), *Report of Study on Drivers of Change for a National Social Protection Scheme in Zambia*. Lusaka: Department for International Development (DFID).

Batten, T.R. (1957), *Communities and their Development*. London: Oxford University Press.

Bayart, J.-F. (1993), *The State in Africa: The Politics of the Belly*. New York, NY: Longman Publishing.

Bekker, S., (1999), 'Territoriality and Institutional Change in the New South Africa', In D.C. Bach (Ed.), *Regionalisation in Africa: Integration and Disintegration.* Oxford: James Currey, pp.103-18.

Blakemore, K. (1998), *Social Policy, An Introduction.* Buckingham: Open University Press.

Boeree, C.G. (1998), 'Personality Theories: Abraham Maslow.' www.ship.edu/~cgboeree/maslow.html, (Retrieved, 14/09/2005).

Bowden, P. (1988), *National Monitoring and Evaluation.* Aldershot: Avebury.

Bureau of International Labour Affairs (2004), Appendix D: 'Zambian Implementing Environment and Key Institutions and Organisations Addressing the Education of Child Labourers.' www.dol.gov/ilab/grants/sga0207/appendix-d.htm, (Retrieved 06/09/2004).

Burnes, B. (1992), *Managing Change.* London: Longman Group.

Chan, S. (1985), 'Humanism, Intellectualism and the Left in Zambia', In K. Osei-Hwedie and M. Ndulo (Eds.), *Issues in Zambian Development.* Roxbury, MA: Omenana, pp. 285-295

Chikulo, B.C. (1985), 'Decentralisation in Centralism: An Analysis of the Zambian Experience 1964-1981', In K. Osei-Hwedie and M. Ndulo (Eds.), *Issues in Zambian Development.* Roxbury, MA: Omenana, pp. 341-354

Chukuwka, A.B. (2000), Poverty and Social Development in Africa, In B., Laabas (Ed.), *Building and Sustaining the Capacity for Social Policy Reforms.* Aldershot: Ashgate Publishing Ltd, pp. 46-87.

Clifford, W. (1966), *Social Case Work in Africa.* Lusaka: Oxford University Press.

Colclough, C. (1991), 'Structuralism versus Neo-liberalism: An Introduction', In C. Colclough and J. Manor (Eds.), *States or Markets? Neo-liberalism and the Development Policy Debate.* Oxford: Clarendon Press, pp. 1-47.

Colonial Office (1943), *Draft Report on Juvenile Welfare in the Colonies.* London: Colonial Office.

___(1945), *Social Welfare in the Colonies.* London: Colonial Office.

Colson, E. and M. Gluckman (1951), *Seven Tribes of British Central Africa.* Manchester: Manchester University Press.

Compton, B., B. Galaway and B. Cournoyer (2005), *Social Work Processes* (Seventh Edition). Belmont, CA: Brooks/Cole.

Crehan, K. and A. von Oppen (1994), 'General Introduction', In K. Crehan and A. von Oppen (Eds.), *Planners and History: Negotiating 'Development' in Rural Zambia*. Lusaka: Multimedia Publications, pp. 1-14.

Day, P.J. (1997), *A New History of Social Welfare*. Boston, MA: Allyn and Bacon.

Department for International Development (DFID) (2001), *Sustainable Livelihoods Guidance Sheets, 5.1 - Policy Reform*. London: DFID.

Department of Social Welfare (2005), 'Brief on the Department of Social Welfare' (Unpublished), Lusaka.

Department of Youth Development (1994), 'National Youth Policy'. Lusaka: Department of Youth Development.

Devereaux, S. and S. Cook (2000), 'Does Social Policy Meet Social Needs?' *Institute of Development Studies (IDS) Bulletin*, 31 (4), pp. 63-73.

Directorate of Public Health and Research (2002), 'Situation Analysis of Mental Health Services in Zambia'. Lusaka: Directorate of Public Health and Research.

Dubois, B. and K.K. Miley (1999), *Social Work: An Empowering Profession* (Third Edition). Boston, MA: Allyn and Bacon.

Elliot, D. (1993), 'Social Work and Social Development: Towards an Integrative Model', *International Social Work* 36 (93), pp. 21-36.

Estes, R. (1995), 'Education for Social Development: Curricula Issues and Models', *Social Development Issues* 16(3), pp. 68-90.

Estrella, M. and J. Geventa (1997), 'Who Counts Reality? Participatory Monitoring and Evaluation: A Literature Review.' Institute of Development Studies (IDS) Working Paper, 70 (Unpublished).

European Commission (2005), 'Research, Innovation: Sustained Growth in R&D Expenditure in Most EU-25 Nations.' www.ec.europa.eu/research/headlines/news/articles_05_03_14_en.html, (Retrieved 30/05/2007).

Evans, P. (2002), 'Collective Capabilities, Culture, and Amartya Sen's Development as Freedom', *Studies in Comparative International Development*, 37 (2), pp. 54-60.

Fakuda-Parr, S. (2002), 'Operationalising Amartya Sen's Ideas on Capabilities, Development, Freedom and Human Rights: The Shifting Policy Focus of the Human Development Approach.' Position Paper (Unpublished).

Fargins, J. (1996), *Readings in Social Theory: The Classic Tradition to Post Modernism*. New York, NY: The McGraw-Hill Companies, Inc.

Fashoyin, T. (2002), *The Contributions of Social Dialogue to Economic and Social Development in Zambia*. Geneva: International Labour Organisation (ILO).

Food and Agriculture Organisation (FAO) (2003), 'Activities of FAO in Support of Least Developed Countries, Land-locked Developing Countries and Small Island Developing States.' www.fao.org/DOCREP/MEETING/006/Y9308E.HTM, (Retrieved, 20/09/2005).

Fukuyama, F. (1992), *The End of History and the Last Man*. New York, NY: Harper Perennial Publishers.

Gann, L.H. (1958), *The Birth of a Plural Society: The Development of Northern Rhodesia Under the British South Africa Company, 1894-1914*. Manchester: Manchester University Press.

Gaynor, C. (2005), 'Structural Injustice and the MDGs: A Critical Analysis of the Zambian Experience.' *Trócaire Development Review*, pp. 57-84.

George, V. (1988), *Wealth, Poverty and Starvation, An International Perspective*. Hertfordshire: Wheatsheaf Books Ltd.

George, V. and P. Wilding (1985), *Ideology and Social Welfare*. London: Routledge and Kegan Paul.

Ghai, D. and D. Westendorff (1993), 'Improving Social and Development Data,' In D. Westendorff and D. Ghai (Eds.), *Monitoring Social Progress in the 1990s*. Aldershot: Avebury, pp. 1-19.

Gill, D. (1994), *Unravelling Social Policy* (Fifth Edition). Rochester, VT: Schenkman Books, Inc.

Ginsberg, L. (1994), *Understanding Social Problems, Policies, and Programes*. Columbia, SC: University of South Carolina.

Government of the Republic of Zambia (GRZ) (1966), *The First National Development Plan*. Lusaka: Ministry of Finance.

___(1994), *Economic Report 1993*. Lusaka: National Commission for Development Planning (NCDP).

___(1996), *The Persons with Disability Act*. Lusaka: GRZ.

___(2000), *National Gender Policy*. Lusaka: Cabinet Office.

___(2002), *Transitional National Development Plan: 2002-2005*. Lusaka: Ministry of Finance and National Planning.

___(2002), *Draft National Policy on Social Welfare*. Lusaka: Ministry of Community Development and Social Services.

___(2002), *Strategic Plan of Action for the National Gender Policy*. Lusaka: Cabinet Office.

___(2003), *National Policy on Community Development*. Lusaka: Ministry of Community Development and Social Services.

___(2004), *Second PRSP Implementation Progress Report, June-July 2004*. Lusaka: Ministry of Finance and National Planning.

___(2005), *Draft Social Protection Strategy*. Lusaka: GRZ.

___(2005), *National Disaster Management Policy*. Lusaka: Office of the Vice-President.

___(2005), *Millennium Development Goals, Zambia: Status Report*. Lusaka: GRZ.

___(2006), *Fifth National Development Plan 2006-2010. 'Broad Based Wealth and Job Creation through Citizenry Participation and Technological Advancement'*. Lusaka: Ministry of Finance and National Planning.

Graaff, J. and D. Venter (2001), 'Understanding the World System', In J.K. Coetzee, J. Graaff, F. Hendricks and G. Wood (Eds.), *Development: Theory, Policy and Practice*. Cape Town: Oxford University Press, pp. 77-95.

Graham, C. (1997), 'From Safety Nets to Social Policy: Lessons for the Transitions Economies from the Developing Countries', In J. Nelson and C. Tilly (Eds), *Transforming Post-Communist Political Economies*. Washington, DC: National Academy Press, pp. 385-400.

Greenwood, E. (1957), 'Attributes of a Profession'. *Social Work*, 2, pp. 45-55.

Grinnell, R.M. (1993), *Social Work Research and Evaluation* (Fourth Edition). Itasca, IL: Peacock Publishers, Inc.

Grobler, M. (2007), 'The Indigenisation of Social Work in Namibia', In C. Rehklau and R. Lutz (Eds), *Internationale Sozialarbeit: Sozialarbeit des Südens, Band 2: Schwerpunkt Africa*. Oldenburg: Paulo Freire Verlag, pp. 45-58.

Hall, A. and J. Midgley (2004), *Social Policy for Development*. London: SAGE Publications Ltd.

Haq, M. (1995), *Reflections on Human Development*. New York, NY: Oxford University Press.

Hare, I. and B. McKendrick (1976), 'South Africa: Racial Divisions in Social Services', In D. Thursz and J.L. Vigilante (Eds), *Additional Perspectives From Thirteen Countries: Meeting Human Needs* (Volume 2). Beverly Hills, CA: SAGE Publications, pp. 71-96.

Hawthorn, G. (1993), 'How to Ask for Good Government.' *IDS Bulletin*, 24 (1), pp. 24-30.

Hefferman, W.J. (1979), *Introduction to Social Welfare Policy: Power, Scarcity and Common Human Needs*. Itasca, IL: Peacock Publishers, Inc.

Hepworth, D.H., R. Rooney and J. Larsen (2002), *Direct Social Work Practice: Theory and Skills* (Sixth Edition). Pacific Grove, CA: Brooks/Cole.

Heywood, A. (1992), *Political Ideologies: An Introduction*. London: Macmillan Education Ltd.

Ife, J. (1999), *Community Development, Creating Community Alternatives: Vision, Analysis and Practice*. Sydney: Longman.

International Association of Community Development (IACD) (2005), 'The Yaoundé Declaration: The Role of Community Development in Building Civil Society in Africa.' www.iacdglobal.org, (Retrieved 10/07/2005).

International Federation of Social Workers (IFSW) (2000), 'Definition of Social Work.' www.ifsw.org/en/p38000208.html, (Retrieved, 26/01/2007).

International Labour Organisation (ILO) (2005), 'Zambia: Economic Situation.' www.ilo.org/public/english/region/afpro/mdtharare/country/zambia.htm, (Retrieved, 27/06/2005).

International Monetary Fund (IMF) (2003), *Debt Sustainability in Low-Income Countries - Towards a Forward-Looking Strategy*. Washington, DC: IMF.

___(2005), 'A Fact Sheet: Poverty Reduction Strategy Papers' (PRSP). www.imf.org/external/np/exr/facts/prsp.htm, (Retrieved, 28/01/2007).

___(2006), 'A Fact Sheet: December 2005 Debt Relief Under the Heavily Indebted Poor Countries (HIPC) Initiative.' www.imf.org/external/np/exr/facts/hipc.htm, (Retrieved, 28/01/2007).

Jansson, B.S. (1994), *Social Policy:From Theory to Policy Practice*. Belmont, CA: Brooks/Cole Publishing Company.

Jenkins, C. and L. Thomas (2002), 'Foreign Direct Investment in Southern Africa: Determinants, Characteristics, and Implications for Economic Growth and Poverty Alleviation' (Unpublished Paper).

Johnson, L.C., C.L. Schwartz and D.S. Tate (1997), *Social Welfare: A Response to Human Need* (Fourth Edition). Boston, MA: Allyn and Bacon.

Jones, S. (1994), 'Structural Adjustment in Zambia', In H. Hodgson (Ed.), *Negotiating Structural Adjustment in Africa*. London: Heinemann, pp. 25-43.

Kabat, M. (1983), *Management Policy in South Africa*. Cape Town: Oxford University Press.

Kalu, K.A. (2005), 'The Impact of Leadership on Public Policy in Africa: Problems and Opportunities.' www.ccels.cf.ac.uk/literature/publications/2005/kalupaper.pdf, (Retrieved 25/02/2007).

Kandeke, T.K. (1977), *Fundamentals of Zambian Humanism*. Lusaka: National Educational Company of Zambia (NECZAM).

Kaseke, E. (1998), 'Social Welfare in Southern Africa: The Need for Transformation', *Social Work/Maatskaplike Werk*, 34 (2), pp. 144-9.

Lavalette, M. and A. Pratt (1997), *Social Policy: A Conceptual and Theoretical Introduction*. London: SAGE Publications.

Leonard, P. (1975), 'Towards a Paradigm for Radical Practice', In R. Bailey and M. Brake (Eds.), *Radical Social Work*. London: Edward Arnold Publisher, pp. 46-61.

Levine, A. (1987), *The End of the State*. London: Verso.

Lewis, W.A. (1954), 'Economic Development with Unlimited Supplies of Labour', The *Manchester School of Social and Economic Studies*, 22(2), pp. 401-20.

Lungu, J. and C. Mulenga, (2005), *Corporate Social Responsibility Practices in the Extractive Industry in Zambia: A Report for the Catholic Commission for Justice Development and Peace (CCJDP), the Development Education Community Project (DECOP) and the Zambia Congress of Trade Unions (ZCTU)*.

Madison, B.Q. (1980), *The Meaning of Social Policy: The Comparative Dimension in Social Welfare*. London: Croom Helm Ltd.

Mafeje, A. (2001), 'Conceptual and Philosophical Predispositions', In F. Wilson, N. Kanji and E. Braathen (Eds), *Poverty Reduction: What Role for the State in Today's Globalised Economy?* Cape Town: New African Education Publishing, pp. 15-32.

Mainga, M. (1973), *Bulozi Under the Luyana Kings.* London: Longman.

Maipose, G.S. (1989), 'Zambia's Economic and Unemployment Problems: An Analysis of Underlying Factors', In K. Osei-Hwedie and M. Ndulo (Eds), *Studies in Youth and Development.* Lusaka: Multimedia Publications, pp. 19-39.

Mamdani, M. (1986), *Citizen and Subject: Contemporary Africa and the Legacy of Late Colonialism.* Princeton, NJ: Princeton University Press.

Marais, H. (1998), *South Africa: Limits to Change, the Political Economy of Transformation.* Cape Town: UCT Press.

Martinusen, J. (1997), *Society, State and Market.* London: Zed Books.

Masiye, G.P.C., R. Tembo, B. Chisanga and A. Mwanza (1998), 'Social Policy and Research Environment in Zambia.' *Journal of Social Development in Africa*, 13 (2), pp. 34-43.

Mayall, J. (1991), 'The Hopes and Fears of Independence: Africa and the World 1960-90', In D. Rimmer (Ed.), *Africa 30 Years on.* London: The Royal African Society, pp. 22-38.

Mbikusita-Lewanika, A. (2006), 'A Vision of Zambia.' Submitted for consideration to the National Stakeholders' Meeting on the Fifth National Development Plan, 2006-2010 and Vision 2030, Lusaka, 24 to 27 July.

McCalman, J. and R.A. Paton (1992), *Change Management: A Guide to Effective Implementation.* London: Paul Chapman Publishing Ltd.

McKendrick, B.W. (1987), 'The Development of Social Welfare and Social Work in South Africa', In B.W. McKendrick (Ed.), *Introduction to Social Work and Social Welfare in South Africa.* Pretoria: HAUM, pp. 5-19.

___(1990), 'The Future of Social Work in South Africa', *Social Work/Maatskaplike Werk*, 26 (1), pp. 10-18.

Mebeelo, H.S. (1973), *Main Currents of Zambian Humanist Thought.* Lusaka: Oxford University Press.

Mhone, G. (2004), 'Historical Trajectories of Social Policy in Post-Colonial Africa: The Case of Zambia' In T. Mkandawire (Ed.), *Social Policy in a Development Context*. Hampshire: Palgrave Macmillan Publishers, pp. 308-337.

Midgley, J. (1995), *Social Development: The Developmental Perspective in Social Welfare*. London: SAGE Publications.

___(1996), 'Involving Social Work in Economic Development.' *International Social Work*, 36 (96), pp. 13-25.

___(2000), 'The Definition of Social Policy', In J. Midgley, M.B. Tracy and M. Livermore (Eds), *The Handbook of Social Policy*. Thousand Oaks, CA: SAGE Publications, pp. 3-10.

___(2003), 'Assets in the Context of Welfare Theory: A Developmentalist Interpretation.' Working Paper No. 03-10. St Louis, MO: Centre for Social Development, Washington University.

Ministry of Community Development and Social Services (2003), 'Confitea V Mid Term Review: Six Years after Confitea, Status and Future Prospects of Adult Learning' (Unpublished).

Ministry of Community Development and Social Services/Deutsche Gesellschaft für Technische Zusammenarbeit (GTZ) (2004), *The Incapacitated Poor in Zambia. Report on a Study by the Participatory Assessment Group, and Public Welfare Assistance Scheme*. Lusaka: Ministry of Community Development and Social Services/GTZ.

Mkandawire, T. (1998), 'Thinking About Developmental States in Africa.' Paper presented at the United Nations University: African Economic Research Consortium, (AEEC), Workshop on Institutions and Development, Tokyo, 14-15 October.

___(2001), 'How can Social Policies be Used to Enhance Social Capacities for Economic Development without in the Process Eroding the Intrinsic Values of the Social Ends that Policy Makers Purport to Address?' Geneva: The United Nations Research Institute for Social Development (UNRISD).

___(2004), 'Introduction', In T. Mkandawire (Ed.), *Social Policy in a Development Context*. Hampshire: Palgrave Macmillan Publishers, pp. 1-33.

___(2006), *Transformative Social Policy: Lessons from United Nations Research Institute for Social Development (UNRISD) Research*. Geneva: UNRISD.

Moser, C. (2005), 'Assets, Livelihoods and Social Policy.' Paper presented at the Conference on 'New Frontiers of Social Policy', Arusha, Tanzania, 12-15, December.

Mufune, P. (2000), 'Street Youth in Southern Africa'. *International Social Science Journal*, 52 (164), pp. 233-43.

Mufune, P., L.K. Mwansa and K., Osei-Hwedie (1990), 'Conceptual and Theoretical Framework', In K. Osei-Hwedie, L.K. Mwansa and P. Mufune (Eds), *Youth and Community Work Practice: Methods, Techniques, and Skills*. Lusaka: Multimedia Publications, pp. 1-29.

Mukuka, L., W. Kalikiti and D.K. Musenge (2002), 'Social Security in Zambia: Phase 1 Overview of Social Security in Zambia'. *African Journal of Social Work*, 17 (2), pp. 65-96.

Mukwena, R.M. and O. Lolojih (2002), 'Governance and Local Government Reforms in Zambia's Third Republic', In D. Olowolu and S. Sako (Eds), *Better Governance and Public Policy*. Bloomfield, CT: Kumarian Press, Inc., pp. 215-31.

Mutesa, F. and W. Nchito (2005), 'Human Security and Poverty Reduction in Zambia', In K. Muloongo, R. Kibasomba and J.N. Kariri (Eds), *The Many Faces of Human Security: Cases of Seven Countries in Southern Africa*. Pretoria: Institute for Security Studies, pp. 7-36.

Muzyamba, G. (2002), 'Country Statement: The Second World Assembly on Ageing'. Madrid, 8-12, April.

Mwaipaya, P.A. (1980), *The Importance of Quality Leadership in National Development, with Special Reference to Africa*. New York, NY: Vantage Press.

Mwanakatwe, J.M. (1994), *End of Kaunda Era*. Lusaka: Multimedia Publications.

Mwanawasa, L. (2006), 'Speech at the Official Opening of the First Session of the 10th National Assembly' (Unpublished).

Mwansa, L.K., P. Mufune and K. Osei-Hwedie (1990), 'Evaluating Youth and Community Programmes', In K. Osei-Hwedie, L.K. Mwansa and P. Mufune (Eds), *Youth and Community Work Practice: Methods, Techniques and Skills*. Lusaka: Multimedia Publications, pp. 166-79.

Mwansa, L.K. (2007), 'Six Decades of Social Work in Botswana: Challenges of Training and Praxis', In C. Rehklau and R. Lutz (Eds), *Internationale Sozialarbeit — Sozialarbeit des Südens, Band 2: Schwerpunkt Africa*. Oldenburg: Paulo Freire Verlag, pp. 93-108.

National Pensions Scheme Authority (2005), Policy Framework. www.napsa.co.zm/policy.htm, (Retrieved, 10/10/2005).

Ndongko, T.M. (1991), 'The Lagos Plan and Social Development in Central Africa: An Evaluation', In D. Mohammed (Ed.), *Social Development in Africa: Strategies, Policies, and Programmes after the Lagos Plan.* London: Hans Zell Publishers, pp. 25-106.

Ndulo, M. (1985), 'Planning in Zambia: An Analysis of the Third Year Plan', In K. Osei-Hwedie and M. Ndulo (Eds), *Issues in Zambian Development.* Roxbury, MA: Omenana, pp. 14-27.

NEPAD (2001), Strategic Document. www.nepad.org, (Retrieved, 3/08/2006).

Nichols-Casebolt, A., J. Figueira-McDonough and F.E. Netting (2000), 'Change Strategies for Integrating Women's Knowledge into Social Work Curricula.' *Journal of Social Work Education*, 36 (1), pp. 65-78.

Nokkala, M. (2001), 'Simulating the Effects of Debt Relief in Zambia.' Paper prepared for the Wider Conference on Debt Relief, 17-18 August, Helsinki, Finland.

North, D.C. (1981), *Structure and Change in Economic History.* New York, NY: W.W. Norton and Company.

Norton, A., T. Conway and M. Foster, (2001), *Social Protection Concepts and Approaches: Implications for Policy and Practice in International Development.* London: Overseas Development Institute.

Noyoo, N. (1999), 'Good Governance and National Social Development: A Zambian Experience.' *Social Development Issues*, 21 (1), pp. 70-74.

___(1999), 'Socio-economic Reconstruction and Development in Post-Apartheid South Africa.' *Socialist Review*, 27(3+4), pp. 147-57.

___(2000), *Social Welfare in Zambia.* Lusaka: Multimedia Publications.

___(2000), 'Social Development in sub-Saharan Africa: Lessons for Social Work Practice in South Africa.' *International Social Work*, 43 (4), pp. 452-65.

___(2004), 'Human Rights and Social Work in a Transforming Society: South Africa.' *International Social Work*, 47 (3), pp. 359-69.

___(2005), 'Monitoring and Evaluation for Social Development: A Case for Social Work in South Africa', *Social Work/Maatskaplike Werk*, 41 (3), pp. 229-36.

___ and D. Mamphiswana (2003), 'Monitoring and Evaluation: A Tool for Social Development in South Africa', In R. Lutz (Ed.), *Soziale Arbeit in Südafrika: Positionen und Eidrücke*. Oldenburg: Verlag Dialogische Erziehung, pp. 77-91.

Nussbaum, M. (2000), *Women and Human Development: The Capabilities Approach*. Cambridge: Cambridge University Press.

Nyakutemba, E. (1993), 'Structural Adjustment. Getting vocal: Zambian pop star's musical protest.' www.newint.org/issue242/update.htm, (Retrieved, 27/05/2007).

Nyirenda, V.G. (1975), 'Social Change and Social Policy in a Developing Country: The Zambian Case' (PhD Thesis). Los Angeles, CA: University of California.

___(1977) 'Towards a Humanist Approach to Planning and Social Service Provision.' *ZANGO*, 3, pp. 8-16.

Oakley, P., B. Pratt and A. Clayton (1998), *Outcomes and Impacts: Evaluating Change in Social Development*. Oxford: INTRAC.

Obbo, D.K. (1990), 'Methods, Techniques, and Skills of Youth and Community Work: Social Casework, Community Development and Supervision', In K. Osei-Hwedie, L.K. Mwansa and P. Mufune (Eds), *Youth and Community Work Practice: Methods, Techniques, and Skills*. Lusaka: Multimedia Publications, pp. 95-128.

Organisation for Economic Co-operation and Development (OECD) (2002), *Sustainable Development Strategies: A Resource Book*. London: Earthscan.

Osei-Hwedie, K. (1990), 'Social Work and the Question of Social Development in Africa.' *Journal of Social Development in Africa*, 5 (2), pp. 87-99.

___(1996), 'The Indigenisation of Social Work Practice and Education in Africa: The Dilemma of Theory and Method.' *Social Work/Maatskaplike Werk*, 32 (3), pp. 215-25.

___(2002), 'Indigenous Practice: Some Informed Guesses. Self-evident and Possible.' *Social Work/Maatskaplike Werk*, 38(4), pp. 311-23.

___, L.K. Mwansa and P. Mufune (1990), 'Policy and Planning in Youth and Community Work', In K. Osie-Hwedie, L.K. Mwansa and P. Mufune (Eds), *Youth and Community Work Practice: Methods, Techniques and Skills*. Lusaka: Multimedia Publications, pp. 44-73.

Osei-Hwedie, K. and M. Rankopo (2007), 'The Social-Cultural Basis of Indigenising Social Work in Southern Africa', In C. Rehklau and R. Lutz (Eds), *Internationale Sozialarbeit - Sozialarbeit des Südens, Band 2 - Schwerpunkt Africa.* Oldenburg: Paulo Freire Verlag, pp. 19-30.

Parry, N., M. Rustin and C. Satyamurti (1979), *Social Work, Welfare and the State.* London: Edward Arnold Publishers.

Parsons, W. (1995), *Public Policy: An Introduction to the Theory and Practice of Public Policy Analysis.* Cheltenham: Edward Elgar.

Patton, M.Q. (1990), *Qualitative Evaluation and Research Methods.* Newbury Park, CA: Sage Publications.

Pearce, R. (1994a), 'Food Consumption and Adjustment in Zambia', In H. Hodgson (Ed.), *Negotiating Structural Adjustment in Africa.* London: James Currey, pp. 85-97.

___(1994b), 'Structural Adjustment in Zambia', In H. Hodgson (Ed.), *Negotiating Structural Adjustment in Africa.* London: James Currey, pp. 25-43.

Piven, F. and R. Cloward (1974), *Regulating the Poor.* London: Tavistock.

Popple, P.R., and L. Leighnninger (1998), *The Policy-Based Profession: An Introduction to Social Welfare Policy for Social Workers.* Boston, MA: Allyn and Bacon.

Quade, E.S. (1982), *Analysis for Public Decisions* (Second Edition). New York, NY: North-Holland.

Reamer, F. (1999), *Social Work Values and Ethics.* New York, NY: Columbia University Press.

Robbins, S. O., (1990), *Organisation Theory: Structure, Design and Applications.* New Jersey, NJ: Prentice Hall.

Rodney, W. (1972), *How Europe Underdeveloped Africa.* London: Bogle-L'ouveture Publications.

Román-Zozaya, A. (2005), *Development and the Capitalism-capable Society: The Role of the State, Social Policy and Economic Growth.* Oxford: The Oxford Council on Good Governance.

Rose-Ackerman, S. (1999), *Corruption and Government: Causes, Consequences, and Reform.* Cambridge: Cambridge University Press.

Rubin, A. and E. Babbie (1989), *Research Methods for Social Work.* Belmont, CA: Wadsworth Publishing Company.

Rubin, F. (1995), *A Basic Guide to Evaluation for Development Workers*. Oxford: Oxfam.

Saasa, O.S. (2001), *Aid and Poverty Reduction in Zambia: Mission Unaccomplished*. Uppsala: The Nordic Africa Institute.

___(2004), 'PRSP and HIPC Completion Point: Unravelling Zambian Experience.' *Africa Resource Centre*, 2 (2004), pp. 1-4.

___(2007), 'Features and Performance of Local Aid Systems.' www.oecd.org/dataoecd/4/23/34384506.ppt (Retrieved, 27/05/2007).

Sandbrook, R. (1982), *The Politics of Basic Needs: Urban Aspects of Assaulting Poverty in Africa*. Toronto: University of Toronto Press.

Sankara, T. (1988), *Thomas Sankara Speaks: The Burkina Faso Revolution 1983-87*. New York, NY: Pathfinder.

Schubert, B. (2003), 'Social Welfare Interventions for AIDS Affected Households in Zambia. A Backup Initiative Consultancy for the National AIDS Council (NAC), the Ministry of Community Development and Social Services (MCDSS)/GTZ Social Safety Net Project.' (Unpublished).

Schuurman, F.J. (1993), 'Introduction: Development Theory in the 1990s', In F.J. Frans (Ed.), *Beyond the Impasse: New Directions in Development Theory*. London: Zed Books, pp. 1-48.

Scruton, R. (1982), *A Dictionary of Political Thought*. London: The Macmillan Press.

Sen, A. (1999), *Development As Freedom*. Oxford: Oxford University Press.

Seshamani, V. (2003), *Poverty Monitoring and Evaluation by Civil Society in Zambia: Rationale, Objectives, Methodology and Design*. Report Prepared for the Civil Society for Poverty Reduction (CSPR).

Siamwiza, R., A. Sikwebele and R. Makonnen (1993), *Zambia in the 1980s: A Historical Review of Social Policy and Urban Interventions*. Washington, DC: The World Bank.

Smith, T.B. (1973), 'The Policy Implementation Process.' *Policy Sciences*, 4 (2), pp. 197-209.

Smith, B.C. (1996), *Understanding Third World Politics*. London: Macmillan Press.

Smith, M.K. (2006). 'Community work, the encyclopaedia of informal education.' www.infed.org/community/b-comwrk.htm, (Retrieved, 10/01/2007).

Social Safety Net Project (2007), 'Social cash transfer scheme. Social protection in Zambia.' www.socialcashtransfers-zambia.org/pageID_2466950.html, (Retrieved, 27/2/2007).

Stadler, A. (1987), *The Political Economy of Modern South Africa*. London: David Philip.

Statistics New Zealand (2000), 'Survey of Research and Development (R&D).' www.stats.govt.nz/analytical-reports/research-development-2002/survey-of-r-d.htm, (Retrieved, 29/05/2007).

Streeten, P. (1995), *Thinking about Development*. Cambridge: Cambridge University Press.

Swedish International Co-operation Agency (SIDA) (1990), *Review of Swedish Support to Education in Zambia*. Stockholm: SIDA.

Sztomka, P. (1993), *The Sociology of Change*. Cambridge, MA: Blackwell Publishers.

Taylor, I. (2005), 'Can Africa Produce Developmental States?' *CODESRIA Bulletin*, 3&4 (2005), pp. 51-2.

Tembo, R. (1998), 'The State of Social Policy Training in Eastern and Southern Africa: An Overview.' Paper presented at a regional workshop on the status of social policy training in Eastern and Southern Africa, 1-2 June, School of Social Work, University of Zimbabwe, Harare, Zimbabwe.

Thompson, E.P. (1968), *The Making of the English Working Class*. Harmondsworth: Penguin.

Tordoff, W. (1993), *Government and Politics in Africa* (Second Edition). London: Macmillan Press.

Tucon, P. and G. Lungwangwa (1992), *Street Children in Zambia*. Lusaka: Institute of African Studies.

Turock, B. (1991), *Africa: What can be Done?* London: Institute of African Alternatives.

___(1999), *Beyond the Miracle: Development and Economy in South Africa — A Reader*. Cape Town: Fair Share.

United Nations (1986), *Developmental Social Welfare: A Global Survey of Issues and Priorities since 1968*. New York, NY: United Nations.

___(1994), *Human Rights and Social Work*. Geneva: Centre for Human Rights.

___(1996), *Report of the World Summit for Social Development.* New York, NY: United Nations Publications.

___(2001), 'Report on the World Social Situation 2001.' www.un.org/esa/socdev/rwss/overview.html, (Retrieved, 13/01/2004).

___(2005), 'The Millennium Development Goals.' www.un.org/millenniumgoals/, (Retrieved, 24/08/2006).

___(2006), *Social Justice in an Open World: The Role of the United Nations.* New York, NY: Department of Economic and Social Affairs, United Nations.

United Nations Children's Fund (UNICEF) (2004), *'At a Glance: Zambia.'* www.unicef.org/infobycountry/zambia.html, (Retrieved, 10/09/2004).

___(2006), *Africa's Orphaned and Vulnerable Generations: Children Affected by AIDS.* New York, NY: UNICEF.

United Nations Conference on Trade and Development (UNCTAD) (2004), *The Least Developed Countries Report.* Geneva: UNCTAD.

___(2005), *Statistical Profiles of Least Developed Countries.* Geneva: UNCTAD.

United Nations Development Programme (UNDP) (1990), *Human Development Report.* New York, NY: Oxford University Press.

___(1998), *Human Development Report.* New York, NY: Oxford University Press.

___(2003), *Zambia Human Development Report.* Lusaka: UNDP.

___(2004), *Human Development Report.* New York, NY: Oxford University Press.

United Nations Economic and Social Commission for Asia and the Pacific (UNESCAP) (2001). *Report of the Special Body on Least Developed and Landlocked Developing Countries on its Fifth Session.* www.unescap.org/LDC&Poverty/LDC5_ReportofSB.doc (Retrieved, 18/08/2005).

Valadez, J. and M. Bamberger (1994), *Monitoring and Evaluating Social Programmes in Developing Countries: A Handbook for Policymakers, Managers, and Researchers.* Washington, DC: The World Bank.

Walker, M. and N. Badasha (1993), 'Academic Development and the Challenge of Curriculum Change at the University of the Western Cape: An Overview', In M.J. Walker, (Ed.), *Explorations in Change: Case Studies in Academic Development.* Bellville: University of the Western Cape, pp. 1-13.

Weiner, D.L. and A.R. Vining (1992), *Policy Analysis: Concepts and Practice* (Second Edition). Englewood Cliffs, NJ: Prentice-Hall.

Wilensky, H.L. and C.N. Lebeaux (1958), *Industrial Society and Social Welfare.* New York, NY: Russell Sage Foundation.

Wiles, J. and J. Bondi (1998), *Curriculum, Development: A Guide to Practice* (Fifth Edition). Upper Saddle River, NJ: Prentice-Hall, Inc.

Woodroofe, K. (1968), *From Charity to Social Work in England and The United States.* London: Routledge and Kegan Paul.

World Bank (1994), *Zambia: Poverty Assessment Report.* Washington, DC: World Bank.

___(2002), *The World Development Report 2002.* New York, NY: Oxford University Press.

___(2003), *World Development Report 2003.* Washington, DC: World Bank.

___(2004), *Monitoring and Evaluation: Some Tools, Methods, and Approaches.* Washington, DC: World Bank.

___(2006), *Infrastructure for Development.* http://devdata.worldbank.org/GMIS/ida14qa/infrastructure.htm, (Retrieved 18/07/2006).

___(2007), *World Development Report 2007.* New York, NY: Oxford University Press.

Newspaper and news agency reports and articles

Integrated Regional Information Networks (IRIN) (2004), 'Zambia: Lusaka can meet five of its MDGs.' www.irinnews.org/report, (Retrieved, 10/09/2004).

Reuters (2006). 'Zambia's Mwanawasa to cut taxes after divisive poll.' www.za.za.today.reuters.com/news/newsArticle.asp, (Retrieved 27/10/2006).

The Guardian (2007), 'UK lawyers helped Zambia ex-president launder £ 23 m.' www.guardian.co.uk/uk_news/story/0,2072936,00.html, (Retrieved, 5/7/2007).

The Post (2006), 'Nearly half of young women in Zambia and Ghana can't Read - report.' *The Post*, 20 September, p. 2.

___(2006), 'Education still a luxury for many.' *The Post*, 8 October, p. 15.

___(2006), '3 million cases are reported annually — Cifire.' *The Post*, 19 October, p. 2.

___(2006), 'State of libraries in Zambia worries Njovu.' *The Post*, 10 November, p. 5.

___(2006), 'Investors deliberately flouting labour laws to disadvantage Zambian workers' — Mukuma. *The Post*, 16 November, p. 4.

___(2006), 'Govt to await EIA outcome of Legacy Holding Hotel project.' *The Post*, 24 November, p. 12.

___(2006), '85% defilement cases result in HIV infection.' *The Post*, 27 November, pp. 1-2.

___(2006), 'We're able soldiers in fight against HIV/AIDS, declares Cifire.' *The Post*, 27 November, pp. 1-2.

___(2006) 'ZNFU, labour condemns IMF tax proposals.' *The Post*, 19 December, pp. 2 & 4.

Times of Zambia (2006), 'Education of the disabled.' *Times of Zambia*, 3 October 2006.

___(2006), 'RDA out to change Zambian roads.' *Times of Zambia*, 27 November, p. 6.

___(2006), 'From brain drain to forex gain.' *Times of Zambia*, 29 November, p. 5.

Zambia Daily Mail, (2006), 'Zambian economy experiencing best growth rate.'

Zambia Daily Mail, 22 September, p. 4.

___(2006), 'Zambia's corruption record unchanged?' *Zambia Daily Mail*, 7 November, p. 2.

___(2006), 'How the State is tackling the issue of street children.' *Zambia Daily Mail*, 7 November, p. 6.

___(2006), 'Zambia's education sector growing.' *Zambia Daily Mail*, 13 November, p. 5.

Interview

Mulenga, L. (2006)

INDEX

A

African National Congress, ix, 57, 58, 246, 260, 261, 262, 263, 264
African Union, ix, xv, 9, 16, 144
Afrikaner, 225
All Africa Games, xviii, xix, 136
Anglo American Corporation, 68
Anglo-Boer War, 55
Angola, 2, 116, 123, 138, 140, 141, 142, 144, 227, 248, 269
Aristotle, 3

B

Banda, Rupiah, xvi, xviii, 143, 148, 261, 262, 269
Barotseland, 55, 58, 79, 80, 239, 246, 257, 259, 262, 263, 264
Barotseland Agreement of 1964, 58, 80
Botswana, 79, 123, 138, 140, 141, 144, 145, 226, 278
Brain drain, 138, 139, 286
British colonial rule, 55, 226
British rule, 56, 226, 227
Bulawayo, 57

C

Cabral, Amilcar, 119
Catholic Commission for Justice and Peace, 41
Chiluba, Frederick, xx, 65, 66, 67, 68, 128, 131, 136, 138, 156, 157, 160, 200, 231, 235, 237, 238, 250, 252, 265, 267

Citizens, xvi, 1, 4, 6, 13, 14, 69, 71, 88, 91, 99, 106, 109, 112, 119, 126, 136, 139, 140, 143, 146, 148, 149, 153, 165, 179, 193, 200, 201, 203, 204, 214, 218, 238, 248, 256, 258, 263, 264, 267
Citizenship, 3, 4, 24
Civil society, xvi, 2, 9, 11, 22, 26, 27, 31, 33, 41, 63, 93, 100, 106, 108, 116, 146, 154, 160, 169, 175, 178, 183, 200, 204, 205, 206, 218, 225, 231, 244, 246, 248, 250, 257, 267
Civil society Organisations, 10, 136, 176, 204
Cold War, 141, 255, 256
Colonialism, 8, 10, 11, 27, 30, 47, 56, 58, 74, 83, 118, 119, 121, 143, 224, 240, 263
Copenhagen Summit on Social Development, 71
Copperbelt, 19, 162, 175, 235
Corruption, xv, xx, 2, 4, 8, 11, 30, 68, 109, 112, 127, 128, 146, 235, 238, 241, 252, 265, 266, 286
Crisis of post-colonial citizenship, 3
Cuban revolution, 74
Cultural imperialism, 34

D

Democracy, xvi, xvii, 18, 19, 33, 58, 63, 82, 264, 265
Democratic Republic of the Congo, ix, 54, 118, 123
Dependency theory, 74

Development, xvii, 1, 2, 6, 8, 10, 11, 13, 14, 15, 16, 17, 18, 26, 28, 29, 30, 32, 33, 34, 35, 36, 39, 40, 41, 43, 44, 45, 47, 48, 51, 52, 59, 60, 61, 62, 66, 69, 70, 71, 72, 73, 74, 75, 76, 77, 78, 79, 80, 83, 86, 87, 88, 90, 95, 98, 99, 100, 109, 111, 112, 113, 115, 116, 117, 119, 120, 121, 122, 123, 124, 125, 127, 128, 129, 130, 131, 132, 133, 134, 138, 139, 141, 143, 144, 145, 146, 147, 149, 150, 151, 153, 154, 155, 156, 158, 159, 160, 161, 162, 163, 164, 165, 166, 167, 168, 169, 170, 172, 173, 175, 176, 178, 179, 183, 186, 187, 188, 189, 192, 196, 199, 200, 201, 203, 204, 205, 206, 207, 209, 212, 213, 216, 217, 218, 219, 222, 224, 227, 228, 229, 230, 231, 232, 233, 234, 238, 239, 240, 242, 243, 244, 245, 246, 247, 248, 249, 250, 251, 252, 253, 255, 256, 257, 258, 263, 266, 267, 283

Developmental state, xx, 14, 32, 61, 100, 243, 244

Dutch Reformed Church, 225, 226

E

Education, xvii, 1, 3, 8, 10, 16, 22, 26, 34, 35, 39, 45, 56, 59, 68, 70, 71, 83, 86, 87, 88, 90, 95, 102, 109, 112, 119, 136, 138, 145, 149, 150, 151, 152, 153, 154, 168, 170, 171, 173, 180, 199, 201, 202, 203, 214, 218, 219, 226, 227, 228, 237, 239, 241, 248, 257, 267, 282, 286

F

Fanon, Frantz, 119
Federation of Rhodesia and Nyasaland, 56, 261
Foreign Direct Investment, ix, 1, 130, 249, 275
French Revolution, 29

G

Gates, Bill, 158
Gross Domestic Product, x, 1, 66, 72, 88, 128, 153, 156, 247

H

Heavily Indebted Poor Country, x, 1, 12, 31, 109, 124, 244, 245, 266, 274, 282
Heritage Party, xvi
HIV/AIDS pandemic, 11, 23, 172, 177
Human Development Approach, 33, 41, 272
Human dignity, 9, 201, 255
Humanism, 15, 29, 30, 59, 87, 90, 249, 258, 270, 275

I

Ideology, 4, 8, 14, 28, 29, 30, 31, 43, 59, 75, 87, 184, 227, 258
Illiteracy, 3, 239, 250
IMF, x, 1, 9, 12, 22, 27, 31, 63, 65, 70, 75, 81, 88, 89, 91, 118, 121, 206, 207, 274, 286
Independent Electoral Commission, xvii

Institutions, xx, 2, 5, 9, 11, 16, 21, 22, 31, 36, 37, 39, 50, 51, 53, 54, 65, 71, 76, 81, 89, 96, 97, 99, 109, 134, 139, 151, 152, 153, 162, 198, 199, 202, 203, 227, 234, 241, 242, 243, 246, 247, 248, 256

International Labour Organisation, x, 66, 76, 123, 131, 177, 272, 274

J

Jesuit Centre for Theological Reflection, x, 154

Johannesburg World Summit on Sustainable Development, 77

K

Kaunda, Kenneth, xvi, xviii, 30, 57, 58, 59, 60, 61, 62, 63, 64, 68, 80, 81, 109, 131, 141, 142, 143, 147, 148, 150, 151, 155, 157, 200, 206, 235, 236, 237, 238, 246, 248, 252, 261, 262, 263, 265, 268, 278

Kazakhstan, 117

Kwacha., xiii

L

Latin America, 47, 74, 75

Lesotho, 141, 144

Liberalisation, 10, 65, 66, 67, 68, 81, 122, 123, 130

Liberation struggle, xv, 141, 142

Livingstone, David, xix, 55, 56, 135

Lumumba, Patrice, 118

M

Maison des Science de L'Homme, vii

Malawi, 56, 59, 123, 140, 144, 148, 261

Malaysia, 250

Marx, 29, 49, 74, 258

Marxist, 29, 30, 49, 74, 75

Mbeki, Thabo, 9, 16, 229

McNamara, Robert, 76

Millennium Development Goals, x, 16, 144, 176, 206, 273, 284

Mitchell, Professor Bill, vii

Modernisation theory, 73, 74

Movement for Democratic Change, xv

Movement for Multiparty Democracy, xi, xvi, 65, 235

Mozambique, 116, 123, 140, 141, 142, 144, 227, 248

Mugabe, Robert, xv, xvi, 252

Mwanawasa, Levy, xv, xvi, xviii, xx, 2, 19, 30, 31, 67, 68, 69, 124, 125, 126, 130, 131, 132, 136, 139, 154, 156, 157, 164, 165, 175, 176, 238, 250, 252, 266, 278, 285

N

Namibia, 123, 130, 140, 142, 144, 225, 227, 248, 273

National Constitutional Conference, xvi

National Policy on Community Development, 95, 273

Nationalist movements, 8

Nationalists, 239

neo-Marxist development theories, 74

New Partnership for Africa's Development, xi, 9, 229
Nkrumah, Kwame, 10, 239
Nkumbula, Harry M, 57, 58, 260, 261
Northern Rhodesia, 55, 57, 58, 84, 150, 257, 259, 260, 262, 268
Nyasaland, 57, 260, 262
Nyerere, Julius, 15, 30, 141

O

Organisation of Zambians Abroad, xi, 140

P

Parents Teachers Associations, 152
Paris, vii, xi, xv, 12, 79
Patriotic Front, xvi, 20
Plato, 3, 48
Policy-makers, 5, 11, 24, 36, 69, 109, 146, 179, 191, 200, 221, 229, 231, 244, 250, 251, 267
Politicians, xviii, xix, 4, 5, 11, 14, 19, 31, 34, 68, 69, 128, 129, 137, 146, 157, 231, 238, 241, 244, 249, 250, 251, 267
Politics, vii, xv, xvii, 4, 28, 31, 57, 58, 59, 60, 61, 62, 63, 65, 67, 83, 100, 112, 122, 195, 200, 234, 235, 236, 237, 239, 240, 263, 264, 265
Poor Laws of England, 21
Poverty, xv, xviii, 1, 2, 3, 13, 15, 16, 17, 18, 26, 27, 30, 31, 32, 33, 34, 35, 36, 40, 41, 45, 59, 63, 64, 67, 70, 72, 75, 77, 84, 90, 91, 93, 95, 99, 100, 102, 105, 108, 109, 115, 116, 117, 120, 121, 122, 123, 127, 128, 130, 132, 134, 142, 145, 149, 162, 163, 164, 167, 169, 171, 197, 205, 206, 207, 211, 222, 223, 224, 225, 226, 227, 229, 231, 232, 233, 234, 238, 239, 240, 244, 245, 247, 249, 251, 252, 253, 255, 256, 257, 267
Poverty Reduction Strategy Paper, xii, 1, 17, 204, 205, 206, 245, 273, 274, 282
Privatisation, 10, 65, 66, 67, 94, 124
Programme Against Malnutrition, xi, 90
Public-Private-Partnerships, 125

Q

Queen Victoria, 55

R

Racialising the labour market, 87
Reaganomics, 22
Rhodesia, 55, 56, 57, 80, 259, 260, 261, 262, 272
Rodney, Walter, 72, 118, 119, 281
Russian Revolution of 1917, 47

S

Salisbury, 56, 57
Sata, Michael, xvi, xvii, xviii, 19
Second World War, 32, 47, 73, 83, 165
Sen, Amartya, 32, 69, 70, 271, 272, 282
Social change, 13, 21, 22, 41, 47, 48, 49, 50, 53, 54, 55, 63, 69, 79, 211, 223, 224, 258

Index

Social welfare, vii, 9, 23, 26, 36, 37, 38, 39, 40, 59, 84, 85, 86, 87, 92, 93, 94, 95, 102, 171, 183, 193, 194, 195, 198, 209, 214, 222, 223, 225, 226, 227, 257, 258

Socialism, 8

South Africa, vii, ix, xix, 16, 55, 59, 66, 68, 79, 80, 116, 136, 141, 142, 144, 145, 157, 180, 225, 227, 229, 246, 248, 250, 259, 260, 272, 274, 275, 276, 279, 280, 283

Southern African Development Community, xii, xv, 144, 251

Southern Rhodesia, 56, 57, 259, 260, 261

Sport, xviii, xix, 119, 136

Structural Adjustment Programmes, 9, 27, 65, 70, 76, 90, 121, 233, 256

Structuralist theories, 75

Students, v, xix, 63, 95, 150, 151, 180, 227, 236, 237

Sustainable development, 17, 76, 77, 145

Sustainable Livelihoods, xii, 99, 164

T

Tanzania, 15, 30, 123, 129, 141, 144, 145, 278

Targeted Food Security Pack, xii, 91

Thatcherism, 22

Third World, 73, 74, 75, 76, 282

Third World countries, 74, 75

Traffic jams, xviii

Tribalism, 3, 11, 68, 235, 236

U

United National Independence Party, xii, xviii, xix, 57, 58, 59, 61, 62, 63, 86, 87, 90, 128, 150, 155, 157, 172, 177, 235, 236, 237, 246, 248, 261, 262, 264

United Nations, viii, xviii, 10, 16, 23, 32, 33, 34, 35, 36, 39, 40, 59, 71, 74, 77, 98, 115, 116, 120, 121, 122, 130, 143, 147, 149, 153, 162, 164, 165, 166, 176, 177, 178, 184, 203, 206, 210, 229, 231, 258, 277, 283, 284

United Party, xii, xvi, 81, 262

United Party for National Development, xvi

United Progressive Party, xii, 81

Universal Declaration of Human Rights, 98, 165, 232

University of Johannesburg, vii

University of Zambia, v, 68, 138, 150, 151, 235, 236

Utopians, 48

V

Vietnam, 250

W

World Bank, vii, 1, 3, 6, 9, 12, 22, 27, 31, 64, 65, 70, 75, 76, 81, 88, 89, 91, 109, 118, 121, 130, 152, 172, 174, 186, 205, 206, 233, 243, 282, 284, 285

Z

Zaire, 9, 236

Zambezi River, 161, 257, 261

Zambia African National Congress, xiii, 57, 261

Zambia Congress of Trade Union, xiii, 68, 275

Zambia National Broadcasting Co-operation, xiii, 64

Zambianisation, 86

Zimbabwe, xv, xviii, 56, 79, 82, 116, 117, 123, 135, 140, 142, 144, 145, 226, 248, 261, 283

www.ingramcontent.com/pod-product-compliance
Lightning Source LLC
Chambersburg PA
CBHW070233230426
43664CB00014B/2289